T CENTURY

QUIRY

es sponsored by
nstitute, located
vanced study of
es and projects.
ries of contem-
stian faith and
nd culture. The
iqueness of the
that relate the
, and practical

om research by
logical Inquiry
es, publications
nsored by CTI.
this series will
theology in its

ENSON,

of God
el Welker

1:
on Life
r J. Paris

THEOLOGY FOR THE *21* ENTY-FI

CENTER OF THEOLOGICAL

Theology for the Twenty-first Century is a s
the Center of Theological Inquiry (CTI), a
in Princeton, New Jersey, dedicated to the
theology. This series is one of its many initia

The goal of the series is to publish in
porary scholars into the nature of the C
its witness and practice in church, society,
series will include investigations into the
Christian faith. But it will also offer stud
Christian faith to the major cultural, soc
issues of our time.

Monographs and symposia will result
scholars in residence at the Center of Th
or otherwise associated with it. In some c
will come from group research projects sp
It is our intention that the books selected f
constitute a major contribution to renewin
service to church and society.

WALLACE M. ALSTON, JR., ROBERT
AND DON S. BROWNING
SERIES EDITORS

What Dare We Hope?
by Gerhard Sauter

The End of the World and the Ends
edited by John Polkinghorne and Mich

God and Globalization, Volume
Religion and the Powers of the Comm
edited by Max L. Stackhouse with Pet

professorship at the University of Aberdeen. He is known especially for his pioneering volume, *Globalization: Social Theory and Global Culture,* and for his multiple essays and editing of collected works that have, as have few others, defined this field of study.

WILLIAM SCHWEIKER. Now Professor of Theological Ethics at the Divinity School, University of Chicago, he previously studied at the University of Iowa and the University of Chicago. He is a senior series editor, with Jürgen Moltmann and Michael Welker, of International Theologie; and author of *Responsibility and Christian Ethics* and *Power, Value, and Conviction.* His current research is on the nature and history of "property" in economic, philosophical, jurisprudential, sociological, ethical, and theological reflection, under a grant from the Lilly Endowment.

DONALD W. SHRIVER, JR. President emeritus and Professor of Applied Christianity at Union Theological Seminary in New York, Dr. Shriver is a graduate of Yale Divinity School and the Harvard Divinity School. He is the author of several works on conflict and the possibilities of the just resolution of conflict: *Rich Man, Poor Man; Spindles and Spires;* and *Forgiveness and Politics: The Case of the American Black Civil Rights Movement.* His newest book is the award-winning international study *An Ethic for Enemies: Forgiveness in Politics.*

MAX L. STACKHOUSE.. After earning an M.Div. and Ph.D. from Harvard University and teaching at Andover Newton Theological Seminary as well as in India, Southeast Asia, and Eastern Europe, Professor Stackhouse was called to the Stephen Colwell Chair of Christian Ethics at Princeton Theological Seminary, where he also directs the Project on Public Theology. Among his works on global issues are *Public Theology and Political Economy; Creeds, Society, and Human*

CONTRIBUTORS

YERSU KIM. A South Korean, Dr. Kim earned a B.A. from Harvard College and a Ph.D. in philosophy from the University of Bonn. He taught in several posts and was president of noted academic societies in Korea as well as serving as the secretary-general of the Afro-Asian Philosophical Association. In 1995, he joined the Social and Human Sciences Sector of UNESCO in Paris, and soon became director of the Division of Philosophy and Ethics. He leads the program to draft an "Ethics Charter for the Twenty-first Century." His books include *Philosophy of Justice* and *Language and Culture,* and he is the recent recipient of a Festschrift.

PETER J. PARIS. A Canadian by birth, trained at the University of Chicago, and having taught at Vanderbilt and several schools in Africa, Professor Paris is internationally recognized for his studies of African and African American leadership. At Princeton Theological Seminary, he occupies the Elmer Homrighausen Professorship of Christian Social Ethics and serves as liaison with the Princeton University African American Studies Program. He is a past president of the American Academy of Religion. His most recent book is *The Spirituality of African Peoples.*

ROLAND ROBERTSON. Known to many as the dean of scholarship on globalization, Professor Robertson came to the sociology department of the University of Pittsburgh after teaching and writing in England for many years. Recently retired from that position, he has assumed a distinguished

6. **Public Theology, Hope, and the Mass Media:** 231
   Can the Muses Still Inspire?
   David Tracy

   Introduction, 231 • Example One: Rationality and Modernity and the Import of Jürgen Habermas for Theology, 232 • Example Two: Debates on Postmodernity and the Recovery of Religion as Participation, 240 • Images of Eschatological Hope: Fragments and Their Gathering into Covenant, 248

Selected Bibliography 255

Index 277

3. Responsibility in the World of Mammon: 105
Theology, Justice, and Transnational Corporations
William Schweiker

Globality and Persons, 107 • The World of Mammon,
110 • The World of Economic Globalization, 117 •
Mammon and the Ecumene, 125 • Responsibility in a
World of Mammon, 128 • The Mission of the Churches,
138

4. The Taming of Mars: Can Humans of the   140
Twenty-first Century Contain Their Propensity
for Violence?
Donald W. Shriver, Jr.

What Almost Happened (1963), 140 • Our Violent Century, 143 • Theology and Nonviolent Politics, 151 •
Peacemaking Theory, 159 • Three Approaches to Conflict Resolution — And a Fourth, 161 • The Contribution
of the Churches to Global Peacemaking, 167 • The Most
Difficult Ethical Question, 172 • The Kosovo Test, 177

5. Faith, Feminism, and the Family in an Age of   184
Globalization
Mary Stewart Van Leeuwen

A Theological Framework: Family as a Mixed Blessing, 185 • A Historical Framework: Feminism as a
Mixed Blessing, 201 • Modernity, Gender, and the Family in Non-Western Societies, 208 • Competing Models
of Gender and Family Relations for the Twenty-first
Century, 211 • The Human-Capabilities Approach to
Development, 219 • Recovering the Idea of Family as
a Creational Sphere, 225 • Theological Themes Once
More, 229

CONTENTS

Contributors   xi

General Introduction   1
   Max L. Stackhouse
   The Project, 1 • The Tasks of Theological Ethics, 9
   • Globalization and "The World" 19 • Theological
   Views of Globalization, 25 • The Powers and Spheres
   in Globalization, 31

1. Globalization and the Future of
   "Traditional Religion"   53
   Roland Robertson
   Introduction, 53 • Globalization, 53 • Inventing Tradition, 57 • Relativization and Culture, 59 • Authenticity
   and Globalization, 63 • Collective Memory and Tradition, 66 • Conclusion: The Future, 67

2. Philosophy and the Prospects for a Universal Ethics   69
   Yersu Kim
   The Globalization of Problems, 70 • The Crisis of Values
   and International Response, 72 • The Western Synthesis,
   76 • The Search for Common Values: Tentative Steps, 78
   • International Commissions, 79 • Religious, Political,
   and Cultural Institutions, 80 • Global Common Values
   in Action, 84 • The UNESCO Universal Ethics Project,
   86 • Prospects toward the Ethics Charter of the Twenty-
   first Century, 100 • The Task Ahead, 103

Trinity Press International, P.O. Box 1321, Harrisburg, PA 17105
Trinity Press International is a division of the Morehouse Group.

Cover design: Tom Castanzo

Library of Congress Cataloging-in-Publication Data

God and globalization : religion and the powers of the common life / edited by Max L. Stackhouse with Peter Paris.
    p.   cm. – (Theology for the twenty-first century)
    Includes bibliographical references and index.
    ISBN 1-56338-311-X (pbk.)
    1. Christian ethics. 2. Globalization – Moral and ethical aspects.
3. Globalization – Religious aspects – Christianity.   I. Stackhouse, Max L.
II. Paris, Peter J., 1933.   III. Series.

BJ1275 .G63 2000
261.8 – dc21

                                                              00-020203

Printed in the United States of America

02   03   04   05   06   10   9   8   7   6   5   4   3

God *and* Globalization

VOLUME 1

RELIGION
AND POWERS OF
THE POWERS THE
COMMON LIFE

Edited by
Max L. Stackhouse
with Peter J. Paris

TRINITY PRESS INTERNATIONAL
Harrisburg, Pennsylvania

GOD AND GLOBALIZATION:
THEOLOGICAL ETHICS AND THE SPHERES OF LIFE

MAX L. STACKHOUSE, GENERAL EDITOR
WITH PETER J. PARIS, DON S. BROWNING,
AND DIANE OBENCHAIN

Sponsored by
The Center of Theological Inquiry
Princeton, N.J.
1999–2001

The world is presently going through a monumental social, political, and economic shift that has implications for faith, ethics, human understanding, and for human well-being. It is clear that the categories of analysis by which most of us have understood the social worlds around us are at least partially obsolete. How are we to understand the new, complex global civilization toward which we are being thrust? What are the ways that religion, theology, and ethics, in close interaction with our social, political, and economic situation can help guide globalization?

The contributors to this set of volumes have sorted the "powers and principalities," "authorities and dominions" that are shaping the multiple spheres of life in our world and have proposed creative new perspectives on a massive range of pertinent issues that lie at the intersection of religion and globalization. The volumes provide insights into ethics, religion, economics, and culture that will interest not only theologians, ethicists, and clergy of many traditions but also academics, social scientists, professionals, and those in business and technology who seek to understand the move toward a global civilization from a social and ethical point of view.

Vol. 1: *Religion and the Powers of the Common Life*
Edited by Max L. Stackhouse with Peter J. Paris

Rights; Christian Social Ethics in a Global Era; and *Covenant and Commitments.*

DAVID TRACY. Having both his S.T.L. (licentiate) and S.T.D. (doctorate) from the Gregorian in Rome, Professor Tracy has been at the Divinity School of the University of Chicago since 1969, and visiting lecturer at Trinity University in Ireland, the University of Lund in Sweden, the University of Beijing in China, and Hartmann University in Jerusalem. He will give the Gifford Lectures in Edinburgh, Scotland in 2000. Among his many books are *Blessed Rage for Order: The New Pluralism in Theology; Analogical Imagination: Christian Theology and the Culture of Pluralism;* and *On Naming the Present.*

MARY STEWART VAN LEEUWEN. A native of Canada, Professor Van Leeuwen is resident scholar at the Center for Women in Leadership, Eastern College, Pennsylvania. She studied at Queen's University in Ontario before earning her M.A. in social psychology and her Ph.D. at Northwestern University, having written her dissertation on cross-cultural research done in Zambia. Her books include *Gender and Grace: Love, Work, and Parenting in a Changing World; After Eden: Facing the Challenge of Gender Reconciliation;* and *Religion, Feminism, and the Family.*

General Introduction

Max L. Stackhouse

The Project

It is a great delight to introduce these four volumes. Working with one of the finest teams of Christian scholars ever assembled to address one of the most fateful clusters of issues for our time is a demanding joy. It is thus a pleasant imperative that I not only start by thanking the authors in these volumes and my coeditors for their rich contributions to this complex, interdisciplinary set of studies, to each other, and to the twenty-first century, but also offer the gratitude of all involved both to the Center of Theological Inquiry at Princeton Theological Seminary for sponsoring this effort and to Trinity Press International for making our efforts available to all.

The design of the project was my own, with the help of treasured friends — Don Browning, Donald Shriver, John Witte, Peter Paris, Diane Obenchain, and Wallace Alston, director of the Center of Theological Inquiry in Princeton, which funded this set of studies. They, and the wider team of authors we assembled, represent a rich mix of resources — some more liberal, some more conservative; some Protestant, some Catholic; some "Western" by birth, some born and raised in non-Western cultures. The project was, at one point, correlated with a conference cosponsored by World Vision and Princeton Theological Seminary, which brought together not only specialists in various academic fields, but specialists in development, aid, relief, and missiology from around

1

the world and from many denominations.[1] I was also able
to present ideas drawn from these studies to interfaith audi-
ences in China, Australia, Fiji, South India and Assam, and
South Africa. I am grateful for the comments of colleagues
and friends in Beijing and Hangzhou, Melbourne and Can-
berra, Suva, Bangalore, Jorhat, Stellenbosch, and Cape Town.
Neither they, nor I, nor any of the contributors agrees with
everything that is said in this set of volumes, nor even with all
aspects of the design of the project; but those who composed
the essays seemed to agree that it was a major intellectual,
moral, spiritual, and collegial adventure to work together. We
have sought to provide fresh resources that can help churches,
seminaries, colleges and universities, other communities of
faith, and, more broadly, the morally and spiritually committed leaders of the emerging international civil society to
identify and face the issues posed by "globalization."

The concerns of theological ethics are primary. We see this
in the title of this set of volumes: "God and Globalization:
Theological Ethics and the Spheres of Life." The issue of
whether God is, is a critical philosophical question, one to
which every serious theology offers reasons for an affirmative
answer and one which philosophy may doubt but can neither
refute or confirm. Theology suspects that philosophies which
deny the possibility of God are superficial and unable finally
to render a normative guide for life. The issue of who God
is, is a critical theological question, decisive in the encounter
of the religions of the world, as we shall see. The question
of how God wants humans to live is a critical theological
ethical issue, one to which the world's great philosophies
and religions offer some common insights and some divergent ones. These are best adjudicated by a philosophically

---

1. Most papers presented at that conference are published in Max L.
Stackhouse, Tim Dearborne, and Scott Paeth, eds., *The Local Church in a
Global Era* (Grand Rapids, Mich.: Eerdmans, 2000).

informed theological ethic. In considering God in conjunction with "globalization," a process that requires an informed social analysis, we are also inquiring into the kind of world that is emerging with specific attention to those social issues that shape our understanding and guide our lives in it. The increasingly globalized world is constituted by many "Spheres" of dynamic activity that acknowledge, utilize, and channel the "Powers" that are in play in them. Our issues have to do with how humanity is to live in the midst of the expanded ability to use the potential of these Powers and to structure the dynamic, pluralistic Spheres that the new complexity demands in ways that accord with values and norms that are not simply "worldly," but which are pertinent both to human flourishing in the world and to our ultimate destiny. The idea of theological ethics in this definition has several presumptions: that the term "God" refers to something about which we can reasonably speak; that this reality is concerned about life, especially human life in the world; and that this life is to be lived under conditions of both finite time and space, with an eye on that which is nontemporal and nonspacial. Today, the world as a historical interaction of people and societies is undergoing a dynamic transformation called "globalization," one that has many implications for the world as biophysical planet and for the world as a philosophical-theological concept. The extent of this change invites, almost demands, a reassessment of those traditions that have not only contributed to the dynamics now reshaping our various societies, but that may enhance or inhibit the capacity to participate in, avoid victimization by, and constructively guide key aspects of what appears to be the creation of a new, encompassing, and highly complex civilization.

Many, of course, would not take up these questions from a theological-ethical point of view. In a lengthy summary of current literature on globalization, Giovanni Arrighi and Beverly Silver do not mention religion, theology, or ethics. They treat the economic, political, and social evidence, with an eye to the effects on national economies, working peoples, and minorities. Pointing toward their conclusion that further historical and comparative studies are needed, they write:

[There is] little consensus on anything but the fact that an era of history has ended. There is no consensus on which state, if any, benefitted most from the confrontation of the Cold War and is now poised to replace the United States as the dominant player in the global political economy. There is no consensus on whether the proliferation in the variety and number of multinational corporations and the formation of global financial markets is undermining state capacities and, if so, how generally and permanently. There is no consensus on whether the world's working class is an endangered species or simply changing color and the countries of its residence. There is no consensus on whether modernization is shoring up civilizational divides, melting them down, or restoring the inter-civilizational balance of power of modern times. Above all, there is no consensus on what kind of world order, if any, we can expect to emerge from the combination of whatever changes are actually occurring in the global configuration of power.[2]

Meanwhile, of course, people have very strong views about these issues. Many are threatened locally by the changes and feel victimized by them, as I found in parts of Fiji, India, and Africa, and are not unwilling to project local experiences and interests onto a global screen. Kofi Annan, secretary-general of the United Nations, recently pointed out that many see "globalization" less as "a term describing objective reality" about the creation of a new social or

---

2. G. Arrighi and B. Silver, *Chaos and Governance in the Modern World System* (Minneapolis: University of Minnesota Press, 1999), 21.

civilizational possibility than as "an ideology of predatory capitalism," which they experience as a kind of siege. Against it, they join a backlash which takes at least three major forms.[3] One form is a growing nationalism, sometimes threatening multiethnic states. The second form, more troubling in view of the history of the twentieth century, is the call for strong leaders — seldom democratic, often overtly antidemocratic — who seek to mobilize these national interests against internationalism. And the third form is the attempt to use globalization as a scapegoat for all the political and social ills that in fact have domestic roots.[4] To many, globalization has nothing to do with religion, theology, or ethics except in changing the way they used to live. They do not know how to control it or to join it. Appeals to religion, religious ethics, or religiously shaped cultural ethics are then used to mobilize sentiment against global trends. Local elites who find themselves swamped by developments they do not understand and cannot negotiate are particularly negative.[5]

Such views seldom help understanding even if they are understandable, yet do point to necessary reforms and cautions in a number of areas. It is more likely that globalization has promising as well as threatening possibilities, which cannot

---

3. "The Backlash against Globalism," *The Futurist*, March 1999, 27.

4. Ibid. We can sometimes see this form of backlash abroad before we recognize it at home. See Mark Juergensmeyer, *The New Cold War: Religious Nationalism Confronts the Secular State* (Berkeley: University of California Press, 1993); and Peter van der Veer, *Religious Nationalism: Hindus and Muslims in India* (Berkeley: University of California Press, 1994).

5. This is true of Christian voices as well as analysts indifferent to Christianity. See, e.g., M. D. Litonjua, "Global Capitalism," *Theology Today* 56, no. 2 (July 1999): 210ff.; *The Cultures of Globalization*, ed. Fredric Jameson and Masao Miyoshi (Durham, N.C.: Duke University Press, 1998); or Paul Hellyer, *Stop: Think* (Toronto: Chimo Media, 1999). Hellyer lists the best available bibliography of attacks on globalization, understood as the increasing influence of the World Bank, the International Monetary Fund, and all who cooperate with "the multinationals" and "capitalism."

be seen clearly without attention to the larger picture and
to certain "public theological" matters. Thus, one purpose
of these volumes is to assess various reactions, and to chart
responses likely to address the realities we all face. The perspective of these volumes does not obscure that globalization
is disrupting many aspects of traditional religion, ethics, culture, economics, politics, and society, but does not only see
religion as a force to mobilize against globalization. Indeed,
we shall find repeatedly that deeper analysis demands that we
acknowledge that people do, or can, know something about
what is holy, and can recognize that holy possibilities are not
entirely absent from globalization. Neither part of this hypothesis has been universally accepted or decisively proven.
However, these ideas have not been decisively refuted or universally rejected either. In spite of a widely held view that
the future will be increasingly secular, the resurgence of religious vitality has puzzled various secularizers to no end, and
it is again becoming clear to a great number of scholars that
religious insights and traditions are a permanent feature of
human life, clearly evident in global trends, and the locus at
which questions of truth, justice, and holiness take their most
intense forms.[6]

However, since not all religious insights are equally valid,
the various claims made about truth, justice, and holiness
must be subjected to critical examination. Thus, comparative

6. Peter Berger, ed., *The Desecularization of the World: Resurgent
Religion and World Politics* (Grand Rapids, Mich.: Eerdmans, 1999),
represents on this point a major trend in current scholarship. From the
standpoint of the philosophical and historical analysis of cultures, see also
the remarkable *The Human Condition and Ultimate Realities,* ed. Robert
Cummings Neville, 3 vols. (Albany: State University of New York Press,
forthcoming), and a discerning review of major new studies in anthropology
that signal a return of interest in religion after several generations of non-
or antireligious focus (Sarah Caldwell, "Transcendence and Culture: Anthropologists Theorize Religion," *Religious Studies Review* 28 [July 1999]:
227–32).

philosophical theology, comparative ethics, and comparative social analyses — and not only appeals to a particular religion — are indispensable in investigating the relative validity of various religious claims about how we should live in this life and the role in this life of that which transcends it. Issues of justice and responsibility, righteousness and compassion, truth and virtue are thus intrinsic to this assessment, for no one authentically can give loyalty or credence to a view or lifestyle that does not evoke, ground, manifest, or sustain these qualities. In an emerging global civilization, theological-ethical issues are again unavoidable. Insofar as we can know these issues with any confidence, we must come to an informed judgment, as many traditions would put it, about how God wants us to live in the global civilization, to respond to it, and to shape it.

We face a complex question in a complex situation. Obviously, the question demands the joining of ethics and theology. In concert with most classical traditions and in contrast to many modern trends that divorced or even opposed the two disciplines, we hold that theology and ethics are mutually supportive, even necessary to each other. Still, we must acknowledge the validity of the modern insight that the two are analytically distinct in a way that allows them to correct one another. Thus, we may use ethics to assess the assumptions and implications of every theologically approved practice and dogmatic claim. We may demand further that valid ethical criteria find ultimate sanction in what is truly universal and enduring, and not only in what is religiously and temporarily "mine" or "ours" at the moment. This is one of the characteristics of "public theology," which works with, but also beyond, confessional and dogmatic theology.[7]

---

7. See my "Public Theology and Ethical Judgment," in *East and West, Religious Ethics: Proceedings of the Third Symposium of Sino-American Philosophy and Religious Studies,* Chinese edition edited by Zhang Zhegang and Mel Stewart (Beijing: University of Beijing, 1998), 132–47 (Eng.

Without these critical principles, theological ethics is tempted
to be little more than an idiosyncratic folkway, and theology
is tempted simply to be the ideological megaphone for what
a group believes or practices.[8]

In this set of volumes, we will focus the theological-ethical
questions by exploring the issues pressed into contemporary
consciousness by the emergence of global business, technologies, ecological awareness, the struggles for universal human
rights, and a host of related developments after the defeat of
militant nationalism in World War II, and after the collapse
of international socialism at the end of the Cold War. These
developments are rooted in historic trends that seem now to
be leading humanity toward the possible creation of a global
civilization that will alter every community and tradition.[9] Of
particular interest to theological ethics as it inquires into such

---

ed., *Theology Today* 54 [July 1997]: 165–79); and "Human Rights and
Public Theology: The Basic Validation of Human Rights," in *Religion and
Human Rights: Competing Claims?* ed. Carrie Gustafson and Peter Juviler
(New York: M. E. Sharpe, 1999), 12–30.

8. See Peter Byrne, *The Moral Interpretation of Religion* (Grand
Rapids, Mich.: Eerdmans, 1998); and Franklin I. Gamwell, *The Divine
Good: Modern Moral Theory and the Necessity of God* (San Francisco:
HarperCollins, 1990). These volumes not only review the contributions
since the Enlightenment of mutually critical thinking in theology and ethics,
but show the contemporary state of discussion.

9. When globalization began is an open question and laden with tensions between naturalist and historical perspectives. Jared Diamond, *Guns,
Germs, and Steel* (New York: W. W. Norton, 1998), suggests that globalization is built into the universal evolutionary process. David Landis, *The
Wealth and Poverty of Nations* (New York: W. W. Norton, 1998), treats
it as a European phenomenon, rooted in the deep social and cultural history of the West — often resisted by political decisions in other parts of the
world. Saskia Sassen, *Losing Control? Sovereignty in an Age of Globalization* (New York: Columbia University Press, 1996), sees globalization as
the wider empowerment of the United States after the collapse of the Soviet
Union, obvious in the global hegemony of U.S. popular culture and in the
new instruments of world governance backed by the United States and its
closest allies. These are not the only, uncontroverted, or mutually exclusive
theories.

issues are the often implicit key moral assumptions and meta-physical convictions that form the moral ecology, the "ethos" of the social environment in which we live. The ethos conditions the minds of ordinary people more than they know, as well as the thinking of the theologian and ethicist more than they often admit. Further, since every viable social context is a network of interactive, interdependent spheres, organized into practices and institutions, we must pay attention to the spheres of activity that shape life, and to what holds these spheres into identifiable units of common action. Thus, theological ethics tries to understand, evaluate, and help guide the spheres of the common life in which the social ecology is manifest as ethos, and to discern how theological ethics should interact with nontheological forces and fields of study beyond ethics that also influence these spheres. These "other" areas are also bearers of values and norms.

Only some of our contributors are theological ethicists; many specialize in other fields. But each has manifested an interest in or a capacity to contribute to the issues raised by theological ethics, a field that always engages the intellectual, religious, and social traditions that shape an ethos.[10]

The Tasks of Theological Ethics

Because of these complex relationships it is necessary at the outset of these volumes to identify the primary tasks of any who engage in theological ethics. The working out of these tasks is a key to the design behind our project. One indis-

---

10. The idea of "ethos" is explored in my *Ethics and the Urban Ethos* (Boston: Beacon Press, 1972). It has been treated as "moral ecology" by Robert Bellah et al. in *Habits of the Heart* (Berkeley: University of California Press, 1985) and in *The Good Society* (New York: A. Knopf, 1991). Historians note that J. S. Mill first tried to develop "ethology" as a descriptive science of morality, but that he did not have the tools of social and historical analysis to do so adequately. However, the effort shows that he knew he needed a concept to go beyond utilitarianism.

pensable task, as already suggested, is to interpret the social contexts of life at the deepest moral and spiritual levels. This task demands close attention to the work of historians, social scientists, and skilled professionals in other areas. Theological ethicists seldom become specialists in a single discipline related to these areas of study, analysis, practice, or reflection, although it is impossible today to do good work in theological ethics without drawing on the research and experience of these fields. The concern of theological ethics at this juncture is to discern accurately the ethos of the areas in which these "experts" study or practice.

An "ethos" is the subtle web of "values" and "norms," the obligations, virtues, convictions, mores, purposes, expectations and legitimations that constitute the operating norms of a culture in relation to a social entity or set of social practices. The values and norms of an ethos may not be agreed upon by all. In fact, they may be sharply contested. At some point, though, they became the scaffolding for organizing of common behavior and moral debate in an institution, movement, organization, or tradition, even if many people hold, as personal convictions, other values and norms.[11] Theological ethics seeks to discern these operating values and norms in behavior and belief, as well as the functioning or regulative structures and dynamics of an ethos. In brief, theological ethics tries to find out what is going on morally and spiritually.

Moreover, ethicists want to know, at the deeper levels of motivation and commitment, what sustains the values and

---

11. Gertrude Himmelfarb, *One Nation, Two Cultures* (New York: Vintage, 1999), does ethics a great service as a historian and cultural critic when she points out that the theologically based Puritan founders of the United States established an order that harbored a now dominant antitheological counterculture, but that still mostly upheld the vision of a democratic civil society under law that they founded. Whether civil society can avoid chaos or tyranny without some such foundation is an open issue.

norms when they are thwarted, violated, or denied by contrary forces, or when these values demand sacrifices contrary to the ordinary interests of those who hold them. To discern what is going on at this level, ethicists become theological in the descriptive or phenomenological sense. They seek, with the more profound social analysts and historians, for example, to articulate the vision of ultimate reality thought to stand behind the ethos. That vision legitimates it and provides its compelling meaning. The theological ethicist will inquire into the explicit or implicit view of what is holy, sacred, or inviolable about values or norms in the ethos of a practice, institution, sphere of society, culture, or civilization. Only some among the many available modes of historical, social-scientific, cultural, or religious analysis are helpful at this point. Some modes comprehend more aspects of complex human actions than others; some examine the basic conceptions of ultimate reality more thoroughly; some offer a deeper portrait of the human condition. "Ethology" studies these contextual factors.

Theological ethics involves a second task, which is the assessment of whether what is going on ought to go on. Are the operating values and norms that ethology discerns valuable and normative? Are the habituated or professed virtues truly virtuous? Are the functioning principles and governing goals valid? To ask these questions is to suggest that all operating values and norms, all examples of ethos as carried by institutions, cultures, societies, or civilizations, are not equal and that it is possible, even if difficult, to recognize the difference between authentic and inauthentic meanings, values, virtues, principles, goals, and ends in organized bodies. Thus, the attempt to do theological ethics presumes that it is possible to evaluate and assess, comparatively and critically, both the values and norms of an ethos and the views of what is holy, sacred, or inviolable as these views legitimate a particular ethos, beyond the task of indicative or descriptive discernment.

The question can immediately be raised, however, as to what, or whose, standards we should use in this evaluation. Much attention has been given to this matter in both philosophy and theology.[12] Some argue that the standards derive essentially from recognizable and constant principles of right and wrong, and others argue that the standards derive from the desired, probable, or actual good or evil consequences of intended behavior, some of which are built into the human condition and some of which are peculiar to various stages of social and cultural development. To note the distinction between the right and the good, and thus wrong and evil, is to introduce one of the deepest debates in ethics. The discussion is also present in jurisprudence and public-policy debates, for it is not clear to all that universal laws or ultimate purposes make full sense in either theory or practice. Even if they do, some wonder how the first principles of right are to be related to ideal purposes in view of the historical actualities that people face daily.[13]

Philosophers over the centuries have demanded that not only theological ethicists, but that jurists and policy makers in every sphere of life be clear about how they come

12. The issue was acutely posed by Alasdair MacIntyre, especially in his *Whose Justice? Which Rationality?* (Notre Dame, Ind.: University of Notre Dame Press, 1988), whose arguments paralleled a series of attacks on, especially, Protestant forms of theological ethics and Enlightenment morality. However, the Leninist and Nietzschian roots of his views were not clear to many at first, especially to pietistic Christians who found in his work a negation of the general values of "modernity," and a rationale as to why they could assert their premodernist and highly particular subcultural values without having to make a case for them in the public domain. His views have been effectively challenged, in my view, by, among others, William Schweiker, *Power, Value, and Conviction: Theological Ethics in a Postmodern Age* (Cleveland: Pilgrim Press, 1998).

13. Interdisciplinary debates about these issues as they bear on globalization appear in D. R. Marpel and T. Nardin, eds., *International Society: Diverse Ethical Perspectives* (Princeton, N.J.: Princeton University Press, 1998); and in C. Gustafson and P. Juviler, eds., *Religion and Human Rights: Competing Claims* (New York: M. E. Sharpe, 1999).

to their definitions of what is right and wrong, good and evil. Philosophers have also noted a constant temptation to try to reduce the right to the good or the good to the right. Subdisciplines of ethics, "deontology" and "teleology," have developed in order to wrestle with these questions, and ethicists have proposed subtle combinations of "rule-teleology" and "act-deontology"; but whether the right defers to and can be governed by the good, or whether the good defers to and can be governed by the right, is seldom finally resolved.[14] The problem is that, for a complete ethic, both the right and the good must be considered, and human systems of thought as well as human judgments and actions rarely are able to combine the two perfectly or with the actual conditions of life.

In Jewish and Christian traditions, this issue can be seen in the relationship of the laws of God to the purposes of God, and in their relationship as aspects of the kingdom of God to actual living in the community of faith and in civil society. The classic biblical tradition, with parallels to Islam on this matter, says that we are to live obediently under the laws of God and to live actively in the world as agents of that God, working toward the fulfillment of God's purposes. Further, some branches of these traditions hold that all humans are able to recognize and seek the kingdom, for it is commensurate with our own deepest nature precisely because we are made in the image of God. Humans thus have some residual capacity to recognize the right and to seek the good in spite of the fact that neither we ourselves nor the conditions under which we live have kept that image undistorted. We may be neither fully

---

14. The now-classic statement of this distinction can be found in Henry Sidgwick, *The Methods of Ethics,* 1st ed. (London: Macmillan, 1874; 7th ed., 1907; reprint, Chicago: University of Chicago Press, 1962). Some of the key issues are stated in William K. Frankena, *Ethics* (Englewood Cliffs, N.J.: Prentice-Hall, 1973). Current debates on Christian views of these issues appear in *Christian Ethics: Problems and Prospects,* ed. Lisa S. Cahill and James F. Childress (Cleveland: Pilgrim Press, 1996).

right nor altogether good, for that capacity may be deeply defaced by sin, rebellion, and ignorance; but that capacity is not utterly destroyed. Since it is given by God, it cannot be destroyed by human action. Indeed, when we are drawn into a relationship with God and into the human associations that God intends for us, we find these capacities revitalized.

To be sure, those not consciously in a relationship with God are also able to recognize the differences of right and wrong because these differences are scripted into the very fabric of life. Such people know, by critical examination of their own and their society's projects, when they are seeking good rather than evil. They can approve the relative forms of righteousness and the proximate possibilities of exemplary goodness in the complexities of sociohistorical life, present in the actions of those who do not believe as well as those who do. Plato made this argument long ago, and it has been echoed subsequently in multiple forms, that possibilities for such goodness are to be honored, protected, and cultivated. But it is difficult to deny that we humans, believers or not, are forever caught up in ethical trade-offs and compromises. When we are honest, we must confess our complicity in "ambiguity" even if we are allergic to the word "sin."

Believers also hold that humans are called and enabled by God to be defenders of the right and instruments of the good, and are in principle able to do this with less distortion precisely because they know themselves to be "sinners," faulty beings who know but do not adhere to the highest standards of right or pursue the best ends. For this reason also, the second task of ethics requires a theological basis, for at certain levels of attitude and behavior, theological ethics points out, humans cannot integrate the right and good in life or in theory without God.[15] The moral confidence of every humanism

15. See, for example, Glenn Tinder, *The Political Meaning of Christianity* (Baton Rouge: Louisiana State University Press, 1990).

must be muted by realism, modesty, and contrition in view
of a holy source of morality, beyond humanity. The issue is
not whether believers are more righteous than nonbelievers, a
very difficult case to make, but whether believers have a better account of why we all are as we are in moral and spiritual
matters, and why we need not despair.[16]

The attempt to find a faith-transcending, critical, secular
base for universal human values and norms beyond religion
has been explored at various times in intellectual history —
most notably in the West among the ancient Greco-Roman
philosophers, again in the Renaissance, and once more in
the Enlightenment. Moreover, in the last several centuries the
West has become aware of very subtle religious philosophies
that have developed in other contexts, those of Hinduism,
Buddhism, and Confucianism particularly. However, it is
more clearly recognized that many of the celebrated "secular" foundations for thought about philosophy, politics,
economics, and science are less secular in their derivation
than their advocates claim.[17] Under close examination it has
become clear that "onto-theological" assumptions always
lurk beneath the surface — sometimes masking interests and
patterns of domination precisely whenever they do not, or
cannot, defend their own foundations or admit that their own
deepest presumptions are theological in nature. They often be-

---

16. In spite of some criticisms posed by contemporary feminist scholars,
this is one of the central and enduring issues posed by Reinhold Niebuhr's
The Nature and Destiny of Man, 2 vols. (New York: Charles Scribner's
Sons, 1939–41).

17. This is not the place for a full argument on this point, but key representatives of the current arguments can be cited. See, for example, in regard
to philosophy and political theory, Joshua Mitchell, *Not by Reason Alone:
Religion, History, and Identity in Early Modern Political Thought* (Chicago: University of Chicago Press, 1993); in economic and social thought,
Robert H. Nelson, *Reaching for Heaven on Earth* (Lanham, Md.: Rowman and Littlefield, 1991); in science and technology, David F. Noble, *The
Religion of Technology* (New York: Alfred Knopf, 1997).

come political crypto-theologies and ideologies, some rather
benign, many temporarily useful, a few positively vicious.
Contemporary "postmodern" thought has exposed many of
the pretensions of these efforts, even if the nihilist element in
the exposé is unable to discern the deepest values and norms,
to evaluate fairly their normative content, or to suggest how
an ethos ought to be sustained, revised, or transformed.[18] This
leads us to still another task of theological ethics.

The third task is prescriptive. It offers guidance about how
we might, insofar as it is possible, form a more valid ethos and
develop those attitudes, institutions, habits, policies, and programs that are in accord with a more ethically viable ethos,
rightly legitimated by a valid theological view of ultimate reality. The allies of theological ethics at this point are less the
social scientist or the historian, the practitioner or professional, and less the philosopher, scientist, or specialist in the
study of religions than the religious leader, the missionary,
and the reformer — the latter often including the "activists"
among those from these other fields who want to use the resources of their fields to improve the world. Theological ethics
always has a place for this prophetic, missiological, and re-
formist dimension, risky as it is. While, at its best, this third
task resists wildly utopian dreams and apocalyptic visions, it
seeks to constrain evil systems and to construct better ones;
it offers the prospects of a deeper, wider, more valid view;
it seeks to improve things for persons and societies; and it
hopes to alter the destiny of souls and civilizations by offering a vision that reaches beyond things as they are. Prophets
and reformers are the ones who help bring others to conviction about a previously unknown or disbelieved point of view,

---

18. See, for example, Mark C. Taylor, *Erring: A Postmodern A/theology*
(Chicago: University of Chicago Press, 1984); and John Milbank, *Theology
and Social Theory: Beyond Secular Reason* (Oxford: Blackwell, 1990). But
also see J. Wentzel van Huyssteen, *Essays in Postfoundationalist Theology*
(Grand Rapids, Mich.: Eerdmans, 1998).

who feel called to persuade others that a different quality of life can be organized on a more adequate moral foundation warranted by a more ultimate framework of legitimacy. These people work, most often, in and through the organizations, religious and voluntary, of civil society, building networks of conviction that, if successful, play themselves out in re-shaped spheres of life and in the establishment of new roles and identities.

It is clear that various religious leaders, missionaries, and reformers have sometimes been imperialistic, using their of-fices or credentials to impose the particularist values and norms of their own ethos on others without first engaging in the careful discernment of other people's contextual ethos or in the critical evaluation of their own. But a case might well be made that religious leaders, missionaries, and reformers have more often been governed by a religious zeal to reform things because they have a discerning ethical framework that allows them to recognize that which needs reform. A sense of holiness illuminates the depths of corruption. On this basis, they have more often sought to constrain the imperialistic im-pulses of those advocates of "self-evident" superiority than they have been a party to them. Still, it must be recognized that religion is potentially explosive. If it had no power to in-fluence life, few would care about it. Those who engage in this proactive, change-oriented task of ethics must see that what they offer is just to all, is based on the most universal realities we can know, and, so far as possible, is voluntarily accepted.

If a religious perspective is propagated without a clear sense of ethics, without a direct reference to what is universally just and to what promotes personal integrity, it is more likely to be explosive. And if it is simply imposed, it is unlikely to claim the loyalties of those it presumes to aid. People have to decide in favor of the message of the religious leader, the mission-ary, the reformer. They have to agree that what is advocated is right and good under God and fitting to the real or potentially

real contexts of life, even if discomforting. Even more, they
have to conclude, after due consideration, that the warrants
for these moral claims are comprehensible and comprehending — valid for them personally and, in some significant way,
for humanity. If the message of the religious leader, the missionary, and the reformer is not convincing, people sooner or
later will cease to attend to it, will decide against it, subvert
it at every opportunity, turn to other authorities, ideologies,
or faiths, and raise every practical and theoretical objection
they can think of.

For these reasons, too, theology is necessary to ethics, and
the third task of theological ethics must work by persuasion
or it will not work at all. Only theologies able to live by
the power of the word, by reasonable communication able to
reach across barriers of culture, civilization, and context and
to call people to conviction, will be compelling. Thus the argument in these four volumes, concluding with a systematic
treatment of "covenant," is designed to show how the etho-
logical, deontological, and teleological aspects of moral living
can become more integrated in various spheres of the common life, can open our vision to a more just global civilization,
and can call us to personal integrity. This implies that, in the
final analysis, a God-based framework for discernment, evaluation, and transformation has something indispensable to
offer if we are to comprehend the moral and spiritual vari-
ables at stake in current globalizing developments, to identify
which ones are potentially right, good, and fitting to the
human conditions, to argue critically and reasonably for them
in public discourse, and to evoke people's commitment to
them.[19]

---

19. In integrating these three tasks, theological ethics relates "common
grace" (or "natural law") to a vision of purpose in community-forming
"covenants" of conviction and to personal dedication of "vocational"
service, as will be argued extensively in vol. 4. How a theological ethic
accenting covenant and vocation can integrate reason and faith in social

Globalization and "The World"

The complexity of theological ethics, manifest in its inter-dependence with other fields and in its several tasks, is compounded when it is employed to study "globalization." The process that we call globalization seems to be creating the conditions for a new super-ethos, a worldwide set of operating values and norms that will influence most, if not all, peoples, cultures, and societies. It is quite possible that most of the contexts in which humans now live, and their roots in particular sets of values and norms, will be modified by a new comprehending context that owes its allegiance to no particular society, local ethos, or political order, even if it is advanced by "Western" influences. Many interpretations of this phenomenon, in fact, see in it the triumph of a "global capitalism" that manifests the interests of the already rich, leads to the exploitation of the less rich, pollutes the environment, commodifies every resource and relationship, creates worldwide inequality, and generates a cultural homogeneity that devastates regional diversity. If this is so, then it will be difficult for many to see in such globalization anything of theological or ethical value. Instead, people will want to resist globalism as our forebears did fascism or communism.

There is little doubt that the global dynamics defining at least our short-term future are today heavily driven by economic factors, although the data regarding the causes and consequences of these processes are less than clear. Besides, to say that the fault is "capitalism" does not tell us what is driving contemporary capitalism. Capitalism may have within it certain "natural laws," but its contemporary forms are not altogether natural or lawful. Further, it is false to say that greed is only manifest in capitalist systems or that these systems sim-

---

and personal life has been suggested in my rather long introduction to *On Moral Business,* ed. M. L. Stackhouse, with Dennis McCann, Shirley Roels, et al. (Grand Rapids, Mich.: Eerdmans, 1995), 10–36, and throughout.

ply unleash greed. Contemporary global capitalism is linked today to a number of dynamics: new forms of organization and management; new technologies; elaborate political-legal arrangements; distinct styles of family organization, education, and child rearing; and social, cultural, and religious values that have a distinctive shape. Where these dynamics are not present, capitalism, especially democratic capitalism under legal constraint, has difficulty taking root. In developing parts of the world, globalization spreads these dynamics into cultures where they did not originate, but their adoption is in substantial measure increasingly voluntary and sometimes even enthusiastic, even in the face of those who seek to mobilize resistance against these "Western" or "American" dynamics.[20]

There is a certain cogency in such perceptions, for it was in the West generally and in America particularly, deeply stamped by centuries of Christianity, that developments fomenting contemporary forms of capitalism and, thus, globalization, were nurtured. Further, it would be dishonest to deny how much the intellectual, social, cultural, economic, and politico-military trends centered in Europe and the United States influence how others live and much of what others can imagine regarding the future. People often feel swallowed or swamped by influences they did not choose. Nor should a view that takes theological ethics seriously be surprised by the sinful presence of arrogance, pretense, greed, and self-centeredness in economic affairs or historical-cultural traditions. For these reasons alone, it is urgent for public theologians based in the United States — especially for those with long sympathetic relationships or with roots in societies outside America, and who are familiar with the

---

20. See Richard J. Barnet and John Cavanagh, *Global Dreams: Imperial Corporations and the New World Order* (New York: Simon and Schuster, 1994); or David Korten, *When Corporations Rule the World* (West Hartford, Conn.: Kumarian Press, 1995).

protests against Western arrogance and concerned about the difficulties peoples face — to take up the questions around globalization. Yet it is also possible that globalization reflects a more pervasive process than some of the protests comprehend, that the moral dynamics behind it are at least more ambiguous, and sometimes better, than the critics allow, and that only a more complex frame of reference than the ones in use among those opposing globalization can deal with the many related developments.

In the first essay of this volume, we find an interpretation of the current state of research and reflection on globalization in the social sciences, especially the implications for religions and cultures. That essay, by Roland Robertson, dean of the scholars of globalization, is followed by an essay on global ethics by Yersu Kim of UNESCO. These essays offer masterful surveys of current nontheological discussions of globalization, which nevertheless are important for our project and which seek to balance both current analyses of globalization and protests against it. Other essays in this and other volumes will also indicate the ways in which the term is understood in various fields of study and from particular points of view.

It would be redundant at this point to summarize the nuanced understandings of what the term "globalization" implies for various peoples and dimensions of human thought and action. However, we can briefly identify some of the key elements in the history of the theological and ethical discussion of globalization. Much contemporary scholarly as well as popular literature refers to a "new world order," echoing a consciousness of change of ethos that parallels changes occurring earlier in the West at the time of Constantine, during the rise of the late-medieval cities, in the age of science and discovery, during the Enlightenment, and in the founding of the United States. One can also find references to the idea in Soviet and Maoist forms of Marxism-Leninism. In each of these historic moments, we find translations of the old Latin phrase: *novus ordo seclorum.* The phrase is telling, for it conveys that the world both is an arranged society with a reliable order, and consists of epochs that bring novelty. The phrase parallels nuances in a term from the Hebrew scriptures, *'ôlâm,* which understands creation as both a God-given, ordered universe and as a historical drama of God's dealings with humanity. These motifs are found also in the Greek terms κόσμος, οἰκουμένη, and αἰών found in the New Testament. They too may be translated "world," the first term with the implication of a created geographical space (cosmos), the second implying the peoples of the whole inhabited earth, and the third implying an age (aeon) subject to change. Taken together, these philosophical-theological terms articulate both a profound sense of a given order for and of life, and awareness of dynamic reconstructions of life in time. The contemporary term "globalization" combines the notions of a worldwide, ordered place of habitation subject to transformation.

Some, however, see globalization as the "end" of something which we can, or must, leave behind us. They define what is "new" in our situation by reference to the demise of something old. Some speak of "the end of Westphalia," by which is meant the end of the sovereignty of the nation-state, in which an established religion served to provide spiritual warrants for a common identity.[21] Others speak of "the end of modernity," referring to the demise of philosophical efforts to establish a secular, cosmopolitan mode of reason by which the laws of the universe and society could be understood.[22] And when still others speak of "the end of history," they mean the collapse of the attempt to see all life, thought, and social development as stages leading to a socialized fulfillment and

---

21. Jean Bethke Elshtain, "International Politics and Political Theory," in *International Relations Theory Today,* ed. Ken Booth and Steve Smith (University Park: Penn State University Press, 1995), 263–78.

22. Stephen Toulmin, *Cosmopolis: The Hidden Agenda of Modernity* (Glencoe, Ill.: Free Press, 1990).

liberation.[23] Given the power of technology and the awareness of ecological danger, some speak more pessimistically of "the end of nature."[24]

Others have their own sense of what order and time we are following, and use the term "postmodern" in various ways — as can be seen, for example, in the arts. Each of these descriptions of "ends" brought claims that the older connections of the common life and theological ethics, of authority and creed, of faith and policy, of metaphysical assumption and social order, are past and, often, should be left behind.

Certainly the Roman church had asserted its "catholicity" while world exploration and trade had been accelerating for centuries. Still, a cumulative shift has taken place. The twentieth century not only saw world wars, hot and cold, for the first time in human history, but also began to think about the possibility of a "world civilization." To be sure, scholars for centuries had debated the merits of cultures and societies other than their own, but only in the last century has the world seen the development of new international institutions, of which the World Missionary Congress (1910) and later the League of Nations (1928) stand as emblems. Such efforts were reinforced by the publication of the *New Schaff-Herzog Encyclopedia of Religious Knowledge* (1908), the *Hasting's Encyclopedia of Religion and Ethics* (1910), and the *Encyclopaedia Britannica* (1912 ed.), which provided information about the world's religions and cultures that during previous centuries was available only in selected circles. The optimism surrounding these projects was soon to be shaken by militant

---

23. This of course refers to the much debated thesis of Francis Fukuyama, *The End of History and the Last Man* (New York: Free Press, 1992), which challenges not only the views of Hegel and Marx, but Nietzsche, all of whom denied the truth of anything nonhistorical.

24. Bill McKibben, *The End of Nature*, 10th anniversary ed. (New York: Anchor Books, 1999), fears a future in which human life is abstracted from and transforming of the "natural" order, no longer structured by or attuned to its pre-given patterns and dynamics.

efforts to establish new imperial social orders on nationalist pagan or secular materialist grounds — one by the proponents of a new *Reich*, another by a new *Soviet*, both with parallels in East Asia, South Africa, and Latin America. But a corner had been turned; these efforts not only failed, they were defeated by developing international, cross-cultural dynamics.[25]

Efforts to cope with newer transnational realities have continued and expanded. It is obvious in law, in the World Court, War Crimes Tribunal, and in remarkably similar constitutions among some 160 nations; in politics, in the United Nations and regional bodies such as the European Union, NATO, Organization of American States, and the Southeast Asia Treaty Organization; in economics, in the World Bank, International Monetary Fund, World Trade Organization, International Labor Organization, and the Group of Eight; and in most professional groups, in medicine, law, engineering, and education, and so on, which all have international associations. Further, practical efforts to control social or natural evils — human rights advocacy, disaster relief, crime and terrorism control, and disease and epidemic containment, for example — reflect a degree of practical transnational moral cooperation not known in previous epochs. Simultaneously, it is difficult to avoid the impact of the expanding networks of communication. Every part of the world is, in principle, now accessible to every other part. Such developments raise an acute question: how are we to understand, respond to, and perhaps guide these developments religiously, theologically, ethically?

---

25. A particularly interesting treatment of how and why these revolutions failed appears in François Furet, *The Passing of an Illusion: The Idea of Communism in the Twentieth Century*, trans. D. Furet (Chicago: University of Chicago Press, 1999). Furet not only suggests a deep affinity between fascism and communism, but also hints that, with these defeats, the historic movements begun by the French Revolution have come to an end.

Theological Views of Globalization

Never before in human history has a civilization been formed and sustained without a religious core. It is doubtful that it can happen now. Efforts to impose a religion by force have been frequent; those who have power know that unless they also gain moral and spiritual legitimacy they will not long have power. Usually, however, a religion is established gradually in the midst of contentious disagreements and divergent schools of thought, each of which claims to foster the transcendent, holy standards on which to ground an ethos and to assess, reform, or revitalize the society should it grow morally and spiritually empty or corrupt. Religions endure by their capacity to provide ultimate meaning and to supply the bases for both personal commitment and social cohesion. A compelling mythology or theology on one side, and a compelling ethic on the other, are fateful for civilizations.

One of the greatest debates of the last century was just on this point, with Marxists, Social Darwinists, secular liberals, and their heirs on one side, and Weberians, social-gospel advocates, Christian realists, and their allies from other religions on the other side. This debate concerned whether an antimythological, antitheological view of life allows us to explain and finally to dispense with religion, or whether religion is necessary to interpret and guide civilization. Since theology and theological ethics are the only disciplines that study religious phenomena, it is critical whether these disciplines are held to be indispensable or not. A critical, related question is whether the resources of civilization now being generated worldwide will be different from all of human history in that the emerging society will not have, or need, a religious core or a theological ethic to interpret, to repeatedly assess, and to guide it. If such a core is needed, what might it be? Several highly regarded scholars have made suggestive first steps toward a theological ethic as it bears on this situation.

Olav G. Myklebust suggests that contemporary concerns for globalization grew out of missiological concerns that developed in the fifteenth century and that intensified dramatically throughout the nineteenth century, with increasing accent on social and ethical matters. The cultural expansion of European influence around the world was fueled, at least in part, by Western Christianity well into the early twentieth century, until many of these efforts were shattered by that century's world wars — notable globalizing forces themselves, although working decidedly against that cultural expansion.[26] Even then, several major theologians addressed the question of how the world could be reconstructed beyond the conflict, and what Christianity could contribute. The Swiss theologian Emil Brunner took up these questions directly.[27] The American theological ethicist Reinhold Niebuhr turned his "Christian realism" in constructive new directions after having mobilized Christians to resist fascism and defend democracy.[28] The Dutch radical theologian Arend Van Leeuwen was one of the first to raise the issues of global processes during the Cold War, and added a major interpretation of how Christianity and its sociohistorical derivatives — democracy, technology, capitalism, and secularization — would

---

26. O. G. Myklebust, *The Study of Missions in Theological Education,* 2 vols. (Oslo: Egede Instituttet, 1955, 1957). No subsequent work has quite matched this history, although it is essentially Protestant in focus.

27. His cross-cultural engagement with social issues and concern for the theological "foundations of civilization," so sharply criticized by Karl Barth, served him well in stating what is required theologically and ethically to reconstruct societies in light of conflict and confessional particularity. See especially his *Christianity and Civilization,* 2 vols. (New York: Charles Scribner's Sons, 1948).

28. See especially his *Structure of Nations and Empires* (New York: Charles Scribner's Sons, 1959). See also Robin Lovin, *Reinhold Niebuhr and Christian Realism* (New York: Cambridge University Press, 1995), and Heather A. Warren, *Theologians of a New World Order: Reinhold Niebuhr and the Christian Realists, 1920–1948* (New York: Oxford University Press, 1997).

likely transform non-Western civilizations and aid in the formation of "a planetary world."[29] In Catholic circles, Pope
John XXIII extended the tradition of the "social encyclicals"
when he not only called a council, Vatican II, but published
Pacem in Terris.[30] Pope Paul VI extended his contributions in
Populorum Progressio and in his address to the United Nations on October 4, 1965.[31] Some themes now seem to have
been modified, but they opened contemporary Catholicism to
renewed social and political influence that can be seen in both
liberation theology in Latin America and in the enormous influence of Pope John Paul II on the extension of human rights
and democracy in Eastern Europe.[32] Also significant is the
work of the "independent" Catholic, Hans Küng. His dia- ✓
logical interaction with the world's religions on questions of
social and ethical life,[33] and his more recent efforts to develop a global ethic, have informed this effort and public
policy.[34] Protestant church leaders, also in dialogue with per-

29. Arend Th. Van Leeuwen, *Christianity in World History: The Meeting
of the Faiths of East and West*, trans. H. H. Hoskins (New York: Charles
Scribner's Sons, 1964). His work partially reflects the rising neo-Marxist
sensibilities of the 1960s, but his accent on the probable continuing influence of the West on other cultures also grated on anticolonialist sentiments
of the period.

30. See D. J. O'Brien and T. A. Shannon, *Renewing the Earth: Catholic Documents on Peace, Justice, and Liberation* (New York: Doubleday,
1997), especially pt. 1.

31. Ibid.

32. In Y. J. Kim, ed., *An Emerging Theology in World Perspective* (Mystic, Conn.: Twenty-third Publications, 1988), we can see how widely these
ideas spread; and in G. Weigel and R. Royal, eds., *A Century of Catholic Social Thought: Essays on "Rerum Novarum" and Nine Other Key
Documents* (Washington, D.C.: Ethics and Public Policy Center, 1991), we
can see the attempt to reclaim the Catholic tradition from the liberationist
views. See also the subsequent encyclical by John Paul II, *Veritatis Splendor,
Origins* 23 (October 1993).

33. Especially his *Christianity and the World Religions: Paths to Dialogue with Islam, Hinduism, and Buddhism* (New York: Doubleday,
1986).

34. H. Küng, *Global Responsibility: In Search of a New World Ethic*

sons of other faiths, met in a number of settings to chart out new directions,[35] while individual thinkers, such as Wilfred Cantwell Smith of the World Religions Center at Harvard, and Tissa Balasuriya of the Centre for Society and Religion in Sri Lanka, wrote pioneering volumes.[36] Still, the area is not fully developed, and the Vatican, the World Council of Churches, and the International Association of Evangelicals, among Christian bodies, as well as the interfaith Parliament of Religions, have put the issues of globalization at the center of their agendas — an agenda that remains unfinished.

One of the most sustained theological discussions of the issues is found in the Association of Theological Schools (ATS), the nondenominational accrediting agency for graduate institutions offering theological degrees in the United States and Canada, which works cooperatively with its international correlate, the World Conference of Associations of Theological Institutions (WOCATI). The ATS has made globalization a priority for almost two decades. Not only have several faculties taken up the matter as a common issue, some have engaged in international excursions and explorations to allow the common encounter with cultures and societies beyond their own. The leadership of Donald Shriver, Jr., William Lesher, and a dozen or so others has kept the matter vibrant,

---

(New York: Crossroad, 1991); H. Küng and H.-J. Kuschel, *A Global Ethic: The Declaration of the Parliament of the World Religions* (London: SCM Press, 1993); H. Küng, *A Global Ethic for Global Politics and Economics* (New York: Oxford University Press, 1998).

35. See Diane Kessler, ed., *Documents from the WCC Eighth Assembly in Harare (December 3–14, 1998)*, especially doc. no. PG1 (forthcoming). For longer traditions on these issues, see Paul Bock, *In Search of a Responsible World Society: The Social Teachings of the World Council of Churches* (Philadelphia: Westminster Press, 1974); and Homer A. Jack, *Religion in the Struggle for World Community* (New York: World Conference on Religion and Peace, 1980).

36. W. C. Smith, *Towards a World Theology: Faith and the Comparative History of Religion* (Maryknoll, N.Y.: Orbis Books, 1981); T. Balasuriya, *Planetary Theology* (Maryknoll, N.Y.: Orbis Books, 1984).

with many adopting the strategies of response summarized by Don Browning: ecumenical cooperation, missionary activity, interfaith dialogue, and service in the struggles for justice and development. More recently, some have taken the debates as an opportunity to accent a concern for "multiculturalism." While several turn to globalization to relativize trends in theology and ethics that they view as narrow and dogmatic, others are especially eager to be sure that minority voices have a place in the larger discussion.[37]

A few scholars, most notably Father Robert Schreiter, have used both social-scientific and theological resources to argue that globalization can best be understood as a transformation like the rise of the ancient dynasties; like the formation of feudalism and the subsequent creation of the modern nation-states, with their rational bureaucracies and scientific-technological attempts to manage the common life; or like the more recent liberation of many peoples from colonialism based on features of "modernity." Globalization in this view is the shift that makes the world an extraordinarily complex yet singular place and that invites a "new catholicity."[38]

The actual consequences of these efforts, however, is difficult to measure. In a report presented to the Globalization Task Force in October 1999, Judith Berling, the project director, reported on the relative success of the member schools in implementing programs related to globalization. A very high percentage (90 percent) of faculty, students, and admin-

---

37. See *Theological Education* 35 (spring 1999), which contains an assessment of the present state of the dialogue, and representative writings by each of the authors. See also Alice F. Evans, R. A. Evans, and D. A. Roozen, eds., *The Globalization of Theological Education* (Maryknoll, N.Y.: Orbis Books, 1993), for a spectrum of views as an accent on globalization was developing.

38. R. Schreiter, *The New Catholicity: Globalization and Contextuality* (Maryknoll, N.Y.: Orbis Books, 1996). See also his earlier *Constructing Local Theologies* (Maryknoll, N.Y.: Orbis Books, 1985), and *Reconciliation* (Maryknoll, N.Y.: Orbis Books, 1992).

istrators affirmed in interviews that their institutions were involved in a world church community, but that the training of students in global issues was only "somewhat evident." The most striking finding for purposes of our project, however, was the response — the most negative in the study — to whether "students (are being) educated in the economic/social factors of ministry in a globalized world." This finding was reinforced by the fact that, when asked to rank thirteen realities of globalization, respondents listed the "expansion of Western culture throughout the globe" last. Berling speculates whether "ATS schools distance themselves from the Western capitalistic juggernaut sometimes identified with globalization (as in the charge from some . . . that globalization is just another form of Westernization)."[39] She is surely correct, and the result likely reveals both an unwillingness of much Christian leadership to take responsibility for aspects of social life which the tradition has helped generate and sustain, and a profound uncertainty as to how, theologically and ethically, the current social and economic dynamics should be understood and guided. Indeed, some forms of theology and ethics flee such questions or blind students to them, just as some forms of social and economic analysis ignore the role of religion and morality in what they study.

This set of volumes intends to extend and refine the projects that others have begun, and in some measure to correct any distortions. The volumes do so by drawing out the implications of a neglected set of motifs deeply rooted in religious history generally and specifically in the Christian tradition, and by relating them to the social, economic, and cultural realities that must be confronted. Already reference has been made to the multidimensionality of globalization, of the many

---

39. Judith Berling, "Our Words Are Beginning to Make It So: ATS Schools on Cross-cultural Relationships and Globalization," photocopied report discussed October 23, 1999, especially p. 11.

forces bringing it about, and of the spheres of life influenced by it. One of the distinctive contributions of these volumes is the attempt to identify the "Powers" that animate the social, cultural, and material forces moving toward a global ethos. This series draws on several closely related but recently neglected motifs in religious life to define the organizing principles for our interpretations, evaluations, and constructive proposals regarding globalization and its emerging ethos. The identification of the moral and spiritual powers and the examination of the sociohistorical embodiments by which they are organized and channeled — the "Spheres" — determined how these studies were selected and presented. Theological-ethical concepts of "covenant" and "calling" are, as will be argued, decisive for how the powers may be ordered and guided into life-enhancing spheres.

The Powers and Spheres in Globalization

The Powers

While it is properly impossible for many to believe in nonsubstantial persons in the form of angels or demons, spirits or devils — flitting around and making things happen in life — it is equally impossible to deny that moral and spiritual forces influence life for better or for worse. The reality of such "spiritual energies" is no less true for contemporary humanity than it was for peoples living in ancient "animistic," "polytheist," or "mystical" cultures, although the ways in which we think about these energies, perhaps even encounter them, have surely changed.

The analysis of such forces has been taken up in the last century by a number of socially engaged theological ethicists, sometimes because they were dissatisfied with the reductionist and materialist, nonspiritual, and amoral views of "forces" in the common life developed by postreligious and antitheological social and historical thinkers. Sometimes the reason was that sectarian readings of Christian scriptures drove some to think that all of modern culture was possessed by evil powers that had to be avoided. Many were also dissatisfied with forms of privatized piety that became so preoccupied with subjectivist forms of spirituality that they were blind to social problems.[40] Against these tendencies, the analysis of spiritual powers has generally gone in three directions: toward a reinvestigation of what ancient texts which refer to these issues must have meant; toward an analysis of psycho-spiritual and socio-moral potentialities that claim people's loyalties and respect in various societies; and toward a fresh interpretation of dimensions of life obscured by contemporary theory, including religion itself. These efforts have been reinforced by the fact that world religions are in resurgence.[41]

In Walter Wink's award-winning trilogy on the powers, we find an artful summary of the last century of historical scholarship on these issues.[42] Many of his findings are largely confirmed by more recent surveys in historical and linguistic

40. I refer, of course, to the traditions of post-Pietistic and post-dogmatic as well as post-Marxist scholarship developed since Max Weber and Ernst Troeltsch. The neo-Marxist view was reasserted not only by populist movements of de-colonialization after World War II, but in magisterial fashion by the annals school led by Fernand Braudel, *Civilization and Capitalism*, 3 vols. (New York: Harper and Row, 1982–84), and still championed by Immanuel Wallerstein. In some ways, we intend to refine the traditions from Weber and Troeltsch, as developed by Talcott Parsons, Robert Bellah, Peter Berger, and more theologically rooted authors represented here.

41. For divergent views of how to view this resurgence, but with agreement that we are in the midst of one, see, e.g., Peter Beyer, *Religion and Globalization* (London: Sage, 1994); John Witte, Jr., ed., *Christianity and Democracy in Global Context* (San Francisco: Westview, 1993); Samuel P. Huntington, *The Clash of Civilizations and the Remaking of World Order* (New York: Simon and Schuster, 1996); and Don A. Pittman et al. *Ministry and Theology in Global Perspective* (Grand Rapids, Mich.: Eerdmans, 1996).

42. W. Wink, *Naming the Powers: The Language of Power in the New Testament; Unmasking the Powers: The Invisible Forces That Determine Human Existence;* and *Engaging the Powers: Discernment and Resistance in a World of Domination* (Philadelphia: Fortress Press, 1984, 1986, 1992).

scholarship, now made easier because of computers' capacity to correlate and contrast key terms — where they are used and with what frequency.[43] Wink announces early that he had to abandon his initial, naive assurance that the terms for the "powers" in the New Testament could be "rendered without remainder into the categories of modern sociology, depth psychology, and general systems theory."[44] While some knowledge in these areas proved useful, and while these sciences point to realities that others ignore, the more important finding is that there is an inner and an outer dimension to any human organization. Many such analogies have been attempted, although each only points in the general direction of what Wink is trying to convey. Somewhat like the relationships of mind and brain, of emotion and chemistry, of electrical current and machine, or of "software" and "hardware," every "power," Wink argues, "tends to have a visible pole, an outer form — be it a church, a nation, or an economy — and an invisible pole, an inner spirit or driving energy that animates physical manifestations in the world. Neither pole is the cause of the other. Both come into existence together and cease to exist together...." He says that "the Powers generally are only encountered as corporealized in some form...." Still, "the implications of this view for healing the split between one-sided materialism and one-sided spiritualism are...extremely far-reaching."[45]

The idea of "moral or spiritual energies" has become obsolete in many learned circles, especially in view of theories of mechanical and organic causation that dominated much

---

It is not necessary to agree with his analysis of contemporary society to recognize the importance of his historical work.

43. See the extensive entries on each of the key terms in K. van der Toorn et al., eds., *Dictionary of Deities and Demons*, 2d ed. (Leiden: Brill; Grand Rapids, Mich.: Eerdmans, 1999).

44. Wink, *Naming the Powers*, 3.

45. Ibid., 5.

thought in the last couple of centuries. Still, attempts to identify and name forces that give spiritual impetus to primary
human activities have not ceased. No serious philosopher
or theologian believes that angels, ghosts, or devils lurk as
powerful personal presences behind every important psychic
or social dynamic. But that some understandings of these
metaphysical substances bring acute conceptual difficulties
cannot obscure the parallel fact that the meaning and character of pervasive and formative dynamics cannot be exhausted
by material and biological understandings. No one knows for
certain what percentage of life can be explained by mechanical and organic factors. Strong arguments can be made that
the percentage is high, and these arguments show themselves
in the enormous interest in "power analysis." But what makes
life interesting is the intellectual and convictional structures
that interact with these mechanical and organic factors, that
transcend them in distinctive ways, that give them an ethical orientation, that alter them by intentionally intervening in
their ordinary patterns, and that see in them possibilities that
these factors themselves do not naturally contain or generate.
The transcendence that allows humans to analyze the material and organic factors and their causation, the intentions
that reach beyond what is, to imagine what might be, and
the meanings or relationships to which people dedicate their
lives, suggest that "moral and spiritual energies" are more
than myth and are critical to personal and social life.

How shall we identify these "spiritual energies," and how
shall we study them? We have no interest in the "paranor-
mal" studies that some undertake. What can be found in the
dynamics and patterns of life, often most visible in the midst
of social change,[46] is more interesting. The varying organiza-

---

46. A remarkable example is Amy L. Sherman's study of economic transformation in Guatemala, *The Soul of Development* (New York: Oxford
University Press, 1997).

tion of these volumes suggests several approaches for studying them. In the first volume, we draw on mythic terms from a variety of cultural-linguistic traditions, but which are used in Western traditions to identify indispensable life-giving potentialities that, at the same time, are necessary for any human society to flourish and subject to serious distortion. These terms point to mundane and necessary realities that are also mixed with "moral and spiritual energies" — dynamic forces that invite, or even capture, people's loyalties and that shape both habituated folkways and formal institutions, and thus the ethos of every society.

The idea of "spiritual and moral energies" can be found in all world religions. Certainly, there are many terms for the powers in world religions as well as in specifically Christian sources. The Greek term for the powers, ἐξουσία (*exousia*), appears in the New Testament, for instance, more than one hundred times, and is often linked with official leaders, but more often with the symbolic power of the offices and roles they play in the common life — that is, with principalities, authorities, or dominions. Each of them manifests a distinctive "dynamic" energy, or δύναμις. What is distinctly theological about these offices is that they can become corrupted or distorted when they become preoccupied with their own value and declare independence from any transcendent source or norm. They then become threats instead of blessings to life and can only be restored to right order and good purpose by being re-related to their source in ways that reconstitute their norms.[47]

Christians believe that Christ redemptively reestablishes a relationship between God and the world, which is alienated from its source and norms. This relationship not only includes people, but also these powers. Other religious traditions, which will also be taken up in this series, especially

---

47. See Wink, especially *Engaging the Powers*.

in volumes 3 and 4, have alternative accounts of the nature, character, origins, destiny and possible treatment of the spiritual, social, and psychological powers that shape institutions and that constitute an ethos. What we can learn about these powers from other traditions and whether a biblical view, particularly a Christian theological-ethical interpretation of the powers, can aid other religious traditions are questions to be examined in these studies and, hypothetically at least, answered in the affirmative. This is because we suspect profound connections between globalization, seen as a dramatic historical process gaining ground in our time, and the more enduring meanings of the "world." As understood in Christian theological ethics, the world is, in substantial measure, ruled by powers that shape its ethos. That world cannot be avoided analytically, existentially, or ethically. We can identify the clusters of the most potent "powers" shaping globalization. We call them the *principalities, authorities,* and *dominions.*[48] By referring to them, we can identify the moral and spiritual dimensions of the common life that constitute key aspects of globalization. The first three volumes will be organized around these powers, each one of which establishes a distinct sphere — a cluster of practices and institutions that operate to keep these powers functional, ordered, and effective. Each power has also developed, in modernity, a "discipline" by which it is studied, cultivated, and extended.

The Principalities

The most basic and pervasive powers are the *archai* — the principalities (from the Greek: ἀρχαι; Latin: *principia*) —

---

48. In volume 2 we shall also make reference to the emerging "regencies" of late modernity, a translation of the biblical term for "thrones" (from the Greek: θρονος, Latin: *cathedra*), the seats of power or socially constructed support systems from which power is exercised in the various spheres of life by those principalities, authorities, and dominions who claim, or are given, moral and spiritual legitimacy. They are not themselves primary Powers, but are derivative loci in which the Powers exercise their influence.

which refer not only to basic energies that give impetus to some aspect of reality, but to the organizing principle of a process. The most important principalities in regard to globalization can be identified as Mammon (Aramaic), Mars (Latin), Eros (Greek), and the Muses (Indo-Aryan). Inevitably, these principalities will be shaped by an understanding of that which brought them into existence and to which they are in some sense accountable. In Semitic and other theistic traditions this is usually identified as the Creator God (Hebrew: *'ēl bōrē'*, translated into derivatives of the Old Romantic *creier* = one who fashions, engenders, or forms, plus the Old Teutonic **guðo* = what is invoked as pervasively present and powerful). Sometimes a society is thought to be created by primeval beasts or entirely by human agency, but these ideas soon assume divinelike characteristics in myth, ritual, and cult.

The point is that every society has and needs to have these powers, and to have them organized into:

1. A viable economy in order to provide the food, shelter, clothing, and opportunity for work and property for people to survive. Today, this sphere is most extensively studied by economics.

2. A system of gaining, legitimating, and using coercive authority to control violence from within and beyond a society, and to foster common well-being. This sphere is studied by political science.

3. An ordered way of dealing with human sexuality, interpersonal relationships, and the demands of nurture, development, and emotional fulfillment. These issues are studied primarily by psychology.

4. A means for communicating information, thought, feeling, aesthetic awareness, and conviction. Today, various cultural-linguistic studies dominate the study of the fine arts and the mass media.

5. An identifying center of being, meaning, and morality that bonds people and the powers together in a shared system.

It has become conventional to call human efforts to identify and represent such power "religion" or "the religions," but the terms are general and disputed, as we shall see especially in volume 3.[49] The terms are most frequently used in these volumes in this way: "religion" is one of the indispensable features of the common life; "religions" are the attempts to identify and cultivate life in response to the finding and commissioning Creative Power, variously conveyed and understood through symbols of transcendence, by which life, meaning, and morality are ultimately sustained; and "theological ethics" is an indispensable discipline by which a critical, publicly accessible discussion about the normative importance of key interpretations of the Creative Power can take place. This basic power, which may also appear in the garb of a principality, gives impetus to the religious aspect of reality that we call "Religion," in distinction from "religion," as a manifest historical reality in much of human life and to "religions" as separate strands in that history.

Today we also face a sharp disagreement as to what disciplines should study these matters and where such study belongs in human understanding. We shall try to keep theological ethics open to the interdisciplinary study of religion and religions, seeking to find out whether or in what ways nontheistic as well as theistic traditions may point to ultimate reality and enable humans to define basic priorities in personal and social life.

---

49. The roots of the terms the term "religion" are disputed: it is not known whether the Latin comes from *ligo* = to bind or bond together, or from *lego* = to commission or bequeath as a legacy, as in a will or testament. Some scholars, however, see the root as *lig*, meaning to pay attention, to give care, and appearing in the negative as *nec-legere*, to neglect.

Those who write social history or the history of religions, and those who focus on how societies and cultures work in a more analytical, structural, or functional way, especially in the twin disciplines of sociology and anthropology, give helpful perspectives on how things work in a society, as the sociologists say, or a culture, as the anthropologists say. They all, at the deepest levels, will identify religion as the bonding activity that both holds civilizations together and that commissions people to transcend mere interests, although differing views of what should hold civilization together means that religions can also be divisive. Today the study of these questions is governed by the highly pluralistic and decidedly nontheological disciplines of "religious studies," but these can be seen as complementary, not contrary to what is presumed here.

The Spheres

We call these particular powers "principalities" because no civilization exists without their viable integration. To use, guide, contain, and regulate these principal powers — Mammon, Mars, Eros, the Muses, and Religion — people carve out "spheres" of social activity, clusters of institutions that house, guide, constrain, and, in certain ways, permit, even encourage, these powers to operate. Each sphere is regulated by customary or legislated rules, and each is defined by its own specification of ends and means, as these accord with the nature of the activity and its place in the whole society or culture. Each sphere develops methods of fulfilling its own standards, ways to mark accomplished goals, definitions of excellence, and standards for success. Each sphere may involve a host of organizations and practices — in economic life, for example, these practices range from the village market, to the partnership, to the family firm, to state-run factories, to the giant corporation, to the international financial market.

Such levels of complexity exist for all the spheres, meaning

that while each "power" has a "sphere" in which it is pre-
dominant, it is very difficult to make each sphere a closed
system. Only totalitarian societies try; after a while, they
always fail. The dynamic in each sphere means that parts
of the system can draw resources from beyond themselves
and influence the environment. No sphere supplies all that
it needs within itself, although some hearth societies, political regimes, and religious communities have attempted to be
self-sufficient. Over time, however, encounter and exchange
result. Each sphere must draw from what is around it; the per-
meability of each sphere means that each is always influenced
by powers beyond itself. Economic life, to pursue the example above, is shaped not only by government and technology,
but by the fact that people fall in love at the factory or office,
which alters work habits, and sometimes leads to marriage
and families, which further alters both earning and spend-
ing patterns. Similarly, an erotic attraction is not only shaped
by psychodynamics and familial history but by the economic
(and cultural and political and religious) factors in the social
context in which it takes place. If any one of these spheres
begins to be dominated by an external power, distortion is
inevitable.

Thus, each sphere will have its own functional requirements, which can be recognized cross-culturally and cross-
historically, and will inevitably take on distinctive institutional forms. But spheres do so variously from society to
society according to the relative influence of other powers
and spheres and the dominant values and norms present in the
wider ethos. The result is a blend of the functionally necessary,
the socially constructed, and the morally and spiritually legit-
imized, with Religion guiding the latter in all spheres. Indeed,
central to the contribution of this set of volumes is that "Religion" is one of these indispensable and relatively independent
spheres, central to all serious social theory and particularly
important in a globalizing era. Religion points at its best to

that which holds the whole together; it is decisive for shaping the ethos by which the spheres of society may cohere with one another and become coherent internally, both morally and spiritually. The particular powers and spheres that we call the "principalities" interact to form the basis of society. Each has its own constituency, yet each must serve the public or the others will not lend support. To be sure, the disciplines that study these powers and spheres are methodologically reductionistic in their attempt to explain as much of social reality as possible solely within their own terms. Psychological, economic, or cultural interpretations are, for example, offered as the "explaining" forces shaping, say, politics or religion. But they cannot do so fully.[50]

At the same time, each sphere has its own temptation to moral or spiritual disintegration, not only functional distortion. No civilization can flourish without an ordered way to produce and distribute wealth, but all the great religions recognize that individuals and groups always face a temptation to put their ultimate trust in material possessions. Money may not be the root of all evil; its absence under contemporary conditions may either be the cause or the effect of evil. But the love of money translates legitimate claims on goods and services into both the idolatry of Mammon and the exploitation of the neighbor, as William Schweiker argues in chapter 3 of this volume. He writes of the formation of the modern corporation, which has given Mammon a new home, and the expansion of the market, which has given it a wider field in which to play, as marks of globalization, and recognizes their

---

50. Previous studies pressed in this direction. See my *Creeds, Society, and Human Rights* (Grand Rapids, Mich.: Eerdmans, 1985) for a view of the "spheres." Relating "powers" to the spheres in global terms is a recent development. See also my articles, "The Vocation of Christian Ethics Today," *The Princeton Theological Seminary Bulletin*, n.s., 16, no. 3 (1995): 284–312; and "Theology and the Economic Life of Society in a Global Era . . . ," in *Policy Reform and Moral Grounding*, ed. T. W. Boxx (Latrobe, Pa.: Center for Economic and Policy Education, 1996), 47–68.

potential contributions. But he argues that, thus far, these
developments have also encouraged the commodification of
goods that ought not be bought and sold. The buying and
selling of sex or of marriage partners, of votes or political
authority, and of access to educational, legal, medical, or religious services distort the common life, blur value boundaries
between specific spheres, and denigrate principles of right and
good that make for covenantal life. Such activities are enormous temptations in an era in which geo-economics seems to
have superseded geopolitics.

Similarly, no society fails to designate a police or military
force as bearers of arms for enforcing ordinary justice and
keeping the peace. But every society, and many persons within
the society, are also tempted to place their confidence in military prowess, conquest, and command. Mars threatens every
powerful political system both as idol and as ungovernable
violence. Donald Shriver, Jr., who has thought deeply and
written widely about the violence of the century just past,
points in chapter 4 to key theological, ethical, and social developments that could reduce the bloodletting in the global
era to come.

Moreover, all societies have some means for guiding sexual
desires and confining sexual behaviors. Institutions and moral
boundaries reward or punish behaviors and press people toward particular forms of intimate relations between men and
women and between parents and children. Indeed, fertility or
the celebration of sexual ecstasy on the one hand, or celibacy
and the disapproval of sexuality on the other, have become
cultic in various cultures and subcultures. Ironically, both un-
channeled or hypercontrolled Eros destroy generations. The
lack of justice in male-female relationships has brought about
a worldwide feminist movement that is examined by Mary
Stewart Van Leeuwen, one of the world's premier Christian
feminists, in chapter 5.

In addition, no society can flourish without poetry and

song, painting and sculpture, dance and drama. At the very least, language, sign, and symbol are necessary. But both art and culture suffer when tempted to worship creativity or the artifacts created. The Muses can become empty and vain, conveying little more than self-celebration. In our time, the mass media have heightened the influence of the Muses. Mass media are creating a worldwide net of unceasing image and sound and a public more vast than previously imagined — beyond boundaries of polity, culture, or established society. In the process, media are also multiplying voices, perspectives, and competing interpretations and narratives, reinforcing a fragmentation of meaning and the displacement of traditional, unifying narratives by thinner, flatter, more obviously virtual images or fragments of images. This new public is theologically and philosophically examined, in chapter 6, by David Tracy, one of the key scholars in recent "public theology."

I have argued that no sphere has been able to order any of these principalities, and no civilization has been able to hold the spheres together without a more or less shared religious awareness that offers guidance throughout the sociocultural ethos. While, in one sense, Religion is but one of the principal powers, with its own moral and spiritual energy, it is also a sphere that points to that ultimate creative power that encompasses and that is in some sense present in every sphere. Christian theology recognizes this truth when it speaks of the Creator God as "Father" and believers as "brothers and sisters," or when it refers to that God as "King of Kings and Lord of Lords," as Provider of bounty in the harvest, as inspirer of song and poetry. This moral and spiritual energy can become the source of horrendous idolatry and domination. Other principalities may recognize the power of Religion and attempt to coopt it to sanctify their own ends. That religion has been used as a weapon in political and family life, or for commercial or artistic ends, is well-known. Further, the

norms and values in a particular religion may encourage or
inhibit temptations to attach itself to Mammon, Mars, Eros,
or the Muses, or to manipulate them for the benefit of specific religious groups. All of our authors are alert to these
dangers; yet all see in one or another aspect of "public theology" something necessary for the ethical formation of the
global society. However, the sphere of Religion will not be
treated distinctly in this volume. Rather, its pervasiveness appears in religious references and theological terms in essays in
this and the next volume. Focused treatment of Religion and
religions will wait until volume 3.

The necessity of these five prerequisites of human society,
and the capacity of any one both to become distorted and to
claim total human loyalty, invites us to use symbolic terms
in referring to them as "moral and spiritual powers." These
powers point to "spiritual energies" that not only appear in
every known society, but are part of what it means to be
human. These powers everywhere bear values and are valued
in themselves, or are seen to be the source of value contami-
nation. We humans are, primally, economic, political, sexual,
cultural, and religious creatures, constantly needing to integrate our lives in, through, by means of, and in terms of
the necessities of wealth, power, potency, creativity, and piety
that are part of our inner possibilities and part of the fabric of every viable society. People live amid multiple forms
of intelligence, in several realms of potential justice. Every
society needs spheres that cohere and sustain meaning and
value. These principalities combine and recombine in our
loyalties, our behaviors, and our social environments, relating the spheres in which values and norms dominate, in
ever-changing ways.

Volume 1 treats these principalities in the context of the
emerging global civilization, and not only in terms of archaic
and pervasive spiritual energies or the modern social sciences,
but also in terms of basic theological and ethical questions as

they relate to our globalizing world. Are these principalities built into the structure of creation and thus part of the intent of the Creator? Are they given by God? If so, are they operating in accord with the divine intent, in recognition of the reality and depths of brokenness that attends existence? Or are the principalities so disordered or distorting that we must abandon them, or suffer their slow destruction with resistance and passive regret? Can they be redeemed or must they be avoided? Above all, how can, how ought, such issues be discussed in public discourse? As we shall see, these questions pertain to all the powers considered, including the "authorities" and "dominions" to which I now turn briefly, to preview subsequent volumes.

The Authorities

I have suggested that the principalities are decisive for every society and that at least five spheres are present. They are therefore important for analysis of the global situation, but they are not the only powers. Complex civilizations, ancient and modern, developed additional, highly refined spheres beyond these principalities. These additional spheres of spiritual and moral energy have gained increasing authority as increasingly complex societies have gained influence. They have, in the view of many, substantially displaced Religion as the central moral-spiritual force that guides, integrates, and regulates society. For some, these authorities have either relegated Religion to the optional inner convictions of individuals, or displaced Religion even there.[51]

---

51. A number of informative and highly regarded studies bearing on globalization make no substantive reference to religion. See, e.g., Paul Kennedy, *Preparing for the Twenty-first Century* (New York: Random House, 1993); Stephen K. Sanderson, ed., *Civilizations and World Systems* (London: Sage, 1995); Jared Diamond, *Guns, Germs, and Steel: The Fates of Human Societies* (New York: W. W. Norton, 1997); Saskia Sassen, *Globalization and Its Discontents* (New York: New Press, 1998); or Ian Shapiro

The "authorities" (Greek: ἐχουσία; Latin: *potestas*) are powers that are dependent on the principalities in that they cannot flourish without a viable base, but are also independent of the principalities in that they have command over areas of life that the principalities cannot fully control. Authorities are not necessary to every society in the way of the principalities, for less complex societies have existed for centuries without clearly differentiated spheres to deal with what, in complex societies, are often identified as "the professions" — especially education, law, and medicine. Each authority requires advanced training, certification by examination, the existence of institutional spheres beyond the principalities, and codes and associations rooted in "universalistic" values to regulate behavior — especially with regard to the clients, students, or patients who entrust these "experts" with access to their property, mind, or body. Traces of these powers may be present in less complex societies, and no society is entirely ignorant, lawless, or without healing practices; but specific spheres are not always fully differentiated or defined by distinct institutional formation or governed by distinct sets of moral and spiritual values that reach across cultures. It is a remarkable change when a society built fundamentally on the principalities develops universities and professors, law courts and judges, and hospitals and doctors. When these are introduced as authorities that can override principalities, it is often only with great intellectual, moral, and spiritual confusion, and people feel both a considerable alienation and a new sense of possibility. Further, if people lose confidence in one of these differentiated spheres, they tend to revert to the principalities — to home schooling, to vigilante law, to traditional medicines, and to ethnocentric cultural expressions. Richard Osmer, John Witte, Jr., and

---

and Lea Brilmayer, eds., *Global Justice,* Nomos 41 (New York: New York University Press, 1999).

Allen Verhey, each widely recognized for his work in relating theology and ethics to, respectively, education, law, and medicine, are among the authors in volume 2.

To these three classic professional authorities, we have added three other spheres which also exercise enormous moral and spiritual influence today, ordering society, commanding personal loyalties, and shaping the professions. One of these is science, but it is seldom "pure science" that moves a society toward globalization. Science everywhere, ancient and modern, wants to know how things are, and in spite of tremendous gaps in knowledge that remain, globalization is in part a product of scientific knowledge. But, as we shall see, it is not the knowledge of how things are as the capacity and willingness to alter the world around and within us that marks the global reality. We live increasingly in a technologically reconstructed world and must take responsibility for how and in what directions we remake our world and ourselves. To be sure, science has become installed in education and is a dominant reality in the contemporary research university. But science has also become the handmaiden to technology which has had and is having a distinctive role in globalization. The recognition of technology as a major profession is not entirely new. Architecture is one of the oldest professions, and its excellence can be recognized by the endurance and beauty of many wonders of the world, by aqueducts, canals, fortifications, and temples. Today, engineering has turned not only to the control of the exterior environment, but to the control of social processes through management and communications, and to the inner genetic structure of human beings. Many have felt ambiguous about the spirit of "techné," as the French Christian theorist Jacques Ellul called it. That ambiguity will be examined in volume 2 by Ron Cole-Turner, a specialist in theology and biogenetics.

The reaction against increasing intervention in the biophysical universe has brought a remarkable resurgence of concern

for "nature." Quite different from classical natural law theories, and distinct from the laws-of-nature theories of the
Enlightenment, the sense of the earth as a living system that
we might disrupt or violate in ways that would destroy civilization has emerged in our time in fresh theories of ecology.
A perspective on nature as a current "authority" is offered by
the noted theologian Jürgen Moltmann.

To the classic professions, technology, and "nature," we
add still another authority, one little noted in much of the
literature on globalization. The charismatic leaders of movements designed to change the world may be rooted in a
religious tradition, but they often transcend particular religious identification and embody moral qualities that become
treasured internationally, beyond the culture and society in
which they developed. Every society and culture has had its
heroes and great philosophical and religious figures. Moses,
Jesus, Augustine, Thomas, Luther, and Calvin, of course, but
also Plato, Aristotle, the Buddha, Śankara, Ramanuja, Confucius, Meng-tzu, Mohammed, and Maimonides, for example,
have attracted attention across several societies and cultures,
serving not only as heroes of faith and learning, but as personal exemplars and moral role models. In most traditions,
the roster of the saints is long.

Further, great military or political leaders have left their
tracks in history books and consciousness — Alexander the
Great, Julius Caesar, Napoleon, and the dozens of imperial
leaders of Asia and Africa. Still, in the last couple of centuries
another kind of exemplary figure has gained higher visibility.
Certain moral heroes have become living icons of the values
that many embrace and take as a source of authority. Albert Schweitzer and Mahatma Gandhi, for example, played
this role in the early part of the twentieth century. Winston
Churchill and Eleanor Roosevelt did for those who fought in
World War II. Mother Teresa and the Dalai Lama play a comparable role for some today. Often these personalities become

not only advocates of, but symbolic personalities for, key values ignored by the "contemporary knowledge" as purveyed by educational institutions, neglected by "the justice system" as codified in law, and obscured by definitions of "health" as practiced in medicine. As we will see in the essay by Peter Paris, several key figures, such as Martin Luther King, Jr., Aung San Suu Kyi, Desmond Tutu, and Nelson Mandela, serve internationally as "authorities" that became emblems of such a global morality. Many of these exemplary figures usher in a moral consensus that forms a new ethos and transcends any enforced ethnocentric value pattern.

One of the remarkable things about these iconic authorities is that each has established or revitalized a social movement, creating in the process an ethical sphere driven by a distinctive "spirit." Frequently connected with religion, but not restricted in their influence to the doctrines, rituals, or metaphysical insights of any single religion, they all expanded the range of voluntary associations — what the United Nations has come to identify as NGOs, nongovernmental organizations — communities, and institutions that cannot be identified with any principality nor with any of the "professional" authorities.[52] In a number of critical analyses of contemporary, complex societies, it is clear that not only the professional associations and interest groups of the classic professions, but a host of "para-ecclesial" organizations are near the core of every vibrant civil society. The para-ecclesial groups help communities otherwise swamped by the vast forces of globalization find their voices and state their

---

52. See D. B. Robertson, ed., *Voluntary Associations: A Study of Groups in Free Societies* (Richmond: John Knox Press, 1966); James L. Adams, *Voluntary Associations,* ed. J. R. Engel (Chicago: Exploration Press, 1986); R. Wuthnow and V. A. Hodgkinson, eds., *Faith and Philanthropy in America* (Baltimore: Jossey-Bass, 1990); and Julie Fisher, *Non-Governments: NGOs and the Political Development of the Third World* (West Hartford, Conn.: Kumarian Press, 1998).

concerns and, above all, bring moral and spiritual insight to society in ways that change the principalities and authorities. Leaders of these groups often evoke and provoke the profession of values among ordinary people and enlist the help of professionals, prompting the alteration of ethical norms in the common ethos and not seldom in the structure of society itself. In volume 2 we treat the ways in which the spirit of the professions and these groups has become formed or distorted, seeking to identify the guiding and regulating influence they have in globalization.

The Dominions

In every past and existing society, what integrates the principalities into a working whole, and what gives distinctive shape to the development of the authorities in complex societies, is Religion. The primal, often tribal, religions organize the principalities and authorities differently from a Hindu, Confucian, Buddhist, Islamic or Christian society. We must recognize that there are varieties in the tribal religions — the traditional religions of Northeast India are not entirely like those of central Africa, Latin America, or the Bering Strait. Nor, for example, is Korean Confucianism the same as Confucianism in classical China or contemporary Singapore, any more than Islam is the same in Egypt, Iran, Afghanistan, and Indonesia. Still, these deep and enduring religious traditions have identifiable characteristics that dominate civilizations over many centuries and bend the principalities and authorities in distinctive directions.

In volume 3, we examine the religions that provide potentially viable possibilities for the future. Not all religions are equal in this potentiality. After all, the ruins of great temples and holy sites exist on every continent, and some sincerely held living religious traditions are unlikely to exercise more than local influence; they are not likely to provide "dominion" in a global civilization.

The term "dominions" (Greek: κυριότητες; Latin: *dominii*) derives from *kyrios,* which means "lord," "master," or "those who exercise sovereignty" over social, familial, economic, political, and often professional powers, and who do so by manifesting extraordinary spiritual and moral dignity and gravity. In biblical times, the term was sometimes applied to angels, the nonphysical bearers of messages of salvation. The great religions are often identified by the founder or by a figure, called a Lord, who exemplifies the fundamental spirit of that religion. The distinctive characteristics of several great traditions and the way they have shaped the ethos which they formed and continue to dominate will be the topic of volume 3, and will demand an account of the ways religions have been studied in the past several centuries.

Diane Obenchain will help us understand the ways in which "religion" has been studied in post-Enlightenment scholarship, and a series of scholars will focus on particular religions. John Mbiti, a leading interpreter of African religions, will help us see key relationships among globalization, aspects of Christianity, and the primal religions; Sze-Kar Wan illumines key themes that show parallels and differences between Confucianism and Christianity; Thomas Thangaraj offers a penetrating interpretation of Hinduism; Kosuke Koyama offers a striking set of contrasts and potential convergences between Buddhism and Christianity; and Lamin Sanneh explores the ways in which Mohammed is not only seen as the fulfilling prophet of the Abrahamic, Jewish, and Christian traditions, but also plays the role of social model. All these essays relate the traditions to contemporary patterns of globalization.

A key question in these authors' work, and in the final volume to follow, will be how Christian theology and ethics does, can, and should develop its own resources to face these complex traditions. The new context of a global society demands revisiting the issues once thought settled and posing fresh questions not yet clearly identified. How can we develop a faithful theological ethic to interpret and guide the common life in a situation in which we must interpret and assess, embrace or resist, what other religions assume, imply, advocate, or demand in regard to the ordering of the principalities and authorities?

At this point, we turn again to a basic consideration: Since no enduring civilization — indeed, no viable society within a civilization — has developed without a dominant religion at its core, and it is unlikely that a globalized civilization, or the structures of civil societies likely to populate it, can develop in creative directions without one either, it makes a great difference which religion becomes dominant, how it does so, and how it treats other traditions. Today, the commonly accepted study of religions is "nontheological" and "nonevaluative"; yet one of the tasks of theological ethics in our era will surely be to evaluate the patterns of religious belief and practice not only within the Christian tradition but in the world religions, specifically as they influence the necessary institutions of the common life in an increasingly complex and religiously plural society. By drawing the insights of those who know both theology and these traditions into a multilateral conversation with specialists in the theological and ethical meanings of the principalities and authorities, we may find ways to better understand the possibilities at hand. If successful, these volumes will help form a genuinely public theology and a global ethic that will invite others to carry the effort further.

– Chapter 1 –

Globalization and the Future of "Traditional Religion"

Roland Robertson

Introduction

I will be arguing that the future for religion and culture generally is bright, even though one finds a widespread view that so-called traditional religions and indigenous cultures are under great threat by globalization. In fact, the concept of globalization is often said to be responsible for the vulnerability of "native" and classical traditions. I will argue, in contrast, that is it not appropriate to blame globalization in this way and maintain that globalization enhances traditional culture. My thesis relates to some of my other writings on religion in the global field.[1]

Globalization

For present purposes, globalization may be defined simply as the compression of the world. This notion of compression refers both to increasing sociocultural density *and* to rapidly expanding consciousness. Globalization itself has been a long-term process extending over many centuries, although only in recent centuries has it, with increasing rapidity, assumed

---

1. See, for example, Roland Robertson, "Religion and the Global Field," *Social Compass* 41, no. 1 (1994).

a particular, discernible form. Globalization is, it should
be clearly recognized, a multidimensional process. In other
words, it is simultaneously cultural, economic, and political.
Moreover, we should not conceive of this process as necessarily leading to global integration in the strong sense of
the word. Density — or, to put it another way, great and increasing interdependence — is not the same as integration.
Integration suggests an increase in normative cohesiveness.
The question of global integration is a complex one, whereas
the issue of globewide interdependence is much more simple.
Whether globalization is leading or will lead to much greater
integration of the world cannot be answered straightforwardly, for there presently are indications of both greater
fragmentation *and* greater global unification.

   We must strongly challenge and, I insist, reject what should
be called the prevalent economistic conceptions of globalization. Economistic (not simply economic) conceptions
reduce globalization to the economic-material aspects of life.
It should be emphasized that this interpretation is of fairly
recent origin. The currently widespread economistic view
has developed rapidly only during the past ten years or so,
whereas a much more comprehensive conception of globalization was being elaborated as long ago as the 1970s. In fact, it
was within the sociology of religion and religious studies that
the idea of globalization was most evident in the late 1970s
and early 1980s. That earlier development did *not* attempt
to explain religious change in economic terms, although the
effort was paralleled by Wallerstein's and others' economistic
interpretation of both modernization and globalization.[2] We
should not, of course, deny the significance of economic factors. I argue merely that they constitute only one aspect of
globalization.

---

   2. See Immanuel Maurice Wallerstein, *The Modern World System*,
3 vols. (New York: Cambridge University Press, 1974, 1980, 1989).

Other factors need careful attention at present precisely because economic issues have been given so much attention in recent years, particularly the growth of the global-market economy, or simply marketization.[3] Interest in the global economy should, I maintain, be balanced by attention to cultural, political, religious, and other dimensions of globalization, which should not be seen as mere consequences of the economic factors. Thus a major conceptual difficulty appears in the claim that globalization is, at one and the same time, a threat to religion and culture because of economics, *and* that globalization includes noneconomic factors critical to all human societies. The former view has become so firmly established in recent years as to constitute a reality that cannot simply be swept away by conceptual fiat, but to many globalization's relation to cultural and religious issues remains unclear.

How and why globalization came in the late 1980s and early 1990s to acquire a mainly economic meaning cannot or should not be explored in any detail here. But we should bear in mind that across the contemporary world, most economists, as well as many politicians, have been successful in establishing the self-serving and misleading view that economics "makes the world go around." In any case, along with the prevalence of economistic conceptions of human life an equally unsatisfactory perspective has developed, which states that the world is being swept by homogenizing forces. This idea is often expressed as "McDonaldization,"[4] meaning that difference and variety are being crushed by irresistible forces of sameness, standardization, and bureaucratic ra-

---

3. Dani Rodrik, *Has Globalization Gone Too Far?* (Washington, D.C.: Institute for International Economics, 1997).

4. Benjamin R. Barber, *Jihad vs. McWorld* (New York: Times Books, 1995); George Ritzer, *The McDonaldization of Society: An Investigation into the Changing Character of Contemporary Social Life* (Thousand Oaks, Calif.: Pine Forge Press, 1993).

tionalism. Again, I cannot go deeply into what I regard as the great weaknesses of this perspective, except to say that many sociologists and anthropologists note that the spread of McDonald's fast-food restaurants involves subtle differences from one country to another.[5] This is true of many phenomena that appear superficially to be forces of homogenization, particularly various brand-name goods and services sold and distributed on a worldwide basis.[6]

I consider the homogenization-versus-hetereogenization dispute as the core feature of globalization. I have in my own work referred to this process as the universalization of particularism and the particularization of universalism. This is where my concept of *glocalization* comes in,[7] about which I shall say more later.

My position on the economic dimension of globalization and homogenization that many have wrongly associated with economics may be summarized as follows. The economistic view that reduces life to economic-material factors is not merely wrong, but it can in part be explained by what has been called "the ubiquitous rise of the economists."[8] Economists — or, at least, free-trade, neoliberal economists — have in recent

---

5. James L. Watson, *Golden Arches East: McDonald's in East Asia* (Stanford, Calif.: Stanford University Press, 1997).

6. John Tomlinson, *Cultural Imperialism?* (Baltimore: Johns Hopkins University Press, 1991).

7. Roland Robertson, *Globalization: Social Theory and Global Culture* (London: Sage, 1992), 173–74; idem, "The Search for Fundamentals in Global Perspective," in *The Search for Fundamentals: The Process of Modernisation and the Quest for Meaning*, ed. Lieteke van Vucht Tijssen, Jan Berting, and Frank Lechner (Dordrecht, Netherlands: Kluwer Academic Publishers, 1995), 50–69; idem, "Globalization: Time-Space and Homogeneity-Heterogeneity," in *Global Modernities*, ed. Mike Featherstone, Scott Lash, and Roland Robertson (London: Sage, 1995), 25–44.

8. John Markoff and Veronica Montecinos, "The Ubiquitous Rise of Economists," *Journal of Public Policy* 13, no. 1 (1993). I would nevertheless emphasize that it is in business studies that one finds the most consistent interpretation of globalization as an economic phenomenon.

decades managed to gain pivotal political offices and/or influence in many countries, primarily through successful attempts to enhance prestige for their discipline, a prestige that, in my judgment, is not warranted. Furthermore, the interpretation of globalization as the rapid spread of sameness is, as I have said, equally inaccurate, as serious sociological and anthropological study — and even business study — clearly shows.[9] On this point, I wish to repeat that we experience trends that simultaneously promote sameness and difference. This simultaneity requires sophisticated tools of analysis.

Inventing Tradition

It is necessary to say something about what has become widely known among social scientists, historians, and those working in cultural studies as "the invention of tradition," an idea that has direct bearing on the "future of traditional religion." The idea of the invention of tradition has become widespread particularly since the publication in 1983 of a book edited by the historian Eric Hobsbawm and the anthropologist Terence Ranger, *The Invention of Tradition*.[10] Contributors to that volume endeavored to show that at the end of the nineteenth century, a period of strengthening of the nation-state, national identities and traditions were widely promoted. In newly unified societies, such as Japan, as well as in older nation-states, such as Britain, we find accentuation of national symbols, monuments, ceremonials, and so on. Some of these traditions were literally "invented" (such as state Shinto in Japan), while others involved highly selective appropriation and valorization of past traditions. It was during this period that the very idea of tradition began to

9. M. de Mooij, *Global Marketing and Advertising: Understanding Cultural Paradoxes* (London: Sage, 1998).

10. Eric Hobsbawm and Terence Ranger, eds., *The Invention of Tradition* (Cambridge: Cambridge University Press, 1983).

acquire its global twentieth-century significance. It is appropriate to say, in fact, that the idea of tradition is a modern phenomenon — a form of *countermodernity* that became a feature of modernity itself.[11] In this same period of the late nineteenth and early twentieth centuries the idea of community began to obtain the great significance that is has now gained, primarily in nostalgic terms.[12]

One might say that at the end of the nineteenth and the beginning of the twentieth century ideas such as national tradition and community were in fact globalized. If this proposition makes sense, then the claim that globalization *threatens* traditional culture is clearly wrong, for globalization has most definitely *encouraged* tradition and the "quest for community." I would go so far as to say that globalization in and of itself entails and accelerates the promotion of traditional culture.[13]

Beginning in the mid–nineteenth century one finds trends toward misconstruing instances of globalization as standing in opposition to globalization. Probably the best example is nationalism. On the rise since the late medieval period and enhanced by the Treaty of Westphalia, nationalism became increasingly widespread during the nineteenth century. Nationalist leaders across much of the northern hemisphere *collaborated* across boundaries to promote national unity and independence. Moreover, the nineteenth century witnessed the growth of national self-determination, which culminated in its promotion by President Woodrow Wilson at the Paris conference following World War I. This political standard was revived after World War II, with the establishment of new na-

---

11. Ulrich Beck, *The Reinvention of Politics: Rethinking Modernity in the Global Social Order,* trans. Mark Ritter (Oxford: Polity Press, 1997).
12. Robertson, *Globalization,* 146–63.
13. Roland Robertson, "Values and Globalization: Communitarianism and Globality," in *Identity, Culture, and Globalization,* ed. Luiz Edwards Soares (Rio de Janeiro: UNESCO, 1997).

tions in Africa and Asia — often after violent struggles against imperial powers in the so-called Third World. Toward the end of the nineteenth century an even more interesting trend, closely related to ecumenicism, began. In 1893 the World's Parliament of Religions in Chicago represented what one might call the international promotion of traditional religions. One cannot overemphasize the significance of this development. For it shows that in an increasingly globalized — or compressed — world, the promotion of indigenous culture had begun to take on a global form. Around the same time, the end of the nineteenth century, the International Youth Hostel movement, as well as the YMCA, YWCA, YMBA (Buddhist), and YMHA (Hebrew) movements — all international, all religiously particular — began. The relevance can be perceived in the combination of globality, or at least internationality, and the promotion of local, communal, and religious values. This movement encompassed various regions, based on the primarily German idea of encouraging young people's involvement in "back-to-nature" activities that braced against the debilitating effects of industrialization and urbanization.

Another much more recent example parallels the earlier developments. Particularly since the early 1980s, when the United Nations placed the issue of indigenous peoples firmly on its agenda, *worldwide* movements seeking to protect or promote the rights and welfare of stateless native peoples have formed. Now tribes from Brazil, India, Central Africa, and North America correspond by E-mail about their special problems and common, often ecological, concerns. Again we find the seemingly paradoxical combination of the "local" with the "global."

Relativization and Culture

This alignment of the global and the local does not, however, eliminate the proposition that traditional, local cultures and religions are under siege. One aspect of globalization does represent a threat to "traditional culture." This can be summarized in one word: *relativization*.[14] Relativization refers to the challenge of coexisting with other — often very different and perhaps antagonistic — cultures. Globalization brings cultures into closer contact and thus often leads to the sense that "one's own" culture is under threat. This relativization has been largely responsible for what has come to be called "fundamentalism." Modern use of the concept arose about one hundred years ago in the United States, when Protestant Christians of mainly British heritage began to perceive themselves as strangers in their own country. At that time waves of immigration from Eastern and Southern Europe, a large part of which was either Catholic or Jewish, and from Japan and China took place. Immigration resulted in pervasive culture shock, not merely for the immigrants themselves but also for many long-standing residents of the United States.

Protestant fundamentalism largely faded from wider public view from the late 1920s until the 1970s, when it reemerged with surprising strength, partly in an unusual alliance of convenience with Jewish movements in Israel. The Iranian revolution occurred in 1979, and soon thereafter the notion of fundamentalism began to be applied to, and largely accepted by, movements that stressed opposition to secular modernity and, often, to globality. These movements attempted to simplify and spiritualize modern life by a return to what were thought of as clear-cut, absolute values and beliefs. Thus, numerous religious movements have been globaphobic.[15]

Insofar as the term "fundamentalism" is a useful sociological concept (and I have serious doubts), it has arisen in

14. Robertson, *Globalization*; idem, "Values and Globalization." See nn. 7, 13.

15. See Gary T. Burtless et al., *Globaphobia: Confronting Fears about Open Trade* (Washington, D.C.: Brookings Institution, Progressive Policy Institute, and the Twentieth-Century Fund, 1998).

close connection with the crucial and unavoidable phenomenon of relativization.[16] To repeat, relativization refers to the
ways in which adherents to cultural traditions come to feel
threatened by existence alongside rival or alien identities or
traditions in an increasingly interdependent world. In my view
relativization demands much more attention than it has so far
received among social scientists, for it is a central — perhaps
the central — sociological and anthropological phenomenon
of the globalization process and of what is increasingly being
described as the global age.[17]

Cultural clashes and tensions are an inevitable feature of
globalization. What should be called the dark side of globalization involves the militance and, indeed, violence that not
infrequently accompanies these clashes. Nothing about globalization should lead people to believe that it is leading to
a more peaceful world; some claim that cultural clashes between civilizations constitute the primary source of current
political and military tension worldwide.[18] However, I do
not believe that globalization is leading automatically to a
more violent or conflict-filled world. Much depends on the
willingness of people to accept peacefully and with understanding many of the challenges posed by unavoidable forces
of relativization. Still, the rise in various parts of the world of
militant antiglobal movements, not least in the United States,
does not cause great optimism. Antiglobal movements that
blame globalization and globewide institutions, as well as
alien cultures, for most, if not all, problems in their own societies contribute to the globalization process by *expanding
and deepening consciousness of the world as a whole*. It is
worth noting that in spite of the popular view that global-

---

16. Robertson, "Search for Fundamentals." See n. 7.

17. E.g., Martin Albrow, *The Global Age: State and Society beyond
Modernity* (Stanford, Calif.: Stanford University Press, 1997).

18. Samuel P. Huntington, *The Clash of Civilizations and the Remaking
of World Order* (New York: Simon and Schuster, 1996).

ization equals "Americanization," some of the most militant
antiglobal tendencies exist in the United States itself. Indeed,
the American form of antiglobalism may well become globalized — leading, perhaps, to the perspective that *anti*globalism
is a form of Americanization!

We are all familiar with the idea that we are, and should
be, "multicultural." But this too is a problematic notion,
in spite of its apparent familiarity. It is important that we
distinguish between multiculturality and multiculturalism.
"Multiculturality" refers to the existence within a nation-
state of a plurality of cultures, which are often sustained by
so-called ethnic groups. (Sometimes the word "polyethnicity"
is used instead of "multiculturality.") "Multicultural*ism*," on
the other hand, refers to the commitment to the supposed
virtues of a plurality of coexisting cultures — an emphasis
on the value of heterogeneity as opposed to homogeneity.
It should be added, however, that the active promotion of
multiculturalism is often undertaken by groups seeking "political space" in particular nation-states, and sometimes to
promote the relativity of dominant values. Essentially, then,
multiculturalism refers to the valued and relatively peaceful
coexistence within a nation-state of different ethnic attach-
ments, religions, lifestyles, and so on. But one of the most
interesting — and, in a way, disturbing — features of so-called
multiculturalism is that it further encourages the invention
of tradition and the invention of subcultures, Canada being
a particularly good example. In some countries movements
claim to have discovered long-lost or suppressed traditions
or invent new ones — an example of which is "Wicca" as if
it were a Druid legacy.

The danger in the strong promotion of multiculturalism
is that it may lead to the splitting of societies into cultural
groups, each claiming its distinctiveness, and to what have
in recent years been called "culture wars." Multiculturalism
can also give rise to anti-immigrant movements. "Culture

wars" are frequently the result of the relativization of cultures (including religious doctrine and ritual), traditions, and identities. But such conflicts, at least militant conflicts, are avoidable to the extent that values can be *generalized* to include (within limits) groups claiming their own traditions or lifestyles within a society. Moreover, in an ever more compressed world, the problems of multiculturality are ever increasingly *trans*national, exceeding the boundaries of nation-states. Ethnic and cultural movements in a particular territory are often promoted by sympathizers in other parts of the world, which is easy to do with current forms of electronic communication. Issues of multiculturality and multiculturalism are rapidly becoming global, not merely national. Formation of an entity such as the European Union, which is supposed to transcend nationality in the conventional sense, gives rise to extranational issues concerning multiculturality and multiculturalism.

More generally, the world at the end of the twentieth century, through diasporas of migrants in various areas, encourages the cultivation of tradition. So-called traditional cultures are often promoted and sustained outside their "home" and must coexist with other cultural formations, often in very different places. Inevitably, the original culture is modified, even though the dedication to authenticity may be intense.

Authenticity and Globalization

I now turn back to the concept of globalization, with reference to the authenticity of traditions. Even though I still believe that "globalization" is a valuable sociological concept, it has — as I have been saying — undoubtedly become a fuzzy and controversial term in recent years. The main problem from an academic perspective is that for many it has become a useful "blame word," often uttered to indicate the ways in

which "authenticity" is being undermined. I cannot explore
the question of authenticity here (crucial as it is), except to
remark that it is also highly problematic. The idea of authenticity often is used in ill-considered ways to justify particular
forms of life without proper regard for the inevitably changing and frequently constructed nature of so-called traditions,
not to speak of the recently developed concept of detraditionalization[19] — which is closely related to the idea of the
invention of tradition. Many features of the late-twentieth-
century world encourage widespread claims concerning the
authenticity — *the essential genuineness* — of systems of beliefs and values. In any case, we must refine the concept of
globalization to avoid the pejorative meaning that it has recently acquired outside the circles of academics who have
considered the concept carefully over a fairly long period.
In other words, we should not give in to those who use the
concept of globalization simply as a slogan, nor to those who
use it in a reductionist manner.[20]

I propose that we think about globalization along the
lines conveyed by the Japanese word *dochakuka* — meaning
something like "global localization" or, more succinctly, *glocalization*. Even though I am not advocating that we should
wholeheartedly substitute glocalization for globalization, I
think we should consider globalization in this light. This
would entail thinking of globalization as including worldwide processes adapted to local circumstances. This means
that globalization is what I call a self-limiting process; insofar as globalization incorporates locality, it necessarily "limits
itself." To make this point differently, globalization and local-

---

19. Paul Heelas, Scott Lash, and Paul Morris, eds., *Detraditionalization:
Critical Reflections on Authority and Identity* (Oxford: Blackwell, 1996).
20. Roland Robertson and H. H. Khondker, "Discourses of Globalization: Preliminary Considerations," *International Sociology* 13, no. 1
(1998).

ization proceed inevitably in tandem. They are *not,* as is so often argued, opposites.

But, it must be heavily emphasized, adaptation to "the local" context, which may include the national, regional, or even larger contexts, will not necessarily mean increasing significance for the "really" local. For undoubtedly the local or the traditional is often "manufactured" or, as sociologists often say, constructed.[21] Such construction has a very long history, reaching back to early map-making and, as I argued earlier, in a much more recent period of the late nineteenth century, to a time in which the entire world was zoned.

With respect to the contemporary period I should mention, in particular, the so-called heritage industry. The concern with the "preservation of the past" — including the very recent past — is guided considerably by market considerations. In this sense tradition has increasingly become subject to commercial interests, which are also closely connected to the huge industry of contemporary tourism. This industry combines an emphasis on uniqueness and authenticity with a standardization of tourist practice, based on evidence that market considerations play a role in cultural factors as well as on the fact that people will pay for "culture," authentic or ersatz, because they think that it is curious or important. To put it briefly, history and tradition have become consumable objects — part of what is often now called modern consumer culture.

The commodification of religion (greatly encouraged by rational-choice theory) can be seen, for example, in Japan, with the increasing commercialization of shrines and temples in the form of vending machines and souvenir shops. These accept both cash and credit cards and sell drinks,

---

21. Arjun Appadurai, "The Production of Locality," in *Counterworks: Managing the Diversity of Knowledge,* ed. Richard Fardon (London: Sage, 1995).

food, disposable cameras, and trinkets, along with incense and other related religious items. Thus shrines and temples are increasingly competing over what might be called — at least from a Western standpoint — their "extrareligious" attractiveness. But a clear-cut distinction between the religious and the secular is not a "natural" feature of Japanese society. One should be careful not to impose, in too facile a manner, concepts which have arisen in one part of the world on another civilization.

It may seem strange that I have stressed the global construction of locality. But conceptions of "the local" are not possible without an awareness of a larger, extralocal context in which locality is placed. Moreover, ideas about "the local," "home," "community," and so on have recently spread over most of the world. These notions have been a central theme of globalization. There is, to put it even more sharply, *a cult of the local;* this phrase indicates that the valorization of locality, home, and community is *globally* sustained. The cult of locality is part of a global culture.

My argument in this respect is very similar to — indeed, it has been partly inspired by — Durkheim's thesis of about one hundred years ago, concerning what he called the cult of the individual. In the face of the rapidly increasing celebration of individualism in Western societies Durkheim insisted — correctly in my judgment — that, far from being antisocial, increasing emphasis on the individual is a socially sustained phenomenon. To put it more bluntly, individualism is a *social* phenomenon and is only sensibly conceivable as such. The same kind of reasoning underpins my conviction that the local is best seen as a global phenomenon.

Collective Memory and Tradition

At this point I turn briefly to yet another aspect of tradition. We live in a world in which the issue of *competing collective memories* has become a prominent feature of global life. There is much competition — indeed, conflict — concerning the ways in which past events, such as wars, should be commemorated. The same applies to the celebration and interpretation of traditions and identities. This means that the writing of history and the maintenance and reinterpretation of traditions have become more subject to manipulation and contestation. One should not think that the "political manipulation" of what is frequently called collective memory is something entirely new. It has been occurring throughout recorded history. But since the nation-state began to be seen as the major "container" of human beings and societies in the mid–eighteenth century, collective memory has been particularly subject to careful and conflictual calibration. This tendency has been increasingly evident during the twentieth century. Controversies about the national and international commemorations in 1995 of the end of World War II, and the events which preceded it, demonstrate this tendency well.

As I have said, some sociologists now use the concept of *detraditionalization* to highlight the extent to which tradition currently appears as less a controlling idea than a phenomenon available for reconstruction — indeed, for invention. At the end of the twentieth century, the idea of tradition is undergoing fundamental changes. When we speak about the future of traditional religion and culture we should bear these changes firmly in mind. Indeed, the extensive concern with the future of traditional culture is itself an indicator of the instability of the theme of tradition.

Conclusion: The Future

At the beginning of this essay I suggested that the future of traditional culture and religion is bright. By this I meant that we should not think that traditional culture or religious traditions are disappearing, for in certain ways they are being enhanced.

This claim will certainly not satisfy "traditionalists." Nonetheless, I must repeat that not only do we live in a world in which traditional culture and religions receive increasing attention, but one in which these are highly manipulable. The question of authenticity will remain for the foreseeable future, in the sense that some will cling to the theme of authenticity and inauthenticity, while others will acknowledge that this theme is largely redundant — that it cannot be retrieved. This is, in fact, my own position.

Thus the future of traditional culture and religion is "good," so long as we fully acknowledge that we all live in a heavily compressed world of *difference within sameness,* and that traditions are increasingly subject to manipulation — indeed, to invention, largely because of relativization. In this respect I noted that traditional culture and religion have become unavoidably commodified. These ideas are not simple to appreciate. But I hope that I have taken helpful steps toward registering some of the complexities of the future of traditional culture and religion.

– Chapter 2 –

PHILOSOPHY AND THE PROSPECTS FOR A UNIVERSAL ETHICS

Yersu Kim

We stand at the twentieth century's end in a situation of extraordinary openness. The forces of the techno-scientific economy are threatening the very foundation of human life, even while they create unheard-of material bounties for a minority of humanity. These same forces are giving rise to ever more complex social, political, and moral questions. At the same time, the ideas and institutions that over the past several centuries had served humanity so well in its tasks of survival and flourishing seem increasingly irrelevant, unimportant, or even counterproductive. People are abandoning old loyalties and building allegiances shaped by rapidly shifting ideas and hopes. The last part of the century is, in the words of an eminent historian, an era of "decomposition, uncertainty, and crisis." As Eric Hobsbawm has written:

> The future cannot be a continuation of the past and there are signs . . . that we have reached a point of historic crisis. . . . We do not know where we are going. We only know that history has brought us to this point.[1]

---

1. Eric Hobsbawm, *The Age of Extremes* (New York: Vintage Books, 1996), 584–85.

The Globalization of Problems

The first clear signs of uncertainty and crisis came in the ecological crisis that accompanied the first oil shock in the early
1970s. Politicization of energy resources by oil-producing
countries had abruptly exposed the fragility of the "golden"
years of postwar economic development, which had seemed
to promise eradication of poverty and full employment to almost all the countries of the North and to some countries
in the developing world. The oil shock, combined with the
ideas of writers who in the 1970s advocated limits to growth,
highlighted the global nature of the crisis. The best-known of
these documents, the so-called Club of Rome Report, issued a
warning that, if growth trends in world population, industrialization, pollution, food production, and resource depletion
were to continue unchanged, the limits would be reached
within one hundred years.

The global nature of the crisis lay not only in that it affected
practically all parts of the world, due to the increasingly integrated and global character of the world economy. It was
global, first and foremost, in that the problems were of a
nature that, while they were experienced locally, they could
only be dealt with by concerted global action across the borders of nation-states, traditionally the basic units of political
action.

Several attempts were made during the 1970s to arrive
at a comprehensive statement of the world's problems. The
report of the Club of Rome, mentioned above, may have
received the most attention, but there were other earnest
attempts at a comprehensive inventory by the International
Institute of Applied Systems Analysis, the World Model Institute, the Russian Institute of System Studies, and the Batelle
Institute, among others. But no other listing of global problems approaches the comprehensiveness of Aurelio Peccei's
The Human Quality (1979). That list includes:

- uncontrolled human proliferation
- societal chaos and divisions
- social injustice
- hunger and malnutrition
- widespread poverty
- mania for growth
- inflation
- energy crisis
- international trade and monetary disruptions
- protectionism
- illiteracy and anachronistic education
- youth rebellion
- alienation
- uncontrolled urban spread and decay
- crime and drugs
- violence and brutality
- torture and terrorism
- disregard for law and order
- nuclear folly
- sickness in and inadequacy of institutions
- corruption
- bureaucratization
- degradation of environment
- decline of moral values
- loss of faith

- sense of instability

- lack of understanding of the above problems and their interrelationship

The Crisis of Values
and International Response

As the sense of uncertainty and crisis deepened, it became increasingly clear that the ideas, assumptions, and institutions on which modern society had been founded were no longer adequate to deal with many of the problems facing humanity. The crisis was increasingly seen as one of ideas, beliefs, and values that had been the foundation of the modern society, which now faced new historical realities engendered by the accelerating process of globalization. Nation-states, the cornerstones of modern political development in the West since the middle of the seventeenth century, were being pulled apart by the contradictory forces of economic globalization and ethnic fragmentation. Since Westphalia, the national state had come to be seen as the only valid form of political-social organization. It now seemed woefully inadequate to deal with the new wave of global, transboundary problems. The model of political authority at the root of modern society was based on the supremacy of national states and interests, and not on the idea of global responsibility and governance.

Throughout the 1970s and 1980s the international community was beginning to appreciate the global dimension of the developing crisis. Over a period of seven years the United Nations established three independent commissions to report on aspects of what was coming to be recognized as a common crisis. The Independent Commission on International Development Issues (known as the Brandt Commission) was established in 1977. In 1980, the Independent Commission on Disarmament and Security Issues (the Palme

Commission) was constituted, while the Brundtland Commission on Environment and Development came into being in 1984.

In the 1990s the UN convened a remarkable series of world conferences, all addressing problems of global magnitude. It was acknowledged that solutions exceeded the capacities of individual member states and depended on a concerted international effort. The conferences were:

- World Summit for Children (1990)

- UN Conference on Environment and Development (1992)

- World Conference on Human Rights (1993)

- International Conference on Population and Development (1994)

- World Summit for Social Development (1995)

- Fourth World Conference on Women (1995)

- Second UN Conference on Human Settlement (Habitat II) (1996)

The international community convened other conferences, including:

- UN Global Conference on the Sustainable Development of Small Island Developing States (1994)

- International Conference on Natural-Disaster Reduction (1994)

- Ninth UN Congress on the Prevention of Crime and the Treatment of Offenders (1995)

- Ninth UN Conference on Trade and Development (UNCTAD IX) (1996)

All of the conferences focused on global well-being and sought to link the problems people face at the community level with policies and actions at the international level. Conferences were predicated on the recognition that the world is facing problems that cannot be resolved only at the national level. Together the meetings formed a cohesive series dealing with interrelated issues such as environmental protection, the well-being of children, human rights and the rights of women, population, unemployment, crime, trade, food, security, and human settlement. While they built on common ground that previous world conferences and conventions had created, there was an increasing demand for implementation of possible solutions along a common framework. The conferences reflect the increasing acceptance of shared values, goals, and the strategies to achieve them. The call for a "common framework" for initiatives presented reflects the growing convergence of views that democracy, development, and respect for human rights and fundamental freedoms are all interdependent and mutually reinforcing.

Thus, along with producing plans for action and exploring possible expansion of normative guidelines, these conferences played a role in the emergence of global principles such as human-centered development, the priority of poverty eradication, and justice expressed as the inseparability of civil and political from economic and social rights. The clearest example is Agenda 21, the "Rio Declaration on Environment and Development," which produced not only concrete conventions on climate change and biodiversity, but principles to guide international action on the environment:

AGENDA 21 PRINCIPLES

- Human beings are at the center of concerns for sustainable development. They are entitled to a healthy and productive life in harmony with nature.

- Scientific uncertainty should not delay measures to prevent environmental degradation where there are threats
  of serious or irreversible damage.

- States have a sovereign right to exploit their own resources but not to cause damage to the environment of
  other states.

- Eradicating poverty and reducing disparities in worldwide standards of living are "indispensable" for sustainable development.

- Full participation of women is essential for achieving
  sustainable development.

- Developed countries, in view of the pressures their societies place on the global environment and of the
  technologies and financial resources they command,
  acknowledge the responsibility they bear in the international pursuit of sustainable development.

Common themes reappear in the final documents of all
these meetings. The 1990 Children's Summit produced a
document whose principles are clearly indicated in its title:
"World Declaration and Plan of Action on the Survival, Protection, and Development of Children." The 1993 "Vienna
Declaration and Programme of Action" emphasized a holistic
approach linking development, democracy, and human rights.
The International Conference on Population and Development likewise stressed that poverty reduction, environmental
protection, and the promotion of gender equality work as
"mutually reinforcing" factors to slow population growth.
The World Summit for Social Development's "Copenhagen
Declaration," transcending cultural differences, united social, economic, political, and cultural concerns in its "ten
commitments" to enhance quality of life. The Fourth World

Conference on Women in Beijing addressed twelve areas in which women are systematically excluded from enjoying their nationally and internationally recognized rights and freedoms. These conferences focused attention on two of the most basic components of human well-being.

At the same time, a reappraisal of the factors that augment quality of life began to call into question the link between simple development and well-being. Dramatic urban growth, mass unemployment, social disintegration, and historically unprecedented polarities of wealth and poverty are consequences of development. According to studies such as UNICEF's *Giving Children a Future: The World Summit for Children* (1990) and *State of the World's Children*as well as the 1996 report of the Independent Commission on Population and Quality of Life, economic growth is not necessarily associated with improvement in quality of life. For benefits to be realized, allocation and distribution of resources require ethical orientation to what are almost universally shared aims and values.

The Western Synthesis

The symptoms of uncertainty and crisis that mark this *fin de siècle* are, in an important sense, a reflection of the inability of nation-states to deal effectively with the new historical situation. But one could argue that even this inability reflects a crisis in the synthesis of ideas and values that had taken the West several centuries to develop. Based on the ideas of individualism, rationalism, scientism, and teleology of progress, the Western synthesis provided a point of reference as societies endeavored to industrialize and modernize. The synthesis had such preeminence in the minds and affairs of people that nations and societies were practically unanimous in accepting Westernization as the only means of ensuring a viable future. Under the banner of modernization, they abandoned customary truths, values, and ways of life, and accepted the degree of Westernization as their measure of progress or regress.

Today the Western synthesis of ideas and values no longer seems like a sure guide to human survival and flourishing. After the demise of socialism and the gradual retreat of the welfare state — the mixed economy of Keynesian and Asian-values provenance — advocates of the neoliberal economic model in today's globalizing economy do seem to be exhibiting a certain triumphalism. They seem, however, unable to deal with the growing impoverishment of much of the South, as well as with mass unemployment and the growing pauperization of a significant segment of the Northern population.

Many countries in the Third World, having won independence from their former colonial powers, pursued industrialization. In need of the capital and the know-how, they were heavily dependent on the developed world. Today the largest portion of the budgets in many of these countries goes toward servicing their loans; some countries pay up to 70 percent of their GNP for this purpose. Nearly one-third of the population in developing countries lives in absolute poverty, while one hundred million children are homeless street dwellers. Even in richer countries more than one hundred million people live in poverty, and the ranks of the poor are growing.

It is clear that the benefits of globalization do not extend to all countries or social groups. Indeed, the dramatic extremes of wealth and poverty born of globalization menace both democracy and social stability in various regions. For many globalization signifies a race to the bottom, not only in wages but in standards of environmental regulation and social legislation. By empowering economic over political entities, globalization has given rise to historically unprecedented heights of regional financial instability. This

global state of affairs casts doubt on the once dominant
and persuasive cultural model that guided many nations'
development.

The Search for Common Values:
Tentative Steps

It is against this backdrop of fragmentation and uncertainty
for human well-being that the search for common ethical values and principles must be seen. Efforts to frame possible
solutions to the global problems in comprehensive, ethical
terms began to crystallize in the 1990s. Among international
organizations, commissions, academic, religious, and political
institutions, as well as among individual thinkers and advocates, we are witnessing vigorous attempts to arrive at new
syntheses of ideas and values that would be acceptable across
cultures and societies and relevant to the tasks of human
survival and flourishing. We are also witnessing an almost
explosive emergence of the so-called one-issue NGOs; these
organizations, emerging from cultural disarray and political
disempowerment of national governments and other public
bodies, often express a new awareness of values.

It must not be forgotten, however, that the new concern with values also has its negative side: the revival of
chauvinisms, the proliferation of sometimes hazardous new
religious movements, and the growing strength of various
forms of fundamentalism. Whether negative or positive, value
awareness is intimately connected with the realization that
the global problems that render our traditional values, ideas,
and institutions impotent must be dealt with in a creative and
novel way. It represents the realization that an important, if
not the most important, part of such an effort must be forging a new cultural synthesis of ideas and values necessary to
deal with the problems of human survival and flourishing in
an age of globalization.

International Commissions

In recent years, a number of studies have drawn particular attention to the need to articulate universal norms, values, or principles that could serve as the basis for peaceful and productive interaction among nations and societies, for prevention of conflicts and crises, and for collective efforts toward peace and prosperity.[2]

"Our Global Neighborhood"

Our Global Neighborhood, the report of the Commission on Global Governance, came out strongly in 1995 for a "global civic ethic" as the foundation for cooperation among different societies and cultures facing common global problems. Such a global ethic comprises a minimum of core values shared by all cultures and religious traditions, and a set of rights and responsibilities constituting a "civic code" based on these core values. These values include respect for life, liberty, justice, and equity; mutual respect; caring; and integrity. The values derive in one way or another from the principle of reciprocity known as the Golden Rule — that people should treat others as they would themselves wish to be treated.

The report then presents a list of rights and responsibilities based on these core values and representing the minimum for building a global civil society. The rights include the rights to a secure life; equitable treatment; opportunity to earn a fair living; participation in governance at all levels; equal access to information; and, finally, equal access to the global commons. The responsibilities, on the other hand, include considering the impact of our actions on others; promoting equity, including gender equity; protecting the interests of future generations; safeguarding the global commons; preserving humanity's cultural and intellectual heritage; being

---

2. Full bibliographical data for the publications discussed here can be found in the bibliography beginning on p. 255.

active participants in governance; and working to eliminate corruption.

"Our Creative Diversity"

Also in 1995, the World Commission on Culture and Development, chaired by Javier Pérez de Cuéllar, former secretary-general of the United Nations, published its report, *Our Creative Diversity*. The report makes a plea for a "global ethics" — a core of shared ethical values and principles — that would provide the minimum moral guidance the world needs in dealing with global issues. Conflicts can be limited and cooperation facilitated if people can see themselves as bound and motivated by shared commitments. Since all societies need moral principles for their self-regulation, social order, and international relations, there is no reason why ethics should stop at national borders.

The commission maintains that global ethics could provide the minimum requirements any government and people should need, while leaving room for political creativity, social imagination and cultural pluralism. Such an ethics could be composed of (1) human rights and responsibilities; (2) democracy and the elements of civil society, such as free, fair, and regular elections, freedom of press and information, and the freedom of association; (3) protection of minority rights; (4) commitment to peaceful conflict resolution and fair negotiation; and (5) equity within and between generations.

Religious, Political, and Cultural Institutions

The Parliament of the World's Religions

In 1993, representatives of more than 120 religions of the world, meeting in the Parliament of the World's Religions in Chicago for the first time in one hundred years, adopted a "Declaration toward a Global Ethic." The text of this declaration was drafted by Dr. Hans Küng, the German Catholic theologian who has for a number of years been at the fore-front of the effort to forge a global ethics acceptable to all religions and adequate to deal with a fundamental crisis in global economy, ecology, and politics. The starting point of the declaration is the recognition that a consensus within re-ligious teachings speaks directly to current global problems. This consensus serves as the basis of a global ethics — a minimal, fundamental consensus concerning binding values, irrevocable standards, and fundamental moral attitudes.

The 1993 declaration confirms the existence of two princi-ples which represent a "fundamental demand" of all religious and ethical traditions, namely, that every human being must be treated humanely, and that one should not do what one does not wish done to oneself. Further, these principles are seen as giving rise to broad moral guidelines found in most religions of the world. They are a commitment to a culture of (1) nonviolence and respect for life; (2) solidarity and a just economic order; (3) tolerance and a life of truthfulness; and, finally, (4) equal rights and partnership between men and women.

The InterAction Council

In 1997, some thirty former heads of state and government who constitute the InterAction Council submitted a draft of a "Universal Declaration of Human Responsibilities" to all heads of state and government and of the United Nations and UNESCO. They did so, wrote Helmut Schmidt, who has been the moving force behind the declaration, "in a hope that the United Nations will adopt our proposed declaration, or at least its spirit, on the 50th Anniversary of the 1948 Human Rights Declaration."

The declaration, drafted by Dr. Küng and a group of ex-perts over two years, consists of a preamble and nineteen articles ordered under five headings. These headings are fun-damental principles of humanity (four articles); nonviolence and respect for life (three articles); justice and solidarity (four articles); truthfulness and tolerance (four articles); and mutual respect and partnership (three articles). The document also includes a conclusion. The structure and content of the declaration are essentially those of the declaration adopted by the Parliament of World's Religions in 1993, expressed, however, in quasi-legalistic format and language befitting its occasion and sponsorship.

The ethical values and standards identified in the proposed declaration are seen as necessary elements for the creation of a better social order and for the realization of human aspirations for progress. Based on the perception that "exclusive insistence on rights can lead to endless dispute and conflict," the declaration seeks to balance freedom with responsibility, but also to reconcile ideologies, beliefs, and political views, in apparent reference to the debate between Western proponents of human rights and proponents of the so-called "Asian values." The declaration's provision on freedom of the press in article 14, which emphasizes a special responsibility for accurate and truthful reporting, has been the subject of critical debate. Against the intention of the declaration's sponsors to supplement the "Universal Declaration of Human Rights," some in the media have said that it would dilute the 1948 document.

The Institute for Global Ethics

For Rushworth Kidder, the founder of the Institute for Global Ethics (USA), ethics is rapidly becoming as much a survival issue as the nuclear threat, environmental degradation, the population crisis, the gap between haves and have-nots, and the need for education reform. In *Shared Values for a Troubled World,* Kidder identifies a number of cross-cultural core values: love, truthfulness, fairness, freedom, unity, tolerance, responsibility, and respect for life.

Kidder's method is sometimes called "Delphic." He interviews individuals of high moral influence and sensitivity on what values or sets of values could form a global code of ethics that would help humanity to deal with its problems. The interviewees include a Buddhist monk, a former president of Harvard, a Chinese author, an American philosopher, Mozambique's former first lady, and the director-general of UNESCO. They form the source from which the above eight values originate. Kidder says that these values could help meet a pressing need for shared values. From them, he writes, we may build "downward" to the level of goals, plans, and tactics.

The Third Millennium Project

The Third Millennium Project of Valencia, Spain, in cooperation with UNESCO and ADC Nouveau Millénaire, presented a "Declaration of Human Duties and Responsibilities" to UNESCO in April 1999 to commemorate the arrival of the year 2000. The document was drafted by a "high-level group" chaired by South African Justice Richard J. Goldstone and including Richard Falk, Bernard Kouchner, Ruud Lubbers, Joseph Rothblat, and Wole Soyinka, among others. The declaration was the result of congresses hosted by Valencia on "Human Responsibilities and Duties in the Third Millennium: Towards a Pax Planetaria" (January and April 1998) and "The Universal Declaration of Human Duties and Responsibilities" (December 1998).

The avowed aim of the "Declaration of Human Duties and Responsibilities" is to help the international community rededicate itself to the implementation of human rights and responsibilities by making clear the relationship among rights, duties, and responsibilities. Reaffirming the universal significance of the "Universal Declaration of Human Rights" and the related covenants, the drafters of the Valencia Declaration consider that the realization of rights and freedoms depends on the assumption of the political, moral, ethical, and legal duties and responsibilities implicit in human rights and funda-mental freedoms. These rights and freedoms are recognized by all relevant players in the global community, including states, intergovernmental and nongovernmental organizations, the private sector and other representatives of civil society, com-munities, peoples, and individuals. Hence the need for an explicit formulation of duties and responsibilities.

The declaration consists of a preamble, twelve chapters, and forty-one articles, spelling out in great detail the duties and responsibilities of different players in different sectors of the international community. The twelve chapters of the dec-laration consist of general provisions (articles 1–2); the right to life and human security (articles 3–9); human security and an equitable international order (articles 10–15); meaningful participation in public affairs (article 16); freedom of opin-ion, expression, assembly, association, and religion (articles 17–20); the right to personal and physical integrity (articles 21–25); equality (articles 26–30); protection of minorities and indigenous peoples (articles 31–32); rights of the child and the elderly (articles 33–34); quality of life and standard of living (articles 35–36); education, arts, and culture (articles 37–38); and finally a right to a remedy (articles 39–41).

Common Values in Action

Business and Finance

In practice, sets of international ethical norms and principles are already operating and evolving in many sectors of soci-ety. In international business and finance, the Bretton Woods institutions, including the IMF and the World Bank, or the World Trade Organization set rules and regulations which the members of these organizations ignore only at their peril.

Multilateral agreements cover services such as banking, in-surance, and intellectual property rights. They bind national governments, limiting their domestic-policy choices. The principles underlying these rules and regulations are competition, profit, deregulation, and transparency. The failure so far of countries in the Organization for Economic Cooperation and Development to reach an agreement on a Multilateral Agreement on Investment (MAI) indicates the difficulty of attempts to agree on globally valid codes of conduct, even limited to a particular sector.

International Governance Agencies

For further illustrations of global ethics in action today, one may point to the dominant values-based orientations of many agencies that are global in scope, for example, the United Nations and its agencies, such as UNESCO, UNICEF, and the World Health Organization. The UN charter and the "Universal Declaration of Human Rights" articulate these values, endorsed by signatories. There are also the so-called Third Sector organizations, representing "international civil society." Many of these NGOs advocate or implement particular values, such as Médecins Sans Frontières or Amnesty International. A recent study estimates that nonprofit organizations in just twenty-two countries form a $1.1 trillion sector, employing nineteen million. Considered collectively, their key values include voluntarism, care, and social justice.

Global Academic and Cultural Conventions

Academic, scientific, and professional organizations, as well as the press, sometimes have precisely defined codes of ethics as they exchange knowledge and information worldwide. Their dominant values include truthfulness, right to intellectual property, and free flow of information, which from time to time may come into conflict with national legislation. A similar situation exists in arts, sports, and entertainment, in which performances have been globalized by the mass media. These fields are governed by agreed standards and practices, supported by common appreciation of aesthetic qualities.

Globalization is also strengthening the transnational dimension of crime. International mafias, drug cartels, and terrorist organizations have been among the first to take advantage of relaxation of border controls and advances in communication and transportation. Their operations across national frontiers are based on implicit codes of behavior, the breach of which is bound to be met with due consequence.

The UNESCO Universal Ethics Project

The main problems affecting the future of the human race are tending to become more interconnected, and at the same time more widespread. Dealing with them requires a minimum of common understanding and shared values. In a multipolar world of heightened individualism and a possibly unprecedented splintering of perceptions, it is more than ever necessary to look for the acknowledgment, or rather the emergence, of a common substratum of values which would make economically, socially and culturally viable coexistence possible on a worldwide scale.

— "UNESCO Medium-Term Strategy," 1996–2001

UNESCO has a history of concern with universal values and standards, dating to its 1945 constitution, which states:

that the wide diffusion of culture, and the education of humanity for justice and liberty and peace are indispensable to the dignity of man and constitute a sacred duty which all the nations must fulfill in a spirit of mutual assistance and concern; that a peace based exclusively upon the political and economic arrangements of governments would not be a peace which could secure the unanimous, lasting and sincere support of the peoples of the world, and that the peace must therefore be founded, if it is not to fail, upon the intellectual and moral solidarity of mankind.

The organization's historic vocation was to enlarge that common ground of intellectual and moral solidarity, to delve into the problems that imperil the future of humanity, and at the same time to facilitate better communication and co-operation among nations and cultures. With the creation of the Division of Philosophy and Ethics some years after its founding, the organization was able to focus more closely on cross-cultural moral principles residing in all traditions and civilizations.

As part of the movement, emerging in the 1980s, in support of global shared values, UNESCO began cooperation with the transdisciplinary *Encyclopedia of Global Problems and Human Potential,* an innovative and systematic study of universal problems and the corresponding values to which they relate. In 1986, UNESCO asked the Club of Rome for an international investigation into the ethical values of the twenty-first century. This resulted in *In Search of a Wisdom for the World: The Role of Ethical Values in Education,* which examined the transmission of values and the intersection of traditional and modern value systems. In 1987 a survey-based document, *The World at the Year 2000,* charted the regional distribution of individual and collective values such as freedom, health, material affluence, tolerance, equality, productivity, honesty, and power. The report concluded by emphasizing the primacy of education, the promotion of democracy, and economic, social, and cultural changes essential to facing crises of the next century.

More recently, this dynamic has appeared in UNESCO's Culture of Peace and in its Bioethics and InfoEthics Programs. UNESCO's 186 member states have repeatedly voiced their support for such initiatives. For example, a 1989 General Conference resolution recalled "UNESCO's role in reflecting *universal ethical aspirations* and also the importance of philosophy and the human sciences in the analysis of the *moral principles* governing cooperation among peoples, human solidarity, respect for human rights and the promotion of peace." Likewise, every consultation of member states and partner organizations has endorsed the Division of Philosophy's various programs to promote ethical and civic values. One example from the 1996–97 program: "The great majority of replies emphasized the Organization's ethical mandate. In order to 'avoid new and even deeper splits within the international community' UNESCO should promote *'universal values'* such as respect for human dignity, equity, justice, tolerance, equality, peace and solidarity."

Based on this history, on the perception of a pressing need for common values, and building on the recommendations in the report of the World Commission on Culture and Development, the UNESCO Universal Ethics Project was launched in early 1997. UNESCO, as the global organization for intellectual and cultural cooperation and the only outpost of philosophy in the United Nations, is in a unique position to lead a worldwide discussion on universal values. The UNESCO Universal Ethics Project was conceived so that UNESCO, as coordinator and facilitator, would provide, first, the philosophical gridwork to shape and support the project; second, the international forum in which philosophers and ethicists test the viability and coherence of their ideas; and third, the intergovernmental platform where breakthroughs in universal ethics could be considered and acted upon.

After a year of preparations, an international meeting of experts under the title "Prolégomènes pour une éthique universelle" was convened in Paris in March 1997, in cooperation with La Maison des Sciences de l'Homme. Twelve philosophers, ethicists, theologians, and political philosophers who have been at the forefront of universal ethics participated. The meeting was designed primarily to lay a conceptual and philosophical foundation for universal ethics. It consisted of two parts: a meeting at which work by individual philosophers was presented to the public, and a series of brainstorming sessions, closed to the public, which saw lively exchange on the project's goal, methodology, and conceptual feasibility.

The second meeting of the Universal Ethics Project took place in December 1997 in Naples, Italy, in cooperation with the Istituto Italiano per gli Studi Filosofici. Some thirty philosophers, ethicists, anthropologists, political scientists, economists, sociologists, jurists, and biologists participated. They included Hans Küng, Karl-Otto Apel, Rudd Lubbers, Hong-Koo Lee, Tu Wei-ming, Hassan Hanafi and Henri Atlan, among others. Formal presentation and discussions focused on the interrelated questions of the meaning of universality in the age of cultural diversity and on the ethical implications of globalization.

The two meetings, together with research and reflection by the members of the UNESCO Division of Philosophy and Ethics, have contributed substantively to shaping both the structure and content of the Universal Ethics Project. They have been instrumental in elucidating the following aspects of the project: aims, feasibility, methodology, the problem of universality, the relation of ethics to human rights, and now the effort to generate a new structure of universal ethics for our new century.

Aims

The participants in the first meeting of the Universal Ethics Project agreed that it should identify basic ethical principles for the emerging global society of the twenty-first century. The job would entail putting together ideas, values, and norms that would help humanity deal with such global problems as poverty, underdevelopment, deterioration of the environment, the population explosion, corruption, extremism in

religions and in other forms, intolerance, and social exclu-
sion. This agreement, supported by most of the participants
in the second meeting in Naples, is noteworthy in that it puts
the Universal Ethics Project squarely on the side of "ethical
maximalism."

The ethics that would result if the proposed outline in *Our
Creative Diversity* were followed could very well be called
maximalist. It would not only contain a few existing general
principles that could serve as foundations for elaboration, but
would also contain extrapolated values which may not be
accepted by all cultures. Only a maximalist morality, or a
"full-blooded" or "thick" ethical doctrine, in the phrase of
Michael Walzer, would be capable of providing a more or
less complete account of what we ought to do and how we
ought to live.

A minimalist ethics, on the other hand, is not free-standing.
It would not furnish cross-cultural standards of conduct. Sissela Bok, a minimalist, identifies three clusters of moral values
that could be accepted across communities: first, the positive
duties of mutual care and reciprocity; second, a limited set of
negative injunctions concerning violence, deceit, and betrayal;
and third, the norms for certain rudimentary procedures and
standards of what is just. The minimalist values, thus pared
down, are not sufficient as a full-blooded ethics. Rather, they
represent a minimum basis for a common language of critical
inquiry and dialogue across cultural boundaries. They offer a
possibility for extension into more comprehensive maximalist
requirements and ideals.

The issue between the maximalists and the minimalists is
whether it is possible to build "downward" from a few abstract principles to ethical values and principles that would
be adequate for a good life. Bok, together with Stuart
Hampshire and, in some sense, Rushworth Kidder, seem to
think so, while for Walzer a minimalist morality *necessarily*
expresses the maximalist morality in which it is embed-

ded. It is not a free-standing morality, and it can only be abstracted temporarily from the maximalist morality. For Walzer, acceptance of a moral minimum implies acceptance of a full-blooded morality.

Feasibility

The participants in the Paris meeting further agreed that there are rational grounds for optimism about the feasibility of the UNESCO Universal Ethics Project, a position largely shared by participants in Naples. This consensus is all the more remarkable considering the lingering positivism that questions the validity of all propositions concerning norms and values, and considering the cultural relativism that emphasizes the historical particularity of all values and norms. As is well-known, many so-called postmodernists such as Michel Foucault and Jean-François Lyotard, as well as neopragmatists such as Richard Rorty, deny, for different reasons, the possibility of universally valid ethical values and principles.

Despite these difficulties, we have been able to document a growing search for universal ethical values and principles both at collective and individual levels. This search is gaining such momentum that it can be said to constitute a key element on the international agenda. The 1998 "State of the Future" report, sponsored by the American Council for the United Nations University, lists "encouraging diversity and shared ethical values" fifth among fifteen of humanity's opportunities at the end of the twentieth century. The report states that "global ethics are being debated and studied as never before."

Such a search has been encouraged by a great shift in doctrine in philosophy and the natural and social sciences. Transcending the once dominant abstinence which characterized philosophical reflection on norms and values, philosophers are questioning the positivistic doctrines of meaningfulness, incommensurability, and untranslatability among cultures and languages, and seeking to give universality a new meaning in the context of cultural diversity. Biologists, neurologists, and anthropologists are exploring the universals in the physical and cultural constitution of human beings and societies.

Over and above these changes in doctrine, what gives relevance to the search for common ethical values and principles is the growing urgency of the great problems facing humanity. There is "the simple pragmatic need for a renewed global ethic in view of the global issues at stake and of growing global interdependency."[3] Social and natural scientists have been emboldened by a global discourse on human rights and global problems as well as by an embryonic global civil society, embodied in the movements led by nongovernmental organizations. The legitimacy and efficacy of these organizations do not derive from some organized form of coercion. Rather they spring from the urgency of the problems at hand and from the relevance of the values and goals shared and pursued across national and cultural boundaries. This development gives substance to the assertion that, if the twentieth century was a century of social sciences, the twenty-first century will be a century of ethics.

Methodology

Among the agreements reached by the participants in the Universal Ethics Project was a methodological one, which nevertheless contains substantive implications. The methodology that met with the most support combined two approaches. The ethical values and principles that would form the core of universal ethics, according to this methodology, should be identified by both empirical and reflective approaches. The

---

3. Göran Bexell, background paper for the seminar "The Search for Shared Values in Global Governance" organized by the Bank of Sweden Tercentenary Foundation within the frame of the Intergovernmental Conference on Cultural Policy and Development, March 30–April 2, 1998, Stockholm, Sweden.

approach to universal values begins with an empirical search for values and principles widely held in diverse cultures and religions. Küng thus sets out to identify "the minimum of what the religions of the world already have in common now in the ethical sphere" and professes to draw from them broad, ancient guidelines for human behavior.[4] This process involves an understanding of the hermeneutics of religious texts, sociology of religions and morals, cultural anthropology, and other social sciences.

An empirical approach may also, however, begin with an empirically ascertainable fact about human life and extrapolate from this fact. Thus Sissela Bok finds the basic fact of human life in the shared concern for survival. From this starting point, the search for common values can sort moral constraints and injunctions across communities and "pare down" each one from the point of view of completeness, scope, and level of abstraction. According to Bok, survival and prospering are interests common to all human beings, and ethical values and principles can be deduced from these interests. One such principle is reciprocity; another is the prohibition of violence and deceit; a third is agreement on what constitutes justice. These values are "so down-to-earth and so commonplace"[5] that they are easily recognizable across national, ethnic, religious, and other boundaries. In this way, Bok arrives at a set of moral values, which, however, do not constitute a full-blooded ethics in themselves, but merely a baseline consensus from which to undertake and facilitate further debate.

Bimal K. Matilal, an Indian scholar of Eastern religions and

---

4. Hans Küng and Karl-Josef Kuschel, *A Global Ethic: The Declaration of the Parliament of the World's Religions* (New York: Continuum, 1993), 8.

5. Sissela Bok, *Common Values* (Columbia: University of Missouri Press, 1995).

ethics, advocates what might be called an empiricist version of universal morality. According to Matilal, "A minimal universal ethics" can be based on "some empirically given concerns of human beings."[6] Since there are limits as to how much individual moral systems may differ from each other without ceasing to be a moral system, a set of context-neutral rules constitutes the basic moral fabric that holds the members of a society together. He identifies the following as components of a universal ethical system: respect for life, truth-telling (or the prohibition of lying), and the prohibition against stealing and adultery. He believes that justice, social responsibility, and the obligation to choose good rather than evil could be added, since these virtues are necessary for maintenance of any worthwhile social life.

At the same time, a reflective method is an indispensable complement to the empirical approach. Identifying values and principles needed to deal with the problems of survival and prospering requires us to go beyond the merely empirical. A reflective method would allow us in some sense to "derive" ethical values and principles considered necessary in relation to the problems to be solved.

Karl-Otto Apel takes what has been called a proceduralist approach and proposes a "planetary macroethics" to deal with the problems engendered by the advance of science and technology in our age. Such a macroethics, which would be universal, is based on the discourse ethics that Apel and Jürgen Habermas have elaborated. It is in the presuppositions of a fair, argumentative discourse that universal norms can be found. That we are obliged to discuss controversial subject matter by way of argumentative discourse is neither accidental nor contingent: there is no reasonable alternative.

---

6. Bilal K. Matilal, "Pluralism, Relativism and Interaction between Cultures," in *Culture and Modernity: East-West Philosophical Perspectives*, ed. Eliot Deutsch (Honolulu: University of Hawaii Press, 1991).

It is, as Apel claims, "the transcendental-pragmatic *a priori*" of all philosophical discourse.[7]

Apel identifies four presuppositions implied in any argumentative discourse. First, all intersubjectively valid *meaning* is shared among partners of the discourse. Second, the claim to *truth* is presupposed. Third, the claim to *truthfulness* or *sincerity* of speech — speech taken as an expression of intention — must be recognized. Finally, speech is considered to have *morally relevant rightness*.

Since the noncontingent, normative presuppositions of an argumentative discourse are formal and procedural, they do not prescribe the concrete material norms needed in human interaction. A planetary macroethics would be the never-finished outcome of this argumentative procedure, and as such allow for divergent outcomes, leaving room for the pluralism of individual forms of life.

This "transcendental" approach requires not only that the goals be clearly set, but also that the problems be clearly understood. This is why identification of the problems facing humanity plays such an important part in the Universal Ethics Project's agenda. Many of the "proto-" universal ethics contained in the various declarations mentioned above use this transcendental-reflective method: values and principles are advanced in view of given constraints. Essential to the transcendental-reflective approach is that we ask *what values and principles may be mobilized in order to steer technological and economic change for the purposes of human survival and flourishing.* It is clear that some factors are beyond the influence of ideas, values, and principles. It is, however, equally clear that the future may be affected and even determined by humans acting on the basis of normative ideas and

---

7. Karl-Otto Apel, "A Planetary Macroethics for Humankind," in *Culture and Modernity: East-West Philosophical Perspectives* ed. Eliot Deutsch (Honolulu: University of Hawaii Press, 1991), 261–75.

principles. This is why, as Bertrand de Jouvenel points out, that long-term forecasting is naturally and even inevitably normative.

The efficacy of normative ideas and principles in influencing and modifying the given constraints in physical nature and human behavior cannot be explained by a clear-cut causal nexus. It is for this reason that the reflective method makes greater use of conjectures or critical imagination than a purely scientific method. In this context, the Delphic method, which relies on the trained imagination and sensibility of those with greater experience and expertise in a given field, acquires methodological importance in the search for common values.

Universality in Diversity

In view of the given diversity in culture and values, the Universal Ethics Project cannot avoid the problem of how universality should be understood. I have already touched on the deep suspicion regarding all universalistic projects, as well as the alliance between universalistic claims and the hegemonic intentions of certain powers. The idea of universality as transcendent or transcendental, as prevalent in the Western philosophical tradition, today lacks persuasion and is in need of revision and development. This is perhaps one lasting service that relativism has rendered to philosophy. New avenues of thought must be explored and made productive if we are to go forward from the mire of this now-defunct controversy.

A conception of universality in this age of great cultural diversity must meet two demands. On the one hand, it must do justice to the incontrovertible fact that there is — de facto — a wide range of agreement on values across religions, cultures, and societies. On the other hand, the notion of universality must respond satisfactorily to suspicions that political ambitions are indelibly associated with all universalistic projects.

Today there are many vigorous philosophical attempts to

recognize and integrate diversity and relativity within a universalistic framework. Charles Taylor, for one, attempts to throw new light on the relationship between diversity and universality by distinguishing between cross-cultural consensus on certain norms and values and the divergent means of justification. While justification for values may differ from society to society, agreement on the norms themselves can be left unaffected. This situation, Taylor contends, is something like the "overlapping consensus" that Rawls describes in his *Political Liberalism.*[8]

Taylor then goes on to discuss several concrete examples of the convergence of norms in different philosophical backgrounds. One such example involves a variety of reform Buddhism represented by the followers of Phutthathat in Thailand, who are strong advocates of human rights and democratic politics. But their justifications of these principles are not the standard Western justifications centered on the inherent dignity and equality of human beings. Rather, their advocacy is rooted in the fundamental Buddhist value of nonviolence, which is seen to imply a respect for the autonomy of each person and rejection of coercion in human affairs. The principle of nonviolence also generates other consequences, such as the requirement of ecological sensitivity and the need to set limits to growth.

Michael Walzer makes an interesting attempt to *describe* an experience of universality or "a moment or a series of moments of moral affirmation, or judgment, or action that either cross cultural/political boundaries or simply make no reference to them." Walzer refers to the demands for "Truth" and "Justice" articulated by a distant people, and the instinctive assent and understanding of these demands by us who

---

8. Charles Taylor, "Conditions of an Unforced Consensus on Human Rights," unpublished paper presented at the second workshop of the Carnegie Council's project on "The Growth of East Asia and Its Impact on Human Rights," held in Bangkok in March 1996.

are ignorant of their concrete aspirations. The thick morality out of which these values spring may be very different
from ours. Nevertheless, we share with the distant people a
core of meaning and understanding in these demands. Walzer
offers a further example first given by Rousseau: the response of an "uncivilized man" who feels immediate empathy
with another human being in distress. Such "first promptings
of humanity" may be the source and method of an actual
universal morality.[9]

In my own work I have been developing a notion of universality that preserves respect for cultures in their individuality.
Central to this notion is the idea of the cultural synthesis. Cultures in each time and place strive to forge a synthesis of ideas,
values, and practices that would enable them to deal with the
tasks of survival and flourishing within the constraints set
by the natural circumstances and by each culture's knowledge and understanding of these circumstances. As the world
and the culture's knowledge of it change, the synthesis must
constantly adapt to these changing circumstances.

At some moment, the synthesis would be perceived by those
inside as well as outside the culture to have reached an optimal point. This point would represent reflective equilibrium
between the continuing interaction and interchange of ideas
and values, on the one hand, and the recalcitrant but changing environment on the other. A culture, having achieved such
an optimal point, may claim superiority for its synthesis over
all others. The basis of the claim would be that the synthesis
transcends the limitations of its predecessors and competitors,
avoiding their weakness while incorporating their strengths.
Such a claim of optimality should be understood as a claim of
universality. Since such a concept of universality is in constant

---

9. Michael Walzer, "Notes on the Experience of Universality," unpublished paper presented at the second meeting of the UNESCO Universal
Ethics Project, December 1–4, 1997, Naples, Italy, p. 1.

evolution, I propose to regard the concept as a regulative ideal in the Kantian sense.

In providing the philosophical gridwork for universal ethics, efforts must be made to take these and other dimensions of philosophical thought into account. The issue of universality is particularly important for the Universal Ethics Project, because the political and economic uses to which this idea has been put, and sometimes is still being put, have discredited other such projects.

Ethics and Human Rights

One of the most frequently discussed issues in the evolution of the Universal Ethics Project has been the relationship between universal ethics and the existing documents on universal human rights, values, and norms, particularly the "Universal Declaration of Human Rights" and the related covenants. A consensus exists among the participants that these documents should form the starting point of the search for universal ethics. The "Universal Declaration of Human Rights," which recently celebrated its fiftieth anniversary, today enjoys wider acceptance across cultures than ever before. It represents the vanguard of universally shared common values. The international legal framework for human rights, including the 1998 agreement to create an international criminal court, is certainly a great achievement for the international community, one which needs to be further developed and strengthened. As universal ethics aims to identify ethical values and principles for the emerging global society of the twenty-first century, the rights and responsibilities as stipulated in the human rights charter will figure prominently.

It is also clear that universal ethics would be based on values and principles of a different, most likely higher, axiological order than those in the human rights documents. They would be values and principles from which particular rights and responsibilities may be derived. Together they would constitute an ethical statement. Universal ethics cannot therefore aim to be a legal or even a quasi-legal instrument, with some organized form of enforcement. The sole source of its authority would be the relevance and persuasiveness of the values and principles for human survival and flourishing. A declaration with quasi-legalistic intent can give neither appropriate nor adequate expression to such an ethical statement. Ethical values and principles almost always permit their contraries, and an ethical document if expressed in legalistic language and form can always be nullified by a document containing the contrary values and principles. Universal ethics must be expressed in a literary form capable of showing the dynamic relationships among values and principles, including contrary ones. Forging a literary form that would give adequate expression to a universally shared ethical commitment is a major challenge for the Universal Ethics Project.

Prospects toward the Ethics Charter of the Twenty-first Century

How, then, do we proceed to an ethical statement that could serve as a universally acceptable guideline as humanity struggles to deal with the tasks of survival and flourishing in the twenty-first century? The signposts of such a statement have been clearly posited. It is to be a maximalist document containing ethical values and principles adequate for and relevant to the myriad problems facing humanity; these values will be ascertained by empirical as well as reflective methods. Such a document must also be acceptable universally. Universality must not be exclusive, but inclusive in that it is capable of accommodating the cultural diversity that characterizes the world today. Furthermore, it must be an ethical document of higher axiological order than the human rights charter, showing how particular rights and responsibilities enshrined in it could be derived from the values and principles within it.

A necessary first step is to make an inventory of ethical values and principles proposed in other declarations and studies — private and public, national and international, and religious and secular — that have been designed to deal with certain problems facing humanity. Five categories of documents can be named:

1. intergovernmental documents;

2. reports of international commissions and declarations of international conferences;

3. nongovernmental projects and surveys;

4. statements of individuals, mainly participants in meetings related to the Universal Ethics Project;

5. proposals from religious traditions.

Once the values and principles are identified, they will be placed in relation to the problems they are intended to solve. It is clear, however, that the list of problems can vary greatly according to the level of generality and concreteness at which the problems are identified and described. The list can also vary according to the vantage point from which the authors of the documents approach the problems. The participants in the first meeting in Paris, "Prolégomènes pour une éthique universelle," for instance, identified eight such problems, while Aurelio Peccei's list encompasses twenty-seven. The *Encyclopedia of World Problems and Human Potential* claims to have identified 12,203 world problems put forth in international journals and in the documents of some twenty thousand international nonprofit organizations. In order to circumvent the difficulty inherent in this profusion, we have found it useful to make an inventory of problems and issues for which solutions lie only in the realm of ethical values and principles.

What, then, are the basic issues and problems around which the ethical values and principles could be organized?

The following list is one among many proposals and contains several clusters of issues and problems. First is the problem of the human relationship to nature. The dynamic at work involves accommodating unlimited human needs and desires to a limited ecosystem. Our relationship to nature must enable management of our economy while perpetuating nature's ability to sustain our economy. The task is not simply to control nature but to control ourselves as well, so that the economy can fit within the natural ecology. The way we face this challenge relates to the way we see the human person: as a being separate from nature, or as one species embedded in the intricate web of natural processes that contains and sustains all life.

The first cluster of issues leads naturally to a second: the conception of what constitutes human happiness or, to put it another way, what constitutes the meaning of life or human fulfillment. Our views regarding what constitutes the meaning of life are bound to influence the priorities we assign to values and thus the way we behave, both in relation to ourselves and others. An attitude that sees human happiness in the accumulation of material wealth may be contrasted with a holistic perspective, which would enable us to balance satisfaction between different dimensions of human existence: between "inner" and material satisfaction.

Such views are intimately connected with the issue of the relationship between the individual and the community in which he or she has his existential root. The basic problem is the role we assign to individual freedom and creativity on the one hand, and the need for the stability and order of the community, without which no meaningful human existence is possible. The aggressive, individualistic ethics that formed the backbone of modern industrial civilization may require some revision and tempering by greater concern for the human good. The problem of the individual in relationship to the community is a particularly difficult one, since a universal ethics worthy of the name must have a place of honor for individuals and their creativity.

The issue of individualism is intimately connected with the problem of justice, both among individuals at a national level and among nations at an international level. Injustice, nationally and internationally, is the most important source of disruption in the fabric of society, as well as of conflict among nations. At play are the tensions between equality and freedom, between the good of one individual or group and another, and between rights and responsibilities. Many conceptions of justice in social organization have been tried: paternalism, colonialism, utilitarianism, capitalism, socialism, and now market liberalism. They have all been found wanting in fundamental respects, some more than others. Universal ethics must point a way beyond these conceptions of justice.

The Task Ahead

The task, then, is how to integrate the problems and needs of humanity thus identified and the values and principles thus scouted into a persuasive and coherent whole, which can guide humanity in its tasks of survival and flourishing. Such a document should not exhaust itself in listing the ascertained values and principles. It must demonstrate the relationship among these values and principles so that the relationship of foundation and derivation is clear. Further, since the aim is to forge an ethical statement acceptable to all societies and cultures, built on different perceptions and aspirations, it must accommodate the challenge of cultural diversity and polarities of values and principles. Such diversity and polarity reflect not only the living dilemma of action and underlying values; the diversity reflects the real source of conflict among cultures and societies. Integrating diversity within each ethical principle, rather than offering a hasty compromise, enables the participants in the ethical dialogue to sense the dimensions of the conflict and the space within which a consensus can be forged. The document must therefore make clear a relationship of creative tension among conflicting but not irreconcilable values, so that a common vision can emerge in an open-ended, evolutionary process of dialogue and mutual learning.

– *Chapter 3* –

RESPONSIBILITY IN
THE WORLD OF MAMMON

THEOLOGY, JUSTICE, AND
TRANSNATIONAL CORPORATIONS

William Schweiker

As the largest peacetime expansion of the U.S. economy in history got underway, in the 1980s, the Christian churches began to speak out forcefully on economic matters. A "decade of the economic pastorals," as some called that period of pronouncements by Roman Catholic Bishops and Protestant denominational bodies, signaled an awakening of the churches to fundamental changes in the world and our perceptions of it. We witnessed the expansion of international corporations and, thanks to the worldwide media system, the globalization of commercial interests and images. The global economy, a $400-trillion-a-year giant, creates new areas of business that reach beyond national laws and governments. Stock market crashes as well as the flow of capital and jobs around the world have set new patterns of immigration and income distribution. What is more, by some estimates roughly a fifth of the world's population lives in absolute poverty, bringing fear, early death, squalid living conditions, and disease. The fact of world poverty raises profound questions of distributive justice. Little wonder, then, that from the papacy

105

to Wall Street there has been intense concern about and reflection on the moral, political, and economic features of global developments.

Theorists of globality, as the idea is called, say our age is marked by a compression of time and space and also by the intensification of consciousness through the awareness of human diversity. The speed of communication as well as the movement of peoples (often forced movement) seems to make the world "shrink" so that many speak, in popular terms, of the global village. Roland Robertson argues that globalization "involves comparative interaction of different forms of life." The reflexivity of globalization, sparked by this awareness of diversity, "is a heightening of civilizational, societal, ethnic, regional and, indeed, individual self-consciousness."[1] Robertson is right to understand globalization in cultural terms: globality is about human meaning as well as social process; we have to explore human values and identities as well as institutions. In a similar way, but focusing on the mobility of people and money, political economist Saskia Sassen notes that the "global city is a strategic site for disempowered actors because it enables them to gain presence, to emerge as subjects even when they do not gain direct power."[2] In thinking about "globalization" we must consider social processes and institutions, but also cultural forces and human persons in their manifold struggles to orient their lives.

---

1. Roland Robertson, *Globalization: Social Theory and Global Culture* (London: Sage, 1992), 27. On this theme also see Richard Osmer, "The Teaching Ministry in a Multicultural World," in *The Spirit and the Modern Authorities,* ed. Max L. Stackhouse with Don S. Browning (Harrisburg, Pa.: Trinity Press International, forthcoming), which will follow the present volume in this series.

2. Saskia Sassen, *Globalization and Its Discontents: Essays on the New Mobility of People and Money* (New York: New Press, 1998), xxi.

Globality and Persons

Sassen and Robertson voice concerns driving the present inquiry, namely, how to further the dignity of persons as moral subjects and, conceptually, the need to understand "globality" not only in sociological but also cultural terms as these bear on the worldly reality of economic life. Christian faith, I show below, has always had a highly differentiated and reflexive conception of "globality" through its idea of "world." This complexity is economically specified, importantly, in the discourse of "mammon." The ethical advantage of theological discourse in thinking about the globalization of economic forces is its intimate connection of "world" and "mammon" to beliefs about justice, something too often missing in discourse about globality. It is the connection among world-mammon-justice that I intend to examine and further in the course of the argument.

Christian conceptions of "world" are systematically related to beliefs about the dignity and capacities of agents, divine and human. The very idea of "world" in Christian faith is related to and dependent on agents (divine, human, institutional) who create and shape reality. The world of nature and history, for instance, have worth because God is creator; social systems and cultures are valuable because they are the stuff of human action. This means that justice, substantively defined, is about how to treat agents who make possible the space of life — the world.

What then of economic forces? Here matters of definition are most difficult. Human beings have always engaged in patterns of exchange: barter, trade, and the like. Mythically speaking, Eden is "pre-commercial," but as soon as Adam and Eve enter history as agents, exchange is present. Ancient "economies" were usually agrarian and embedded in special social and cultural relations, often deeply religious and patriarchal in nature. In our situation, having traversed mercantile

and commercial ages, we find highly differentiated and co-
ordinated financial and credit systems as well as high-tech
industries and even postindustrial information flows that are
influencing all aspects of economic life. New kinds of agencies have emerged — the World Bank, International Monetary
Fund, World Trade Organization, as well as the North American Free Trade Agreement — and transnational corporations
collaborate in the making of international law.

What should we call this economic situation? Deploy-
ing the conceptual richness of the Christian conception of
"world," I speak of the "world of mammon" and the "world
of economic globalization" as general sociocultural conditions. But I am also interested in the "agents" acting in and
creating that world. Given this interest, I will focus a portion of the inquiry on transnational corporations as global
economic agents. Because of the link in Christian thought
between "worlds" and "agents," I have been led to designate our economic situation both in terms of the world of
mammon and corporate economy. But when I designate more
general features of economic life, I sometimes use the terminology of commercial culture or market society. The point
is that I am denoting economic forces deeply entangled with
the emerging global reality.

This brings us to the central problem. In economic exchange
there is the constant possibility of losing the means to protect
the ground of those societies, namely, the dignity of persons as
historical agents. The loss of "persons" is a pervasive threat in
systems of commodification that reduce value to one system
of measurement (say, money) and feed human vice, especially
greed. The inability to articulate a robust sense of the worth
of persons is a fact in most commercial cultures.[3] This is a

---

3. Matters of money and exchange and, hence, commodification within
a shared system of measuring value, have been discussed at least since
Aristotle. On this history see Lionel Robbins, *A History of Economic
Thought,* ed. Steven G. Medema and Warren J. Samuels (Princeton, N.J.:

regular feature of economic exchange and not (as some think) peculiar to a capitalist economy. The poor throughout the ages have been driven to sell not only their labor, but also their bodies, children, and futures. We forget that in the ancient (Western) world, slavery was accepted as economic necessity; empires, then and now, were built on the backs of the poor. The current global sex trade, selling of children, and dealing in body parts is a sad reminder of these facts. Grinding poverty means that everything can (must?) become a "commodity" for sale, trade, or negotiation. To demonize capitalism is to miss the deeper problem inherent in economic life as such.

The paradox of the global age is how human beings develop systems of commodification that create immense wealth, shape consciousness, and yet endanger the meaningfulness of life through unjust distribution or rampant consumerism. Understood from a Christian perspective, any and every attack on the worth of persons and God's good creation is to be resisted and transformed. The direction of my argument, accordingly, is to show the way theological ethics can articulate the dignity of persons and play a transformative role in the life of corporate economies. I am engineering a critical interaction between a distinctly theological construal of globality ("world") and trends in current thought about globalization and economy. This cross-fertilization of ideas is crucial to a viable theological ethics of culture.[4]

Princeton University Press, 1998). For a more recent inquiry into these matters, and also the idea of gift beyond the logic of exchange, see Jacques Derrida, *Given Time,* vol. 1: *Counterfeit Money,* trans. Peggy Kamuf (Chicago: University of Chicago Press, 1992). For a parallel argument about "greed" in this series see Kosuke Koyama, "Observation and Revelation: A Global Dialogue," in vol. 3, *Christ and the Dominions of Civilization,* ed. Max L. Stackhouse with Diane Oberchain (Harrisburg, Pa.: Trinity Press International, forthcoming).

4. I deploy the resources of the Christian tradition not simply to speak to the Christian community, but, rather, to engage wider debates about how we can and should live healthy, complex, and responsible lives. For a further

I want to begin by specifying the "world of mammon" as
a shorthand phrase for a theological-ethical interpretation of
our economic situation. This task also requires clarity about
trends in the history of Christian thinking about "mammon."

The World of Mammon

The idea of "world" is systematically complex in Christian
faith. To say that the idea is "systematically complex" merely
means that "world" relates in a nuanced but coherent way
to every other Christian belief. There is a distinct logic to
Christian convictions. First, "world" is bound to the idea of
creation as God's bestowal of being and worth. Creation is
not a matter of exchange or refashioning preexistent "stuff"
on the model of human labor. It is the creation and gift of
being. Christian faith is not metaphysically dualistic; it is radically monotheistic, and this means creation is good. Next,
"world" designates the realm of earthly reality; it is a descriptive term for the conditions of human existence as orderly
(cosmos) rather than chaotic. The ancients could speak of
the "ecumenical" church, meaning thereby the whole civilized "world." In this sense, "world" does not designate the
status of goodness in reality, as creation does, but rather a
sociocultural insight about communal boundaries, patterns of
social intelligibility, and the common good. All human communities enact some "cosmos" or they simply cease to exist.
Yet, third, the "world" also denotes, in terms of conceptions
of sin, that reality which does not know God or Christ and in
fact opposes God's goodness and grace (cf. John 1:10). The
human "cosmos" we actually inhabit is one deeply distorted
by hatred, violence, and injustice. This is why Christians are
to be "in" but not "of" the world. Indeed, one could gain

---

elaboration of this approach to theological ethics see William Schweiker,
Power, Value, and Conviction: Theological Ethics in the Postmodern Age
(Cleveland: Pilgrim Press, 1998).

the whole world and in doing so lose one's soul (Mark 8:36). The world of sin is a reality constituted by denial and destruction and yet driven, unknowingly, to continue its own undoing.[5] Hence, fourth, soteriologically, the "world" is that for which Christ suffered (cf. John 3:16). Salvation is never limited simply to the individual; all creation groans for renewal and liberation. The depth of this conviction about Christ's salvific work extends to the insistence, in ecumenical Christianity, that one can hope in God's glory and in "a world without end." The idea of "world" is thus linked, finally, to eschatological convictions about the reign of God.

The idea of "world" relates a descriptive claim (human societies requires stability and order) to ideas about creation, sin, redemption, and eschatology. The reduction of the meaning of the "world" to any single appraisal — to, say, "the world is utterly fallen"; "the world is obviously 'God's body'" — falls below the complexity of Christian thinking as well as actual experience. Nihilistic despair, just like naive optimism, does not ring true to the subtle realism of this conception of existence.[6] This complex construal of the "world" presents a profound moral, practical outlook. A properly Christian response to social and cultural existence will endorse its goodness as created, resist it as fallen, work for its transformation, and hope in its salvation. Christians are to love the world in its finitude and proper relation to God. The constant danger is to fall into an inordinate love or hatred of the world.

---

5. One might note, for historical purposes, that this is how, in *The City of God*, Augustine thought God punished sinners: the sinner is allowed to remain in her or his sin. The punishment, then, is that God sustains something amid its act of self-destruction.
6. For recent conceptions of moral and theological realism see William Schweiker, *Responsibility and Christian Ethics* (Cambridge: Cambridge University Press, 1995), and also Michael Welker, *God the Spirit*, trans. John F. Hoffmeyer (Minneapolis: Fortress Press, 1994).

This account of the "world" is manifest in Christian responses to "mammon" and thinking about economic justice.
Within the barter and agrarian cultures of the ancient Near
East, the term "mammon" represents the Aramaic word for
riches or wealth. It is derived, probably, from the Semitic root
mn meaning "to be firm, reliable." Mammon is something secure; it is that on which one relies for sustenance and life. In
the New Testament it occurs only in the words of Jesus, but
it is not uncommon in the Targums and Talmud. Throughout
scripture there is the recognition of private property; a divine
command, in the Decalogue, against theft; periodic redistri-
bution of wealth (the Jubilee Year); divine blessing tied to
prosperity and progeny; and, even in the parables of Jesus,
the awareness that a worker is due his wages. Of course,
within Jesus' parables the extravagance of the divine reign is
presented in such a way as to overturn normal patterns of economic distribution. The least are given the most; the faithful
son is not welcomed with the same abundance as the prodigal.
These seeming inversions of justice by extravagant love do not
negate the importance of property.[7] The scriptures acknowledge the rightful place of mammon (wealth, gain, possession)
in human life.

On the other hand, mammon has been seen as a basic threat
to the moral and religious life. Jesus insisted that "you cannot serve God and mammon" (Matt. 6:24 = Luke 16:13). At
issue is that on which persons rely, on what provides security in life. Jesus repeatedly bids his followers to trust in God,
not wealth, for the necessities of life. "For the love of money
is the root of all evil" is a basic theme in scripture. The insight seems to be that sin entails a confusion between means
of human exchange and that in which one ought to trust,

7. On the connection between justice and the extravagance of love see
Paul Ricoeur, "Love and Justice," in his *Figuring the Sacred: Religion,
Narrative, and Imagination,* trans. David Pellauer, ed. Mark I. Wallace
(Minneapolis: Fortress Press, 1995), 315–30.

namely, God's covenantal fidelity. Church fathers, like Tertullian and Chrysostom, railed against the dangers of money. As early as Gregory of Nyssa, "mammon" was taken to be the name of the demon of riches or a Canaanite god. Drawing on a distinction first made in "The Rich Man's Salvation" by Clement of Alexandria, Augustine noted that some things are to be used and others enjoyed. Money is to be used; only God is the fit object of ultimate human love — enjoyment. Confusion at this level is sin, the confusing of what is not God for God. While Augustine deploys the language of "love" and its object rather than Hebraic ideas of covenant, the point is the same as the covenantal argument made in key New Testament texts. By the Middle Ages, and culminating later in Milton's *Paradise Lost,* it is not surprising that mammon was pictured as a demon. And even in nonreligious circles during the Renaissance mammon was personified as greed — for example, Sir Epicure Mammon, the greedy knight of Ben Jonson's *The Alchemist.*

The lesson is that "mammon" evokes fascination, grows into devotion, but can, finally, enslave. It is a threat to the spiritual and moral life, both at the level of specific vices (e.g., greed), but also in terms of faith and loyalty to the divine expressed as covenantal fidelity or the right object of human desire. This is the paradox noted above, namely, that human beings can create systems of meaning that are self-negating. The root of the paradox is not in systems or in things, *but in us.* We can define our lives by a commodity and thus deny our dignity by equating worth with things having only use, exchange, and sign-value. Realizing this fact, the Christian tradition in the West has seen mammon as a basic social "power." It is a sphere of life necessary for human existence, but which can drive to encompass the whole of life and in doing so betray demonic features. Economic activity and valuation must be set within, limited by, and judged according to more basic moral and religious norms and purposes.

In the development of the Western Christian tradition there arose various ways to conceive of the proper context of economic activity. By and large, classical Protestants from Luther and Calvin to John Wesley and Jonathan Edwards tended to continue the biblical insight about covenantal relations. This insight maintained that the norms and purposes of human life arise within oath-created patterns of interaction founded, ultimately, in God's fidelity to creation, Israel, and the church. In order to live out such covenants, persons must fulfill their vocations or callings within spheres of sovereignty, for example, in family life (father; mother; child), the civil sphere (citizen; ruler; soldier), and religiously (church member; leader; missionary). As various scholars note, a covenantal view of life received concrete institutional embodiment through ideas of vocation. In this way, it presents a highly differentiated conception of social life.[8] By means of these vocations persons could be good stewards of natural, social, and spiritual resources.

In Roman Catholic ethics the idea of covenant has played less of a role. The focus of thought, at least since Thomas Aquinas, has been on basic claims of entitlement within a differentiated, hierarchical conception of human ends. The view is that human beings have a natural right to the preservation of their lives (including self-defense) as well as a responsibility to participate in the common, social good. But "life" and the "common good" have to be conceived in terms of related, but distinct, ends or *teloi*. These ends, the natural ends of human existence and also the supernatural end in the vision of God as a gift of grace, are obviously ordered. The pursuit of natural ends — human flourishing as individuals and communities — must serve the purposes of the supernatural ends

---

8. Several of the essays in this series present this view of life. See especially Mary Stewart Van Leeuwen, "Faith, Feminism, and the Family in an Age of Globalization," which forms chapter 5 in the present volume.

of life. This "two-level" conception of reality has been seriously questioned in the modern age, even by contemporary Roman Catholic theologians. Nevertheless, Roman Catholic thought still stresses differentiated conceptions of ends as important for understanding the meaning and dignity of human economic activity as well as its limits. We humans do need bread to live; but we do not live by bread alone!

Obviously, the legacy of Protestant and Roman Catholic thought about the place of labor, exchange, and wealth in human life is too complex to examine in one essay. I will, nevertheless, work ecumenically and draw inspiration from the different sides of the Western Christian traditions. My argument links a differentiated account of social subsystems consistent with features of convenantal thinking with a claim about the good of persons-as-agents in relation to God, a claim that draws on Augustinian and Thomistic insights about the goods of life. In terms of moral theory, at issue is the connection between duties and ends, social norms and sources of value.

Given the historical legacy of Christian thought, that there is a mountain of literature among contemporary theologians on justice and global economics is hardly surprising. Among many theologians there has been a profound suspicion of market economies. The world of mammon and the reality of economic forces have been often painted in terms of fallenness and sin. For Pope Leo XIII, thinkers in the American social gospel such as Walter Rauschenbusch, and current liberation theologians, the market was often seen as a profound impediment to the just distribution of material goods. Other theologians, advocating as did Paul Tillich some form of democratic socialism, also worried about market economies. In its extreme form, these perspectives identified economic injustice with capitalism.

Since the 1980s, there has been a shift in analysis. This shift rests on an acknowledgment of the sinfulness of mammon, but also the insight that the "world of mammon" taken descriptively is the fact of globalized, differentiated social systems. These systems are a more or less orderly reality (a cosmos) needed to sustain human life in our age; they are also (more or less) consistent with democratic politics. More than one scholar has noted that the "corporate economies" and personal rights and freedoms tend to go hand in hand. Protestant theologians, like Max Stackhouse, David Krueger, and others, as well as the U.S.A. Roman Catholic Bishops and moral theologians Dennis McCann and David Hollenbach have reopened the question of the moral assessment of the market.[9] Even Pope John Paul II, in his encyclicals on labor, makes a proper, if limited, place for the growth and expansion of the market.[10] There has been a concern for matters of justice and the common good. David Krueger has put the matter well:

> From a Christian theological perspective, if we affirm the enduring legacy and applicability of the common good for a market-based society in a global economy, then we must be able to define and support the respect in which the economic practices of creating wealth, exchanging goods and services in markets, working for business corporations, and making profits are consistent with and practically supportive of a common good of society that stands beyond private goods and interests.[11]

---

9. See Max L. Stackhouse, *Public Theology and Political Economy: Christian Stewardship in Modern Society* (Grand Rapids, Mich.: Eerdmans, 1987); Max L. Stackhouse et al., *Christian Social Ethics in a Global Era* (Nashville: Abingdon Press, 1995); David Krueger et al., *The Business Corporation and Productive Justice* (Nashville: Abingdon, 1996) and National Conference of Catholic Bishops, *Economic Justice for All* (Washington, D.C.: United States Catholic Conference, 1986).

10. See, for example, John Paul II, *Centesimus Annus* (1991).

11. Krueger, *Business Corporation and Productive Justice*, 40.

Much current work in Christian ethics focuses on the extent to which market societies are consistent with and can be made supportive of democracy and the common good. This focus is to combat the radical consumerism and unjust disparity of wealth too readily seen in such societies.

The World of Economic Globalization

Before turning to questions of justice, we need to explore the "world of mammon" from a different, nontheological perspective. Contemporary societies under the pressure of modernization and globalization are internally pluralistic. By "pluralistic" one means that they are culturally diverse and socially differentiated. In these nations, diverse communities struggle for cultural recognition and viability. No one culture is immune from the impact of others; cultures are not self-contained units. There is a seeming cacophony of voices among and within cultures. Additionally, different social spheres or subsystems (economy, law, education, politics, media, etc.) work by their own logic, rules, norms, and primary purposes. This seems to be the contemporary expression of the insight of covenantal thinking.[12] That is, pluralistic societies, when they function properly, enable the various subsystems, analogous to the differentiation of vocations and spheres of sovereignty, to interact and yet constrain each other. This is to insure that no one subsystem gains a tyrannous relation to the social whole. In this context, "tyranny," as Michael Walzer notes, means the invasion of one subsystem — say, the economy — into all others (say, family), thereby converting and homogenizing values, norms,

---

12. On the functional differentiation of complex societies see Niklas Luhmann, *Social Systems*, trans. John Bednarz, Jr., with Dirk Baeker (Stanford, Calif.: Stanford University Press, 1995). A similar argument, based on Protestant ideas about the "orders of creation" or "spheres of sovereignty," can be found in Stackhouse, *Public Theology and Political Economy*.

authorities, and relations.[13] Commercialism, as opposed to commerce, would pose precisely that kind of situation: it would be a social world in which there could be no "outside" to commerce; everything would be commodified and saleable. This admittedly hypothetical situation would be the extreme negative or sinful instance of the "world of mammon."

Pluralistic societies are one social means to combat such tyranny — when they are functioning properly. Each social sphere must distribute its primary good and also work to check the tyranny of any other sphere in the whole of common life. The intrinsic heterogeneity of pluralistic societies means that every social subsystem has an "outside" with which it must work and contend. In economic life, the primary good is the creation of wealth in order to meet the economic needs of a society, namely, the needs of material well-being and survival. We cannot and ought not expect that economic institutions will deny their primary purpose and continue to survive. Societies need to insure that other spheres check the tyrannous drive of the economy (or law, media, or whatever). This is accomplished by having robust and vigorous social subsystems interacting with each other.

Granting the obvious fact that economies are social institutions, one must see that human "worlds" are also constituted culturally. This requires, I will argue, an "outside" to the value schema of the economy, an outside provided in part by religious discourse. This is especially the case in the age of globalization, when the wedding of market and media enables new ways of self-understanding and identity formation. The global flow of cultural artifacts through commercial means — that is, the new "sign-value" of commodities beyond their manifest use and exchange value (e.g., name-brand products; pictures of pop stars) — shapes human identities.[14] We must,

---

13. Michael Walzer, *Spheres of Justice: A Defense of Pluralism and Equality* (New York: Basic Books, 1983).

14. On the idea of sign-value see Jean Baudrillard, "Consumer Society,"

therefore, move beyond institutional analysis and examine how self-understanding and world-making are structured by and yet animate pluralistic social systems. The economy, especially the global economy, involves a massive network of interlaced influences between culture and society: the economy is one of the social spheres, and yet it also mingles and mediates cultural meanings in a plethora of ways that affect cultures powerfully and unpredictably. This cultural power is paradigmatically seen in transnational corporations, which are economic agents and also vehicles of the imagination.

If we look at transnational corporations in terms of the connection between social spheres and cultural production, what do we see? A corporation is "an artifact with its own internal 'spirit' or 'character' and with legal standing as an agent, an actor, in human affairs." More pointedly, a corporation is "a community of persons designed for efficient production that must base every decision on the question of whether or not it can continue to produce."[15] A corporation has what some theorists call an "internal culture" (a character, ethos, or spirit) even as it is also an economic institution. This double fact about the corporation has led to complex debates about whether or not a corporation is a "moral person" and also to questions about the source and limits of corporate responsibility.[16] We can at least say that a corporation is

---

in *Reflections on Commercial Life: An Anthropology of Classical Texts from Plato to the Present,* ed. Patrick Murray (New York: Routledge, 1997), 447–73.

15. Stackhouse, *Public Theology and Political Economy,* 124–25.

16. On this see Peter A. French, "The Corporation as a Moral Person," in *The Spectrum of Responsibility,* ed. Peter A. French (New York: St. Martin's Press, 1991), 290–304. Also see C. Edward Arrington and William Schweiker, "The Rhetoric and Rationality of Accounting Practice," *Accounting, Organizations and Society* 17, no. 6 (1992): 511–33, and William Schweiker, "Accounting for Ourselves: Accounting Practice and the Discourse of Ethics," *Accounting, Organizations, and Society* 18, nos. 2–3 (1993): 231–52.

an "agent" if not a full "person." It is, legally speaking, an agent of shareholders; philosophically, it is an agent insofar as a corporation has the capacity to shape, influence, and even create reality directed by purposes and by some (complex or simple) means of decision making. Yet corporations lack a robust self-consciousness; they are not personal agents. Corporations are instrumental agents in social goods while also fostering or destroying moral values.

How should we speak of a corporation as a *global* agent? First, "transnational" corporations are "agents" of global reach that face the problems of production and distribution of goods and services. By its very designation, a "transnational" is a community that transcends national, political, legal, and economic boundaries. A "transnational corporation" is an economic entity that has freed itself from embeddedness in a specific nation's economy and culture. Whether or not modern market economies as such are "disembedded" from pre-commercial realities (to use Michael Polanyi's terms), this is clearly the case with transnational corporations. While it may be true that, say, IBM or Nike retains the cast of its "mother" country in terms of management style, tax law, ethos, mores, and so on, these entities are free to incarnate themselves in different and quite diverse cultural contexts. A famous example is Japanese automakers in the United States. Styles of management had to confront deep cultural patterns and to make adaptations, even as American workers had to refashion their self-understandings. The differentiation of social subsystems coupled with the disembeddedness of the corporation are preconditions for transnational corporate agents. And this fact poses grave questions of economic justice. On the global scene, what common good is the corporation to serve?

Second, the liberation of transnational corporate agents from embeddedness rests on widely held beliefs about human existence. Western cultures picture human beings as *historical agents*, that is, as beings with the power knowingly to fashion their world. This self-understanding is partly indebted to the biblical traditions; it is central to what Westerners think grants worth and meaning to human life. Similarly, the idea of persons as historical agents is crucial for the shift to corporate economies and away from tradition-based or authority-planned economic systems. As theorists from Max Weber onward have noted, the person as historical agent is key to the rise and flourishing of commercial culture. Often enough, traditions that accent personal dignity tend toward business societies. Some authors even insist that for Western civilization, "we are at our best in history-making" and, therefore, "we should seek to perpetuate history-making practices in our work, our citizens associations, our cultural activities, our everyday life."[17] Corporate economies presuppose and must also advance a picture of human beings as world-formative agents, as historical beings. This is important not only for the significance of human work, but also in terms of cultural flows: the coupling of media and market means persons around the world are engaged in history-making in and through the images, beliefs, and values of the market.[18]

However, there is a paradox facing corporate economies that is central to the remainder of my argument. The paradox, as noted above, is that the more individuals are rationalized within the economy, the greater the social system undercuts

---

17. Charles Spinosa, Fernando Flores, and Hubert L. Dreyfus, *Disclosing New Worlds: Entrepreneurship, Democratic Action, and the Cultivation of Solidarity* (Cambridge, Mass.: MIT Press, 1997), 175.

18. See John Paul II, *Laborem Exercens* (Boston: Paulist Press, n.d.). Also see John T. Pawlikowski, "Modern Catholic Teaching on the Economy: An Analysis and Evaluation," in *Christianity and Capitalism: Perspective on Religion, Liberalism, and the Economy*, ed. Bruce Grelle and David A. Krueger (Chicago: Center for the Scientific Study of Religion, 1986), 3–24. On global flows see Arjun Appadurai, *Modernity at Large: Cultural Dimensions of Globalization* (New Delhi: Oxford University Press, 1997), esp. chaps. 2–4.

its human presupposition. This is true, in principle, of any economic system. Grinding poverty and vast differences in income and power create situations in which, historically and currently, the poor, especially women and children, must sell not only their labor but, often, their bodies and selves. But as social theorists as diverse as Karl Marx, Alexis de Tocqueville, and Max Weber have noted, this fact of economic commodification is manifest with particular force in capitalistic societies. The irony is that these societies help to create conditions in which personal freedom includes the possibility of freely disposing of oneself. "It is the fate of capitalism constantly to undo its own prerequisites," as Ernst Troeltsch once put it.[19] This is so, since market capitalism (1) presupposes that a person can (freely) dispose of her or his person, and yet (2) commodification in the market and the reduction of all value to a monetary scale pose the question of how much I can sell of my labor, my time, and my body before I have sold off myself. As Patrick Murray astutely notes, the market tempts persons to dispose of themselves as persons.[20] The global spread of the corporate economy means the widening of this fact. The market always threatens to devolve into commercialism where there is no "outside" to commodification. The great weight of the Christian tradition is to insist on the moral priority of persons over institutions and their practices. This has made most Christian thinkers profoundly sensitive to what I will call "Troeltsch's paradox."

Finally, the globalization of economic agents has accentuated a fact present within all cultures. Any culture reproduces itself by informing the lives of its members with some set of beliefs about the world — convictions about what is impor-

---

19. Ernst Troeltsch, "The Essence of the Modern Spirit," in his *Religion in History,* trans. James Luther Adams and Walter F. Bense (Minneapolis: Fortress Press, 1991), 248.

20. On this see Patrick Murray, "General Introduction: On Studying Commercial Life," in Murray, *Reflections on Commercial Life,* 1–38.

tant in human life. I will speak of this set of beliefs as a "table of values," using this phrase to denote three things: (1) beliefs about what is important in human life, what we can and should care about, and therefore how we should deploy our energies; (2) a ranking valued so that some things (say, love) are to be treasured and sought over and above other things also of worth (e.g., a new car); and (3) a fundamental distinction held in a culture between what is to be valued just for itself (intrinsic good) and what can be used to attain intrinsic goods (hence, instrumental values).[21] The greatest force in any society, as Augustine clearly understood, is the cultural power to define and transmit values, to determine what matters and how much it matters and thus to saturate consciousness with those values. With the dramatic advance of the global media system and also the spread of transnational corporations, "economic values," along with money as the measurement of use, exchange, and sign-value, increasingly shape personal and social self-understandings. The "table of values" in societies marked by corporate economies is focused decidedly on wealth and consumption. Granted, corporations facilitate and enact goods other than purely instrumental, economic goods. The corporation fosters personal growth, the development of numerous virtues, a belief in fairness.[22] And yet, because the corporation is defined by its specific economic

---

21. On theories of value see H. Richard Niebuhr, *The Responsible Self: An Essay in Christian Moral Philosophy,* introduction by James M. Gustafson with a foreword by William Schweiker (Louisville: Westminster/ John Knox Press, 1999); Charles Taylor, *Sources of the Self: The Making of the Modern Identity* (Cambridge: Harvard University Press, 1990); and also Friedrich Nietzsche, *The Birth of Tragedy and the Genealogy of Morals,* trans. Francis Golffing (New York: Doubleday, Anchor Books, 1956). One should note — and note well — that the second essay of *The Genealogy of Morals* centers on economic transaction.

22. On this see D. N. McCloskey, *The Vices of Economists — The Virtues of the Bourgeoisie* (Amsterdam: Amsterdam University Press, 1996), and "Bourgeois Virtue," *American Scholar* 63 (Spring 1994): 177–91.

purpose (wealth) and practice (production, exchange), it is always at the risk of reducing or effacing the difference between humane, intrinsic goods and purely economic, instrumental ones. This is, again, the specter of commercialism.

Insight into the cultural power of valuation seems to be important for the two previous points. Transnational corporations are cultural forces — and not only social institutions — insofar as they breed and transmit a "table of values" that informs the self-understanding and world-making of persons and societies. The spread of economic rationality as a cultural force threatens to efface the distinction between intrinsic and instrumental goods. Not surprisingly, within a corporate economy it is increasingly difficult to give compelling reasons why something (say, persons or the common, social good) ought to be respected and enhanced other than speaking of their use-value in maximizing economic utility. Insofar as "money" is one of the languages, the currencies, of cultural reproduction in a market society, there is always the possibility that everything can be made and measured as a commodity. As the anthropologist Arjun Appadurai has noted, the global economy/media provides images and values that enable persons around the world to fashion and refashion their cultural identities. The construction of new identities can be a way of resisting dominant forces — thereby asserting the intrinsic good of a community's way of life — or a means to draw persons within the economic system. In all cases, the "imagination is now central to all forms of agency, is itself a social fact, and is the key component of the new global order."[23]

As cultural forces, transnational corporations must be seen as vehicles of the "imagination": they produce and distribute a table of values (again, beliefs about what matters and how much in human life) that shape understandings

---

23. Appadurai, *Modernity at Large*, 31.

and perceptions of life. By means of this connection to the imaginary, transnationals transform values such that system-specific goods (e.g., wealth production) can endanger the value of persons through commodification. And it is because of this risk of commodification and the supremacy of money as the measure of value that ethicians have sought to give accounts of the human good that economies must serve. The ethical arguments center on the supreme good of persons, or private choices and desire, or the common social good. The pressing question about the transnational corporation is not an economic one, but one about human worth.

Mammon and the Ecumene

I have made three points about transnational corporate agents and also isolated questions of economic justice along the way. These points, we should note, roughly correlate to the meanings of "world" in Christian thought. First, I have noted the "locality" of transnational corporations. They transcend local political and pre-commercial relations. While this point can be made in terms of social theory (i.e., disembeddedness and social differentiation), we should also note that corporations demarcate a cultural space. It is a "space" of human life defined by market processes and values on a global scale. These entities are, quite literally, located in the whole world, the ecumene. This is a simple, descriptive claim about our situation even as it poses, in a new way, matters of distributive and commutative justice. Insofar as we are always, if not totally, economic beings, the space of human life is structured by questions about the fair distribution of goods and services as well as the rightness of processes of exchange.

Second, I have made an anthropological observation. Corporations presuppose human beings as historical agents, and, further, they foster and yet can endanger that agency. At root this is a question of productive justice, both in terms of the presupposition of economic activity (i.e., human beings, through their labor, as producers of things) and also related to how the creation of wealth coheres with basic beliefs about the meaning of our humanity. Theologically construed, this observation is linked to sin and redemption of the world. It is through human productive activity in the creation of wealth that the social world is in part healed or distorted because of the entanglement of production with commutative and distributive justice. A just social order, even as an eschatological ideal, would be a situation in which the dignity of human labor is related to fair distribution and just relations of exchange.

Finally, I have isolated an axiological point correlated to Christian convictions about creation and goodness. Corporations, like all cultures, create and transmit some table of values. That table of values, as many have suggested, always includes intrinsic worth and instrumental value as well as the risk that this difference will be effaced. The pressure of economic relations is in fact to press all values into commodification and utility values that can be measured in terms of "money."[24] It is through the promotion of a table of values that transnational corporations reach beyond local boundaries and also foster and yet endanger the self-understandings of persons. Of course, much more can and needs to be said. This can hardly count as an adequate portrayal of the transnational corporation and corporate economy. But it is enough to raise anew the question of justice.

Before doing so, I must note an odd analogy. It is arguable that prior to this century the main "transnational" forces in the West were the religions and also languages. The ancient ecumene (from *oikos,* the root of terms for "household,"

---

24. Advocating the translation of all values into utility is the project of "rational-choice theory" and neoclassical economics. For a powerful and helpful criticism of this (terrifying) position see Margaret Jane Radin, *Reinterpreting Property* (Chicago: University of Chicago Press, 1993).

"economy," and "ecology") depended, in the Greco-Roman
world, on the spread of Greek and Latin along with political
expansion and conquest. To be civilized — hence, cosmopolitan — required linguistic facility. Likewise, the ecumenical
church transcended political and social boundaries (class,
race, and gender as well as the boundary between Jew and
Roman) and spread throughout local cultures. The church
did so in part because, presupposing human beings as historical agents, it provided the means for communal identity
formation (worship, moral codes) by severing personal ties
with pre-ecclesial reality. Through baptism, the member dies
to the "world of sin" that is governed only by considerations
of power, and also to ties of family, lineage, and so on. Neither
Mars nor Eros is to rule life's meaning, even if faithful existence requires political and familial responsibility. By means
of resocialization, a Christian entered the "household" of the
saints by appropriating the "signs" of the faith (creeds, symbols, narratives, sacraments).[25] Oddly enough, the ecumenical
church and transnational corporations share three cultural/
social facts: (1) the transcendence of given, natural relations;
(2) the presupposition of human beings as historical agents;
and (3) the use of signs (commodities, texts, narratives) expressive of a table of values to shape the identities of agents by
saturating self-understanding with new values and meanings.

There is a crucial difference, however. The church, in principle if, sadly, not always in practice, ardently insists on the
distinction between instrumental and intrinsic worth and that
the human conundrum is to define one's life in relation to
a good outside of the universe of commodities, outside the
realm of sign-value. As Augustine put it, only God is to be
enjoyed in Godself as the highest human good; things of this
world, accordingly, are to be used and not enjoyed as one's

---

25. On this see Wayne Meeks, *The Origins of Christian Morality: The
First Two Centuries* (New Haven: Yale University Press, 1993).

ultimate good. The Christian imaginary is one in which a person's historical identities are formed with respect to the non-reducibility of intrinsic to instrumental worth and lived out in highly differentiated vocations and spheres of sovereignty. Furthermore, expressive of the prohibition of idolatry, the highest good is not reducible to sign-value. Christians have, at least in principle, always resisted the reduction of "value" (what is esteemed or assigned worth) to one system of reference (e.g., money), simply because at least one value precedes all systemic relations, specifically, the unnameable, holy God. God is simply and always "outside" social systems of valuation and spheres of sovereignty; God is, in the root sense of the word, "Holy."

The mission of the church, seen in this light, is to communicate in and through the spheres of society the connection between selves and their own most intrinsic good. It is to provide a table of values about what lies outside of commodification. This is why, as we have seen, the "world of mammon" is so ambiguous in Christian thought. The religious problem is that it is a domain of meaning and value that can contradict and war against the very source of the church's own meaning and value, namely, human agents and God. This happens whenever the "world" tries to define its worth purely in self-referential terms and thus denies its relation to and dependence on persons and the divine. The conundrum of transnational corporations in a market economy, as we have seen, is that it too can contradict the very source of its worth. And on grasping this point, we can return to matters of justice.

Responsibility in a World of Mammon

By focusing on the connection between "worlds" and "agents," our inquiry has led to the insight that the question of justice and transnational corporations must shift focus. It is no longer only a matter of the production and distribution of wealth or the morality of exchange, topics rightly explored by others. The question becomes the place of a substantive sense of justice, and thus a matter of moral worth, in our conception of reality and ourselves. This sense of justice expresses the contrast between intrinsic and instrumental goods and is essential for resisting the commodification of life. We must ask: does the emergence and spread of global economic forces, like transnational corporations, provide any means for sensing the claims of justice as basic to self-understanding and to a construal of the world? This is a profoundly theological query. A Christian interpretation of the world is mediated through beliefs about and experiences of the living God, the God of Jesus Christ. Any cultural force or social institution that nullifies our sense of the reality of justice and mercy is, practically speaking, atheistic and, theoretically stated, nihilistic. If that is true of our global situation, then Christians must advocate ways of containing and constraining transnational corporations. Conversely, if these economic powers do foster, or, at least, do not utterly destroy, a moral construal of the world, then Christian communities can find common cause with them and work for their transformation.

Admittedly, specific judgments about economic powers are often prudential and strategic in nature. There are times when economic agents will be deemed utterly destructive to any sense of justice (e.g., ancient and contemporary forms of slavery). In those cases, the churches must vigorously but peaceably oppose them. At other times and places, economic powers might be agents of moral sensibility. This would warrant a (qualified) endorsement of their moral rightness and purpose. Granting the need for discernment in moral matters, the task of Christians, most basically, is to work for the transformation of the world around them.[26] This moral

---

26. See H. Richard Niebuhr, *Christ and Culture* (New York: Harper & Row, 1951).

stance admits the genuine ambiguity in all things human and yet seeks to work for their betterment. It is consistent with the account of the "world" found in Christian faith.

I have noted how the transnational corporation as a vehicle of the imaginary can aid in the formation of new social worlds, new forms of identity. This provides some means to insure the dignity of persons even within economic practices. But that possibility assumes, of course, that our economic practices have robust images of human worth that can circulate within corporate economies. And this is where contemporary globalized societies are failing most profoundly. The continuation and integrity of the economic sphere requires a contrasting table of value about human worth to that found in these societies.[27] We need, at the level of conceptions of worth, an "outside" to economic norms and purposes. Only through a different axiology in how persons imagine their world will the tyranny of economic commodification be checked as well as "Troeltsch's paradox" contained.

The difficulty is that in highly differentiated societies it seems impossible to conceive of an encompassing good that does not always tread on social tyranny, or, conversely, to provide reasons that are not sphere-specific, that is, not trapped by the logic of any one social sphere (law, economics, or whatever). In complex societies it is difficult to imagine one human good, The Good (as it were), that can orient human social activity. This is not only because of the diversity of beliefs and values among peoples in those societies. It is, more profoundly, the problem of how to avoid tyranny in a conception of what is good, since all conceptions betray their origin within the logic and purpose of a specific social subsystem. It is hardly surprising that many contemporary

---

27. For the importance of counterbalances see Krueger, *Business Corporation and Productive Justice,* 71–72.

ethicists mindful of the social experiments of the last two centuries, when speaking of intrinsic worth, deny such a concept and work with purely subjective or procedural ideas of the good.[28] The "good" is then simply what any particular person or group happens to like or a term to designate fair social procedures. What is lacking is a discourse (a set of concepts, symbols, narratives) able to articulate intrinsic worth — some idea of the human good — in a nontyrannous and also non-sphere-specific way.

The demand of the moment, if my argument so far has been correct, is that we risk specifying some idea in order to provide an "outside" to the values of corporate economy. We can do so, I submit, by pushing further the connection between "world" and "agent." As Walzer notes, the "primary good that we distribute to one another is membership in some human community."[29] Human social life is not only about kinds of world-making — an activity that includes, but is not reducible to, economic activity — but also about defining who peoples that "world" and thus about recognizing or destroying individual worth. Each social subsystem is involved in distributing that primary good, a good (we must note) that is intrinsic in nature. Moral standing in a human community — who counts and is due recognition, respect, and enhancement — is not a means to some other end; it is the presupposition of other social purposes. Economic justice is, of course, about fairness of exchange, distribution of goods and services, or the creation of wealth. Yet justice, substantively defined, is the demand that within each of the social spheres the moral standing of persons as such be respected

---

28. For expressions of these options see Jürgen Habermas, *Moral Consciousness and Communicative Action,* trans. Christian Lenhardt and Shierry Weber Nicholsen with an introduction by Thomas McCarthy (Cambridge, Mass.: MIT Press, 1990), and John Rawls, *A Theory of Justice* (Cambridge, Mass.: Belknap Press, 1971).

29. Walzer, *Spheres of Justice,* 31.

and enhanced. And this requires some way to conceive of the worth of persons *outside* or *prior to* their worth in social practices. Mindful of the role of the "imaginary" in the flows of globalization, the problem, therefore, is not, as many moral theorists believe, the need to establish the rational necessity of God or Good. It is, much more, a hermeneutical, cultural problem, namely, how to saturate self-understanding with beliefs about the worth of persons and the claims of justice. We need symbolic resources that can test and transform the "sign-value" of commodification. Can we await any longer the rebirth of the moral imagination?

Sensing the force of this demand, I have intimated resources for the rebirth of the imagination, namely, the resources of Christian faith and its claims about "world," agents, and justice. I have also isolated an ecumenical social reality that might balance the global spread of the transnational corporation, namely the Christian churches.[30] The central Christian conviction is that all reality exists in relation to God as creator, redeemer, and sustainer and, in light of this fact, bears inviolable worth. This is most pointedly stated in the confession that God became incarnate in an embodied individual, and, additionally, that Christ's spirit is communicated ecumenically in and through the life of the Christian community and its practices. Furthermore, the divine is never translatable into our system of signs, and, morally speaking, this means that human worth, grounded in a relation to God, cannot be commodified or measured within the discourse of any social sphere. It is hardly surprising, then, that *at its best* the church, from the earliest days until now, has always resisted

---

30. For an account of how Christian theological ethics can offer a transformative axiology see William Schweiker, "Power and the Agency of God," *Theology Today* 52, no. 2 (1995): 204–24. For a account of a "multidimensional" theory of value see James M. Gustafson, *A Sense of the Divine: The Natural Environment from a Theocentric Perspective* (Cleveland: Pilgrim Press, 1994).

the commodification of human beings, slavery, the destruction of children, and dehumanizing patterns of social and familial life. We know the failures of Christians by the same standard. The church must transmit this picture of the worth of human life and enable it to penetrate the global, social imagination.[31] The practice of the church ought to limit the domination of life by sign-value.

The force of this argument should not be missed. The insight of the Christian tradition is to insist, unlike so much contemporary ethics, that moral matters are not piggybacked on a more or less neutral view of life. Moral claims are not explainable solely in terms of social conventions. Convictions about what is good, right, and virtuous afford light into reality. Faith in God is a way of interpreting and evaluating the world. Theological ethics does not move from, say, economic and institutional analysis to trace out "ethical implications." I have already noted this fact by outlining the meanings of "world" in Christian faith and how "the world" admits of diverse evaluations. The same point was made in nontheological terms by showing how a cultural question, namely, the enterprise of world-making and self-formation with respect to some table of values, is (logically speaking) prior to while also permeating social systems. Taking our cue from Christian ideas about "world," we have been led to a profound moral and conceptual insight. At the very origins of "worlds" is a question about what bears intrinsic worth, a table of values, and how this is linked to some conception of *historical agents:* God as the creator of space and time; human beings as agents in time forming moral spaces, forming cultures and societies. I have tried to suggest that transnational corporations presuppose this insight about "worlds" but can also endanger human agents. Insofar as they presuppose persons

31. For a similar claim see Stackhouse, *Public Theology and Political Economy.*

to be sources of economic value, then the church can work for their transformation rather than condemnation. Insofar as people always live within social systems, the church is to work to further systems that respect and enhance the integrity of life.

My contention, then, is that Christian faith provides symbolic and conceptual means for thinking about the very presuppositions of economic justice in ways that can form human self-understanding around ideas of personal dignity and the integrity of life. It provides a bulwark against the tyranny of any social sphere and its practices, a wall rooted in the worth of persons, consistent with a specific construal of the world. In this way, Christians have good reason to work for the transformation of economic practices. To put it provocatively, Christian discourse can and ought to work like a curative computer virus within the moral code of a civilization to rewrite that code, making the dignity of persons and the demands of justice basic in a vision of life.

We can now state quite simply what is at issue in matters of justice. In an age in which corporations have become global agents of the imagination, the most pressing question is how we are to see and value the world. If we cannot see or sense the claims to respect and enhancement uttered in the lives of others, moral arguments simply will not help. So in the end, the task of the churches amid a world of mammon is to provide an "outside" perspective to commodification and to form the moral imaginary. To use biblical, prophetic terminology, it is a matter of "knowing justice." Yet given the ambiguous state of the "world," Paul put it even better: what is required is a renewal of mind so that one might prove the will of God (Rom. 12:1–2). The greatest challenge we now face is not creating the institutions for handling globalization. It is, much more, to seek an education in justice.

Of course, issues of justice have been debated over the centuries. At present three major positions dominate thinking about Christian ethics and economics. One position, so-called liberation theology, insists on the priority of distributive justice with equality and community as regulative principles. The second position draws on current economic theory. These thinkers focus on commutative justice and hold fairness and freedom as regulative ideals. Finally, a third outlook seeks the formation of a global society to overcome poverty and marginalization. In this third position the focus is decidedly on productive justice while opportunity and access function as regulative guides for thought and action. The debate among these positions often devolves into questions about how seriously one takes the biblical witness, the validity of empirical claims, or the grounds for pragmatic, prudential judgments. Of course, the Bible, facts, and judgments are all important in theological ethics! But in light of the profound current crisis of meaning centered on human worth, these debates can seem all too academic. What specifically and concretely can we take from this discussion about the question of justice and economic globalization? How might we reach an integrated view of economic justice?

Christians must work to transform the patterns of valuation and the means for self-understanding within commercial societies. This is the very substance of justice. How is that possible and how does it relate to the more proximate and pressing issues of forms of justice? The work of moral transformation is possible, I judge, because Christian faith and transnational economic agents share a presupposition, namely, that human beings are *historical agents*. The notion that human beings are owed moral consideration is not in principle contestable, even if it is always deniable. We begin with a point of consensus, a shared presupposition necessary to render intelligible other forms of social activity. From this simple fact about the subject of justice flow some important insights.

First, the affirmation of human beings as agents warrants,

as John Paul II has seen, the importance of labor in life
and thus as the backbone of productive justice. To demean
or destroy the conditions in which human beings can labor
meaningfully is morally illicit; enabling persons to find fulfilling labor, and thus also the creation of wealth, is required.
The churches, accordingly, must struggle to enable meaningful work as well as the good of productive justice. Yet, second,
this same point — that is, understanding human beings as
historical agents — requires, as many liberation theologians
note, the empowerment of the poor to be a force in their
world. Questions about distributive justice are, to my mind at
least, not only about goods and services; they are more fundamentally about how to respect and enhance persons as agents.
For Christians and many others, goods and services, morally
speaking, draw their worth from their connection to human
agents and not the inverse. Christians must be dedicated to
new patterns of distribution simply because of their commitment to the worth of persons. Finally, commutative justice
must respect and enhance agents within market exchanges.
The morality of exchange is really about the interaction between persons who can knowingly shape their world and the
kind of world they enact through the exchange. Here, too, the
church must work for justice and, specifically, for the manifold ways, through legal or political means or through social
pressure, to insure the rightness of patterns of exchange.

My point, then, is that the forms of economic justice are
ways to respect and enhance the good prior to economic
systems, namely, human beings as historical agents. This substantive moral good is necessarily binding of economic agents
(like transnational corporations) because it concerns a presupposition of their very existence, a presupposition that is,
paradoxically, also endangered by economic activity. We can
think about the morality of economic practices along the lines
of productive, distributive, and commutative justice. These
help us to understand vocations within various spheres of

sovereignty. At issue are *matters of justice,* precisely because these concern the dignity of persons in relation to God. In moral theory, at issue is the relation between values dependent on human choice and a form of worth that choices must respect. Charles Fried has put it well:

> All other values gather their moral force as they determine choice. By contrast, the value of personhood[,] ... far from being chosen, is the presupposition and substrate of the very concept of choice. And that is why the norms surrounding respect for persons may not be compromised, why these norms are absolute in respect to the various ends we choose to pursue.[32]

The various forms of economic justice can thus be seen as ways to allow Christians to live in but not of the "world." Productive justice articulates in economic life the meaning of creation as good; commutative justice enables the world of actual social and cultural exchange; distributive justice reflects in economic life convictions about sin and redemption.[33] It is not possible in this essay to trace the full meaning of these forms of justice! What I have tried to show is that they draw moral force from a relation to agents, to the living God and human beings. As stated at the outset, the demands of justice for Christian faith focus on the very presupposition of worldly value. Religiously understood, justice is right relation between God and all of creation; morally conceived, justice comes to focus on human beings as agents who fashion their

---

32. Charles Fried, *Right and Wrong* (Cambridge: Harvard University Press, 1978), 29. For my own account of the complex relation between the deontic demand of respect and the teleological requirement to enhance the integrity of life, see *Responsibility and Christian Ethics,* esp. chap. 5.

33. This is interestingly reflected in current discussions, drawing on the idea of the Jubilee Year, of the relief of debt for "developing nations" in the year 2000. Theologically construed, what is at stake is sin and redemption in social existence.

world. Economic justice, in its various forms, is about respecting and enhancing the integrity of agents amid the world of
mammon.

The Mission of the Churches

These claims about Christian faith allow us to conclude with
a word about the churches as ecumenical, worldly forces that
can and may and must counterbalance transnational, global
agents. If my argument about justice and the imaginary is at
all compelling, then the root mission of the churches is to
work to inform the moral sensibilities of market societies so
that the respect and enhancement of the integrity of life are
basic to the self-understanding and ethos of a society. One
ought not to be naive about this task. It is, quite simply, un-
ending, and will have to take concrete institutional form (and
constant reform). And, yet, it is the task through which the
churches leave the tracks of moral history under God and for
humanity.

The church always has prophetic, doxological, and sacra-
mental missions. But on the example of disciples gathered
around Jesus, a crucial task of the churches for a global future
is pedagogical. The ethical mission of the church, I suggest,
is to be an academy of justice in the crucible of culture creation.[34] In this way the church's mission draws together in

---

34. On the importance of Jesus as teacher see Hans Dieter Betz, *The
Sermon on the Mount* (Minneapolis: Fortress Press, 1996). In making this
argument, I mean to continue the impulses of historical Protestantism and
Christian humanism as well as strands in current hermeneutical inquiry.
We should never forget the dedication to education and the forming of
schools by Protestants and other Christian humanists throughout the ages.
For the historical background to this claim see Werner Jaeger, *Humanism
and Theology,* The Aquinas Lectures (Milwaukee: Marquette University
Press, 1943). Also see R. William Franklin and Joseph M. Shaw, *The Case
for Christian Humanism* (Grand Rapids, Mich.: Eerdmans, 1991), and
Schweiker, *Power, Value, and Conviction,* esp. introduction.

Christian self-understanding the grand task of shaping civilization with a distinctive faith in the justice of God. This vision of the church's mission is rooted in the confidence that, as creatures of a loving God, human beings can be grasped by truths that raise them above vice and hatred. Is not the most powerful counterbalance to the "crisis of meaning" about the worth of human beings in globalizing societies a simple and yet profound vision of human beings as agents of justice?

– *Chapter 4* –

THE TAMING OF MARS

CAN HUMANS OF THE TWENTY-FIRST CENTURY CONTAIN THEIR PROPENSITY FOR VIOLENCE?

Donald W. Shriver, Jr.

The twenty-first century is sure to see unprecedented new connections among all human inhabitants of this planet. That certainty is full of both threat and promise, as is evident in what we already know about our ecological, economic, information, and political systems. If the threats in these new connections are to turn toward promise, we will have to achieve some transformations of human character, social systems, and cultural ideas. This essay, like others in this volume, concerns the possible role of religion in these transformations. The particular challenge to which I respond is our modern worldwide potential for violence.

For realism, I turn to a bit of history and my own retrospective implication in it.

What Almost Happened (1962)

[Khrushchev:] "When I asked the military advisors if they could assure me that holding fast would not result in the death of five hundred million human beings, they looked at me as though I was out of my mind, or, what was worse, a traitor. . . . So I said to myself: 'To hell with these maniacs. If I can get the United States to assure me that it will not attempt to overthrow the Cuban government, I will remove the missiles. . . . ' I said to my comrades, 'We achieved our goal. Maybe the Americans have learned their lesson. Now they have the time to think it over and weigh the consequences."

While [Soviet officials] were waiting for Kennedy's reply to [Khrushchev's] radio message, a cable arrived from the KGB in Washington. From the time Kennedy had announced the quarantine of Cuba, the KGB had put him under intensive surveillance. They now reported that he had gone to church. Khrushchev and his colleagues argued about the significance of the report. Some Presidium members feared that it was a prelude to a nuclear attack; the president had gone to church to pray before giving the order to destroy the Soviet Union. [Deputy Premier Anastas] Mikoyan thought that Kennedy was probably as confused as they were and was praying for divine guidance. Some suggested that the church visit was disinformation, a deliberate attempt by the Americans to mislead Soviet leaders. . . . Mikoyan observed that this made no sense: how could the Americans plant the story about Kennedy's visit to church as a deliberate deception, when they could not know how it would be interpreted? One or two others challenged the validity of the report on different grounds. "The KGB has been wrong about everything else," they insisted. "Why should we believe them now when they tell us the president has gone to church?"

Khrushchev's message announcing that the Soviet Union would withdraw its missiles from Cuba was re-broadcast over American radio at 9:00 A.M. Washington time. McGeorge Bundy telephoned the good news to the president. Kennedy prepared to go to the 10:00 mass at St. Stephen's Church. Bundy waited for him at the door of the residential quarters of the White House to give

him the text of the message as he left for church....
Mrs. Bundy had arrived with their children, and Robert
Kennedy, in an ebullient mood, passed out chocolates.
In Moscow ... they celebrated with vodka.[1]

Once upon a time, the vast majority of the human species
could afford to think: "What happens in the capital cities
affects us very little." No more. If the personal entanglement
of my generation of Americans in world war did not permit
the lesson to sink in, our memory of the Cuba crisis finally
engraved it on our minds. No man, woman, or child is an
island.

As it happened, the week of October 21–28, 1962, was
a moment of great transition in my life. My family and I
were traveling the New Jersey Turnpike on the way from com-
pleted study at Harvard to a new job in North Carolina, via
a visit to my hometown, Norfolk, Virginia, site of the world's
largest naval base. I calculated later that the nine-hundred-
mile range of the Soviet missiles in Cuba was just enough to
reach that naval base. As it happened, that October 28 was
my parents' thirty-eighth wedding anniversary. In 1992, that
day would become the birthday of our youngest son's first
child. In October 1962, that future father was one and a half
years old.

We now know how close, on that weekend, the world came
to its first nuclear war, and, in my case, how close I came to
having no grandchildren. But the personal and the worldwide
are intimately connected: once John Donne could make the
moral case for the continental connectedness of our island
selves. Now to the moral was added empirical connectedness,
its threat and promise intertwined.

---

1. Richard Ned Lebow and Janice Gross Stein, *We All Lost the Cold
War* (Princeton, N.J.: Princeton University Press, 1994), 141–43.

Our Violent Century

The sad fact is that we humans are emerging from the most violent century in our history. The end of the "seventy-five years war" (1914–89) did not see the end of slaughter in, between, and by organized masses. No one knows for sure how many of us have perished in these conflicts. An estimate of 150 million seems probable.

The key word there is "us." Is it possible, likely, or practical to speak now — or at any previous time — about humanity as a whole? When, in 1940, American presidential candidate Wendell Willkie returned from a forty-eight-hour around-the-world plane journey, he held up his index finger and exclaimed, "One world!" For decades afterward skeptics derided "one-worldism" as a liberal illusion. These skeptics would be assaulted in the next fifty years by gathering reasons for thinking that what happens to Americans, Europeans, Africans, Asians, Latin Americans, Australians, and the penguins of Antarctica happens to them together. Now that economic blessing and bane enmesh them in "globalization," we have world trade and ecological counterparts to the politics of actual and potential world war.

Without question the twentieth century is bequeathing to the twenty-first not only a uniquely fearful precedent of organized violence but also new potentials for building on that precedent. Questionable indeed is whether, on a global scale, we know how to control this violence — our propensity for inventing and using tools for killing.

The ambiguous role of religion, ancient and modern, in this history is my central interest in addressing this cluster of issues. In the sobering retrospect of joint Soviet-American study of the Cuban Missile Crisis, interpretations of what the antagonists *meant* to do turned out to be crucial. It defies conventional Realpolitik analyses of the crisis to realize that, in the midst of Moscow's strategic discussion, the question of what religion might mean to Americans came to the fore as anything but theoretical. It is hard to imagine any more potent illustration of the truth in Kurt Lewin's aphorism: "Nothing is so practical as a good theory." Bad theories can be equally practical, like the idea that religion is useful mostly for the legitimation of collective material interests.[2]

Definitions of "religion" are bound to vary, but basic to the meaning of the word is "meaning" itself. Mircea Eliade said that humans have a basic impulse toward "the transformation of chaos into cosmos," toward the organizing of chaos by giving it forms and norms. Commenting on this definition, Robert Lifton cautions that "meaning" can as easily inform human terror as well as human blessing. "We are meaning-hungry creatures; we live on images of meaning. Auschwitz makes all too clear the principle that the human psyche can create meaning out of anything," as the Nazi doctors managed to do in that awesome, awful place.[3]

Asked afterward what the Cuba crisis taught him, Secretary of State Dean Rusk replied: "It reminded me of the first question in the Westminster Shorter Catechism: 'What is the chief end of man?' The answer is: 'To glorify God and to enjoy Him forever.'" On his own humanistic grounds, Khrushchev must have agreed with Rusk that there was no glory to God or to any human cause in the death of five hundred million

---

2. The Marxian — and much Western social-scientific — theory of religion as a variable dependent on the "real" forces of power and interest was at issue in the Soviets' discussion. Of particular interest is Mikoyan's observation that Kennedy may have been as confused and worried as his counterparts in Moscow, which might have been why he went to church. This sounds like a rare break with Communist theory about religion in the inner circle of Soviet policy making.

3. Robert Lifton, *The Nazi Doctors: Medical Killing and the Psychology of Genocide* (New York: Basic Books, 1986), 459, 453. The quotation from Eliade is from *The Sacred and the Profane: The Nature of Religion* (New York: Harcourt, Brace, 1959), 29–32.

people. This drawing-back from the brink of collective suicide has a religious feel: for what is religion if not the ascription of an ultimate meaning to our lives and our deaths?[4] As is well-known, humans vary greatly in what we consider ultimate. In the world of politics, power is a perennial strong candidate. Charles Maier calls the longing of national leaders and peoples for "the bomb" a modern "sacrament of sovereignty,"[5] and Lifton echoes the same religious language: "[N]uclearism combines morally blind technicism with awed genuflection before all-powerful objects that can do what in the past only God could do: destroy the world."[6]

That thought provokes another: What sort of species can imagine its own extinction and actually invent a tool for effecting it? Who are we that we should think so poorly of our existence? In our time, the question has stolen upon us with great rapidity in the multiplication of mass killings. Deep crisis peered out from the western front in World War I, in the Nazi concentration camps, and in the mass killings that have persisted up to 1999. In act and in theory the question rears up: are some humans only worth killing? (In the Nazi term, is there some life that should be designated *lebens-unwertes Leben?*) Anyone, like me, who is old enough to remember World War II has to concede that little grief came with the firebombings of Dresden and Tokyo or the atomic bombing of

---

4. During his brief tenure as head of the Soviet government in the early 1980s, Yuri Andropov remarked that "God will not forgive us" if the Americans and the Soviets failed to prevent nuclear war. (Scholars fluent in Russian tell me that this remark owes more to a Russian colloquialism than to theology.) Khrushchev himself remarked: "When the military informed me about the destructive power of our nuclear weapons, for several nights I could not sleep. But finally I realized that no one could ever use those weapons. Then I could sleep."

5. Charles Maier, *The Unmasterable Past: History, Holocaust, and German National Identity* (Cambridge: Harvard University Press, 1988), 145.

6. Lifton, *Nazi Doctors*, 495.

Hiroshima and Nagasaki. Ending the war and saving the lives
of Americans was the political axiom of the time. While the
mood of the eventually victorious nations was predominantly
sober rather than idealistic, the label "good war" seems to fit
our generation's memory of the event.

What we cannot forget from that time — but have yet adequately to remember — is how close alleged high cultures
came to the massive dehumanization of enemies and, in the
process, of themselves. Lurking was a devil whose cultural
power still poisons the backroom contingency planning of
many nation-states: we can kill "them" if we "have to." The
deep-down crisis is twofold, one political-pragmatic and the
other ethical-philosophical: (1) How can humans survive into
a distant future? (2) Is our survival important or not?

A book that received much attention at publication and
that deserves more rereading is Jonathan Schell's *The Fate of
the Earth* (1982). The book planted lingering anxiety in the
minds of many careful readers by addressing these questions
in depth. Tearing off nuclear missiles' disguise as "just another
weapon," Schell described their uniqueness as putting into
human hands the power to "end history" in a sense more lit-
eral than Francis Fukuyama intended. Schell and his scientific
sources conceded that no one can be sure that a full-scale nuclear war would end all human life, but testing the hypothesis
would resemble an experiment in how close to suicide one can
come without succeeding. Scientifically reliable results would
come when the experimenter crossed the line into death. If
such information were worth any deaths, it would be so only
because others lived to benefit. What if, in this unique case,
no humans were left?

Schell saw no way to face this blunt question of human survival without resort to fundamentally religious feelings and
beliefs. What he wrote about the prospect of nuclear war
was akin to what many also said and would say about the
environmental crisis:

[A]lthough, scientifically speaking, there is all the difference in the world between the mere possibility that a [nuclear] holocaust will bring about extinction and the certainty of it, morally they are the same, and we have no choice but to address the issue of nuclear weapons as though we knew for a certainty that their use would put an end to our species. In weighing the fate of the earth and, with it, our own fate, we stand before a mystery, and in tampering with the earth we tamper with a mystery. We are in deep ignorance. Our ignorance should dispose us to wonder, and our wonder should make us humble, our humility should inspire us to reverence and caution, and our reverence and caution should lead us to act without delay to withdraw the threat we now pose to the earth and to ourselves.[7]

In March 1945, Secretary of War Henry Stimson, pondering the secret of the Manhattan Project, then four months from its successful "Trinity" test of July, wrote similar words in his diary:

Our thoughts went right down to the bottom facts of human nature, morals, and governments, and it is by far the most searching and important thing that I have had to do since I have been here in the Office of the Secretary of War because it touches matters which are deeper even than the principles of present government.[8]

Unfortunately, in his famous defense of the dropping of the atomic bombs one year later, Stimson spoke little about his perception of "the bottom facts of human nature" or the ambiguity and anxiety which the beginning of the nuclear

---

7. Jonathan Schell, *The Fate of the Earth* (New York: Alfred A. Knopf, 1982), 95.
8. Quoted in ibid., 149.

era had apparently stirred in him in 1945.[9] In the meantime, from the Nazi death camps to the Rwanda massacre
fifty years later, a more basic "bottom" question haunted the
moral imagination of those who have lived in the twentieth
century: Why care if humans survive or not? Especially, why
care about the survival of *all* of us?

If there are convincing answers to this question which have
no tinge of religion, I do not know of them. One of the "topics" of classical systematic theology has been anthropology,
often far down the priority list of core topics. The twentieth
century's experience with destruction should push anthropology to the top of the list. In a rather exotic book written
during World War II, Kenneth Patchen has Albion Moonlight say: "The great question of the twentieth century is not
whether we can believe in God, but whether God can believe in us."[10] Said Schell: "The first principle of life in the
new common world would be respect for human beings."[11]
But a shift into theological justification of human existence
comes hard to Schell, and harder yet to many of his critics,
most of whom seemed to think that we have to take the value
of human being for granted. The trouble is that, with the demonic aid of ideology, governments of our time have recruited
millions to the killing of fellow millions. Ideology can readily
function as the "ultimates" which have had their usual more
ethically regulated home in theologies.[12]

---

9. See Gar Alperovitz, *The Decision to Drop the Atomic Bomb* (New
York: Alfred Knopf, 1995). Stimson was asked by several leaders in the
Truman administration to state the case for the bomb in terms of what, in
the summer of 1945, seemed necessary to them for ending the war with
Japan. Stimson's article in *Harper's* became the official reasoning on the
matter. Alperovitz's research has shown that there was more debate about
the *military* necessity of the atomic bombs than the government wanted to
share widely with the public.

10. Kenneth Patchen, *The Journal of Albion Moonlight* (Mount Vernon,
N.Y.: New Directions Paperback, 1941).

11. Schell, *Fate of the Earth*, 177.

12. Roland Bainton, church historian of Yale University Divinity School,

Theirs may not be the only religious community which should undertake the task, but people of Christian faith and theologians of their churches have no more momentous ethical task now than the restoration of *derivative sacredness* to human beings, to the earth itself, and to a universe beloved by its Creator. Standing in awe before the mystery of earth — the mystery that anything, including ourselves, exists at all — is not as common an experience in the secularized West as it once was. But we see in the history to which I have alluded that, for want of a respect akin to *reverence* for "the other," humans slide easily down the slippery slope of mutual degradation.

From its earliest pages the Book of Genesis makes clear that we humans are tempted to degrade others for allegedly high moral reasons. There we read, in the myth of Cain and Abel, that God put a mark on Cain to protect him from the "just" vengeance of his neighbors, who would righteously follow Cain's example by killing him. The mark was protective — not because his crime was being forgiven but because God willed to put some stopgap limit on the repetition of the crime by others.[13] Even in his criminality, Cain retains a certain human dignity, guaranteed by the Creator against whom he has sinned in the act of sinning against his brother.

In those same early pages, we meet the Hebrew belief that the Creator, having made most of the universe, decided to make humans "in our image, after our likeness. . . . So, God created man in his own image, in the image of God he created him; male and female he created them."[14] Jews and Christians

---

remarked once that the religious beliefs that sent heretics, witches, and political enemies to death in the centuries of Christian dominance of Europe can hardly be compared numerically to the millions killed in the twentieth century in the name of political ideology. The mass murders ordered by Hitler, Stalin, and Mao are the definitive cases in point.

13. See Genesis 4:8–16.
14. Genesis 1:26–27.

have no easy time in the modern world first in believing and then in witnessing to the possibility that over the murder of every Abel on earth stands the Great God of the Universe, outraged and grieving, as though the criminal had assaulted God's own self. "Who are humans that You should be mindful of us?" is a question rightly composed from a mix of faith and skepticism.[15] Especially if one wants to escape divine outrage and grief after murder, it is easy to think that none of us matters all that much: "Am I my bother's keeper?" What if none of us is worth keeping?

If these statements reflect actual "bottom facts" of twentieth-century cultures, then the most embattled claim in several world religions is that in killing a human neighbor one assaults God. Christianity would seem to have the most radical version of this claim by asking what "the King" will say in the final judgment on human history. "Inasmuch as you did it to one of the least of these my brothers [and sisters] you did it unto me."[16]

In their history Christians have both affirmed and contradicted these scriptural claims about this peculiar source of human value and dignity. Among the affirmations have been gestures of care toward all human beings such as appear in the ministries of a St. Francis, a Mother Teresa, a Kagawa, and a Desmond Tutu. The latter once remarked that he was drawn to the Christian faith on the day Father Trevor Huddleston passed Tutu's mother on the street and tipped his hat. A truly fundamental protest against the inhuman begins with such an affirmation, which says that we are all God's beloved children. Otherwise we lack the nerve systematically to uproot all those traditions in our history that make it legitimate to kill a human being. Historically and empirically, the uprooting, if it

---

15. See Psalm 8, which goes on, in much astonishment, to claim that God has made humans "a little lower than the angels," in direct reflection of Genesis 1.

16. Matthew 25:40.

proceeds at all, proceeds irregularly. As I will try to reason be-low — with avoidance of paradox and gross inconsistency — pacifism, from the Christian point of view, is the consumma-tion most devoutly to be wished for the human future. How to take steps toward that future without involving the con-tradictory means of measured violence is the ethical-political problem that will not go away. Can children of God use vi-olence to kill some and to protect other children of God? To that dread question I return at the end of this essay.

Theology and Nonviolent Politics

What both nationalist consciousness abroad and some forms of ethnic consciousness at home have in common is the proposition that listening to strangers is worth-less, since no one can actually understand you but your own group. What is denied is the possibility of empathy: that human understanding is capable of penetrating the bell jars of separate identities. But social peace anywhere depends for its survival on just such an epistemological act of faith: when it comes to political understanding, difference is always minor, comprehension is always possible.[17]

By and large, the theology and ethics associated with much history of the Christian churches has lacked comprehensive treatment of the interconnections of ideas, institutions, and individuals. In practice and in concept, the world needs syn-theses of "mind, self, and society." In particular, the saving of human life from the *organized* violence of war and geno-cide will require new complexes of norms, institutions, and personal character. As Lifton puts it: "Prophylaxis against the genocidal directions of the self... must always include critical

17. Michael Ignatieff, *The Warrior's Honor: Ethnic War and the Modern Conscience* (New York: Henry Holt, 1997), 60.

examination of ideologies and institutions in their interaction
with styles of self-process. . . . The embodied self requires both
constant critical awareness of larger projects demanding allegiance and equally pervasive empathy, fellow feeling, towards
all other human beings."[18]

In a striking appropriation of the philosophy of René Girard, Gil Baillie makes the case that Christians should be
reading human history as the struggle of the Spirit who raised
Jesus from the dead against the repetition of the crucifixion in
our own propensities for murder.[19] The theological claim is
not only the ethical example of Jesus' nonviolent response to
his "legal" execution, but the overruling of this legality by the
Power who means to redeem humans from their sins. There
is a Jobian-Augustinian-Calvinistic spirit in this claim, for it
takes as basic the sovereign rule of God over all reality and all
human history. It stresses the relentless work of the Spirit in
obstructing, undermining, and defying the human propensity
for violence. Anyone willing to look at history through this
lens will be called to realistic perception of good in the world
as well as realistic perception of evil. Christians, in this visual
frame, will not forget that theirs is an ethic not based as much
on moral conscience and moral knowledge as on moral *capac-
itation*. "To all who received him . . . he gave power to become
the children of God."[20] We live in a time when the work of
the Holy Spirit in persons, churches, societies, and world history enables and requires discernment among all who believe
that God is not a theory but an event-maker.

Walter Wink, quoting Gene Sharp, calls attention to a long
list of events over the past several thousand years in which
nonviolence won victories over violence and which qualify

---

18. Lifton, *Nazi Doctors*, 500.
19. See René Girard, *Violence and the Sacred*, trans. Patrick Gregory
(Baltimore: Johns Hopkins University Press, 1977), and Gil Baillie, *Violence
Unveiled: Humanity at the Crossroads* (New York: Crossroad, 1995).
20. John 1:12.

as candidates for the working of God's Spirit in history.[21] Not as dramatic, but indicative of the quiet contribution of pacifism — and of a theology that stresses the Spirit — to political deliberation is an exchange during the Nigeria-Biafra war of the 1970s. The head of the short-lived Biafran state, Emeka Ojukwu, testified to the contribution of Quakers to the amelioration of that conflict — empathy.

> Rugged political negotiators, said Ojukwu, "are likely to dismiss the deaths of fifty people with an 'Oh, well, that happens.' But when you say to the Quakers, 'this is what happened,' there is a silence for a bit. There is a fellow human feeling for the tragedy, which is fully understood, and they then take that into consideration in their responses."[22]

No one who has ever endured basic military training will underestimate the psychological difficulty of asking for empathy for people who have been politically designated as enemies. A poignant memory for me will always be a fellow draftee who, in the midst of infantry training in 1946, said to me what he soon said to the commanding officer, "I know I should have known it before, but in this place they are training us to kill people. I have to apply for a dishonorable discharge, I guess." Punching straw dummies with a bayonet and aiming a rifle at a human-shaped target are supposed to prepare a young civilian for the real thing. Military leaders know that soldiers "have to be carefully taught." Indeed the

21. Walter Wink, *Engaging the Powers: Discernment and Resistance in a World of Domination* (Minneapolis: Fortress Press, 1992), 244–51. Cf. Gene Sharp, *The Politics of Nonviolent Action* (Boston: Porter Sargent, 1973).

22. Douglas Johnston and Cynthia Sampson, eds., *Religion: The Missing Dimension of Statecraft* (New York: Oxford University Press, 1994), 108. See also my essay, "Religion and Violence Prevention," in *Cases and Strategies for Preventive Action*, ed. Barnett R. Rubin (New York: Council on Foreign Relations and the Twentieth-Century Fund, 1998), 169–95.

Niebuhrian hope that Christians will "carry their guns with a heavy heart" may not be militarily functional.

Whether we are counting on nature or on nurture, we should not overestimate the capacity of any of us, including the most religious, for empathy with members of our species who, day after day, die from murder, hunger, war, or other violence. The world's most preventable disease — hunger — kills forty thousand children a day on this planet; it is worrisome that this fact climbs so infrequently onto the agenda of our minds and our institutions. Low indeed on that agenda is empathy for the perpetrators of such evil.

Nonetheless, the belief of Christians and Jews that God "bears our griefs and carries our sorrows"[23] is an invitation to our own practice of empathy, up to our limits. Numbness to the suffering of others is common among those who themselves have suffered much, but by a certain chemistry of grace some use their own suffering as gateways into empathy for the suffering of others. This grace should be celebrated and cultivated among congregations of Christians worldwide. Remarkable, and truly filled with this grace, was the remark of an African American grade-school child to her companion as the two walked through the Holocaust Museum in Washington: "See, other people have suffered too." Jewish American sensitivity to the historic suffering of African Americans is the correlative of this spiritual gift.

It is said that when news of the floods in China in the summer of 1998 reached Chinese around the world, many went to work raising funds for relief, so strongly do many of Chinese origin feel for the land of their ancestors. The principle that Christians must try to follow is empathy without ethnic preference. The struggle to participate in this ethical universalism is and always has been hard. Robert Lifton exemplifies that difficulty when he reluctantly concedes that "the logic of my

---

23. Isaiah 53:4.

position" — that every human ought to be an object of others' empathy — had to apply to his relation to the Nazi doctors, too. "Only a measure of empathy, however reservedly offered, could help one grasp the psychological components of the *anti-empathetic* evil in which many of these Nazi doctors had engaged."[24]

Among Christians, this spiritual discipline has to be conceived as the discipline of our spirits by the Spirit. In what some would consider the most important "bottom fact" about humanity in the New Testament, Paul grounds his faith in the human future in his current experience of "the Spirit of him who raised Jesus from the dead." Cosmos and all humanity are the context for this awesome witness:

> We know that the whole creation has been groaning in travail together until now; and not only the creation, but we ourselves, who have the first fruits of the Spirit, groan inwardly as we wait for adoption as sons, the redemption of our bodies. For in this hope we were saved.[25]

Theologians have not much explored the connection, but the richest of all sources for Christian interpretation of God's will-to-empathy are the classic attempts to speak of the Trinity. A recent conference on violence and religion paid much attention to the importance of the "included third" in both the Christian concept of the divine Trinity and in human politics. Nothing is more common in politics than two parties who "gang up" on a third. But in the image of God as a Trinity, the exact opposite is portrayed: a person is there "understood as a model of intersubjective triadic relation where each contributes to the definition of oneself as another."[26]

---

24. Lifton, *Nazi Doctors*, 501.
25. Romans 8:22–24a.
26. From a report of a conference in Saint-Denis, France, sponsored by

South Africans have a proverb, expressive of *ubuntu:* "A person becomes a person through other persons." The Christian faith raises this social notion of personhood to the highest possible level in believing that the divine can best be defined in images of relationship. In both internal being and external purpose, God is the Great Includer! The power of the divine inclusiveness extends to humanity in the Spirit "who helps us in our weakness," including our weakness in taking on the griefs and sorrows of all our world neighbors. The promise of the Spirit is that our limited capacity to love our neighbors will not frustrate the intention of God to enable us to participate in the divine pathos.[27] The achievement of that intention is not yet; it is as if God is both patient and impatient with the demonstrated limits of human creatures' readiness to honor the divine image in each other: patient with their weakness, impatient with their resistance to the wordless help of the Spirit who "intercedes for the saints according to the will of God."

In our time, there may be no more crucial issue for the Christian theological struggle with "the powers of this world" than over the anthropological question of whether humans are incurably violent. Psychiatrists and politicians take seriously our apparent need to find outlets for aggressive impulses, both in our families and in our not-so-civil societies. Social scientists such as Desmond Morris and Robert Ardrey offer strong documentation of the possibility that humans are by nature wielders of weapons. Colin Turnbull's study of famine among the Ik tends to the conclusion that extreme hunger breaks all human ties, and the histories of politically organized massacres offer evidence for the presence

the Colloquium on Violence and Religion, May 27–30, 1998, in its *Bulletin* 15 (October 1998): 6. Courtesy of Kosuke Koyama.

27. Perhaps the most eloquent modern exposition of the theme of God's pathos is that of Abraham Joshua Heschel. See his early work, *The Prophets.*

of a Cain slumbering in the heart of every Abel. Albert Camus believed that the only innocent place in modern society was the athletic field, where violence has a relatively benign outlet. Though the phenomena of the Mark McGwires and Sammy Sosas may bear out the truth of that belief, Camus may have been more hopeful than empirical: *spectator* behavior at games, not to speak of players, keeps the evidence ambiguous.[28]

Ambiguity of evidence, on this and many another empirical questions, leaves an intellectual vacuum which only moral consciousness can fill. Between Pascal's "grandeur and misery," human agency has some weight to throw on one side or the other. How and *at whom* we throw our moral weight is a question, and honest followers of Jesus will insist on weighing in, first of all, on themselves. Here the theoretical conflicts between the moral analysis of Daniel Goldhagen and Robert Lifton are momentous. Goldhagen attributes to nineteenth-century-rooted German culture a streak of "eliminationist anti-semitism" that the Nazis turned into action. The national need to get rid of Jews, said Goldhagen, became "normality" for the great majority of Germans. But now that modern Germany is democratic, Germans have returned to the ranks of "normal people," who include most of the rest of us.[29] The Goldhagen theory, in sum, lets most living Germans and non-Germans off the moral hook. Quite different is Robert Lifton's sad conclusion from his long interviews with the Auschwitz doctors: "[M]ost of what Nazi doctors did would be within the potential capability — at least under certain conditions — of most doctors and most people."[30] This

---

28. Among the many books by these and other authors, see the essays and bibliographies in the volumes referenced in nn. 19 and 22 above.

29. Daniel J. Goldhagen, *Hitler's Willing Executioners: Ordinary Germans and the Holocaust* (New York: Random House, Vintage Books, 1996–97).

30. Lifton, *Nazi Doctors*, 427.

sober assessment of human nature matches the New Testament view that "all have sinned and come short of the glory of God" and the realism of Jesus that anger at a fellow human has the potential of exploding into murder.[31]

What combinations of (1) personal character, (2) institutional restraints, and (3) dominant cultural beliefs will hinder our potential for violence in the future? If none of us has a definitive answer to this comprehensive question, it behooves us to focus on the question for many years to come. Again, religion, too, must be active in research, imagination, and self-criticism on all three of these dimensions. Too scarce are religious heroes whose lifework touches profoundly on all three. Two such heroes were Dietrich Bonhoeffer and Martin Luther King, Jr. Another is Desmond Tutu. In the mid-1980s, Tutu remarked, "In South Africa it is impossible to be optimistic. Therefore we must hope." It was a religious affirmation, but in the meantime Tutu did more than hope: he presided over church organizations that offered protective cover to the ideology of the African National Congress; he became South Africa's most persuasive advocate of international sanctions against the apartheid government; and when, finally, surprising political change came to South Africa, he accepted chairmanship of a commission charged with public investigation of the crimes of all parties in the struggle over apartheid. In all of this, numerous colleagues testify, the power of Tutu's compassion and integrity as a person have made a vast difference in the way that a violence-prone society is fitfully turning away from its violence. The continuing political task of churches in South Africa is learning new roles vis-à-vis a new government: Will the courage to critique a white-dominated national government be equaled in the courage to critique a black-dominated one?

Hoping against the evidence will always seem irrational to

---

31. Romans 3:23; Matthew 5:21–22.

those who think that facts should determine values and that the notion of a "moral fact" is absurd. Nothing ought more to distinguish religious folk from radical secularists than the former's devotion to Tutu's dictum: "If we hope for what we do not see, we wait for it with patience."[32] Another echo also comes from the Apostle Paul: "For through the Spirit, by faith, we wait for the hope of righteousness."[33]

There are active and passive forms of waiting, however, and on the whole Christian churches have been prone to retreat from the one into the other. We have entertained very modest "hope of righteousness" in the affairs of nations. The facts seem to call for modesty, inclining some theologians to their own versions of Realpolitik. "Wars and rumors of wars" become for them the one prediction of Jesus that history validates.[34] Accordingly, the classical just-war theory of the medieval and modern churches makes a certain peace with war, albeit an uneasy peace.

Our twentieth-century record of massive violence, summarized at the beginning of this essay, casts questions on this modesty. Globally threatened humanity and globally threatened ecosystems call for a global transformation of the characters, the political structures, and the cultural ideas of human beings away from violence toward peace. The efforts of religious and secular thinkers in this direction are the focus of the final sections of this essay.

Peacemaking Theory

When Jesus said, "Blessed are the peacemakers,"[35] he foresaw that wars would come in the human future. But as with another of his often-to-be-quoted predictions — "the poor you

---

32. Romans 8:25.
33. Galatians 5:5.
34. Mark 13:7; Matthew 24:6.
35. Matthew 5:9.

always have with you"[36] — too many Christians have turned
his anticipation of wars into justification for moral complacency, rather than what any exegete should have known: that
the implicit moral judgment on poverty and war is also a
judgment on complacency.

Can humans of the twenty-first century make an epochal
transition from an era of suicidal collective violence to an
era in which interhuman conflicts are nonviolently adjudicated? In the television space-travel fantasy *Star Trek,* set in
the twenty-fourth century, reference is sometimes made to
the pacification of earth some two centuries before, which
opened earthlings to the collaborations of space travel. The
troubling feature of *Star Trek,* however, is its portrayal of
human interaction with other creatures of the universe chiefly
in highly technical, often violent conflict. It is as if this fantasy
of twentieth-century imagination can only project enduring
war onto the rest of the universe.

Other planets and star systems aside, we have to ask if there
will be a transition to peace ahead. Will the coming decades,
rather, see dreary repetition of the deadly disasters of 1900–
1999 and even worse scenarios that our technical and political
powers now facilitate? Suspended as many of us are between
hopes and fears for the lives of our grandchildren, we have to
concede that the transition from fears to hopes cannot bypass
the hard question: Is there a violence that can serve peace?

The "no" answer, promptly forthcoming from pacifists,
will always be a pertinent, cautionary voice in the deliberation that should ensue when others advance a "yes." If the
latter are credibly to justify their yes, they will have to keep
taut the tension between our tentative collective potentials
for good and evil, and the tension between the evil we try to
contain and the evil we hope to *eliminate.*

A transition between these two stages of political soci-

---

36. Matthew 26:11; Mark 14:7; John 12:8.

ety preoccupies many sober actors in the field of "conflict resolution." Its practitioners vary in their beliefs about the degree to which human conflict can be "resolved" by being contained, transformed, or eliminated. But all agree on the purpose of diminishing the human potential for collective as well as personal violence. Below I want to sketch some approaches in conflict-resolution theory to the diminishment of international violence, to focus on violence containment, and finally to propose distinctive contributions to "peacemaking" that ecumenically minded Christian churches should adopt as their agenda for the twenty-first century.

Three Approaches to Conflict Resolution — And a Fourth

Russian-born Anatol Rapoport, a distinguished scholar in the field of conflict analysis, identifies three major models of "world order." The first is "hegemony," in which one collective dominates others by force of arms or by other exercise of irresistible power. This is the "threat system" basic to all imperialisms. The *weakness* of this model for the maintenance of political power is that its dependence on violence may generate counterviolence, especially among subjects willing to die in the cause of imperialism or liberation from imperialism. The 1998–99 wars in Kosovo compose an ambiguous, troubling instance.

The second model is "balance of power," in which all sides reckon with the advantages and rewards of respecting each other's interests by tapping those interests for mutual benefits. This is a "trade system" in which the rewards are both economic and noneconomic, including spheres of profit, influence, and prestige. In the 1966 World Conference on Church and Society, economist Kenneth Boulding suggested that, since politicians had done such a poor job of preventing war in the twentieth century, perhaps it was time to give business and trade a chance, in the hope that by virtue of economic interdependence nations could no longer afford to go to war. The *weakness* of this system is twofold: most power balances are dynamic, changeable, unstable. Further, as in most tradeoffs in politics, some on both sides are usually denied a share in the rewards or feel that the terms of trade are unfair. Finally, few governments will trust economic forces alone to provide security, and publics will tolerate extraordinary sacrifices of economic resources in the name of security.[37]

Both of these models can be subsumed under a philosophy of Realpolitik, but "power" in the second concept is more complex than in the first. Whether "power" is a synonym for violence or, as regards politics, is a word for a more complicated phenomenon is an important question.[38] Those who lose out in a global market, for example, will be tempted to say that economic power can be a form of violence, as when a Korean mother in 1997 suddenly found that the money which last week bought a whole loaf of bread this week bought a half.

Rapoport's third model is "common security," which he calls "an integrated system" based on "induced identifica-

---

37. No one knows exactly how much the United States and the USSR invested in their respective military power over the years after 1945, but one calculation puts the American figure at twelve trillion dollars — an amount sufficient for replacing every physical structure in all fifty states. This figure is approximately twice the current American GNP. The annual proportion of the former USSR's annual GNP invested in military expenditures has been estimated at 25 percent. That of various poor countries is even higher. The point is that, combined with the "threat system," economic interdependence is a fragile moderator of violent international conflict.

38. I follow Hannah Arendt's definition of "power" in her book *On Violence* (New York: Harcourt, Brace, and World, 1969). Violence, she says, may temporarily protect or challenge the power of a government, but enduring political power requires legitimation and consent in the eyes of constituents. "Violence appears when power is in jeopardy, but left to its own course it ends in power's disappearance" (56).

tion of the self with others."[39] At this stage, world order and other social order (e.g., the family) are profoundly akin. The bridge between interpersonal and collective ties is the ability of agents on all sides to identify with the interests, situation, and histories of the "other." The strength of this model is its formula for democratic stability, as in G. H. Mead's remark that "democracy depends upon the ability of voters to vote for someone else's interest in addition to their own." The *weakness* of this model is empirical: cultures and interests impose blinders on the human ability to perceive and respect the cultures and interests of others. At worst these blinders set the stage for misunderstanding that degenerates into understanding just enough of the others to fear and hate them. A kindred weakness relates to morale: a culture that encourages members to appreciate the humanity of the "others" may risk passive betrayal of its own deepest values and weaken its willingness to defend those values in a worldwide competition.

In the early 1960s, Rapoport published *Fights, Games, and Debates,* whose analysis of conflict closely paralleled his three later models of world order.[40] A *fight* is a contest of raw power. In extreme form, fights end in the death of some combatants or their defeat by superior physical strength. A *game,* on the other hand, is more sophisticated: it has rules that curtail the legitimate use of violence. With the exception of deadly games such as those of gladiators in ancient Rome, the rules usually exclude killing as a legitimate cost of winning. One can die playing football, but the rules inhibit that possibility. In economic competition, so long as the competition does not degenerate into a fight, rules of fairness

---

39. Rapoport's discussion appears in his essay *Conceptions of World Order: Building Peace in the Third Millennium,* Occasional Paper No. 12 (Fairfax, Va.: George Mason University, Institute for Conflict Analysis and Resolution, 1997).

40. Ann Arbor: University of Michigan Press, 1960.

and unfairness prevail, sometimes in alliance with a legitimated threat system — for example, the police, legislature, and courts. Whether or not economic power can be a kind of violence remains a question to remember.

Politics at all levels involves many fights and games. But the most sophisticated and distinctly human conflict, as proposed by Rapoport, is the *debate,* a form of competition whose characteristic instrument is *words.* At one point or another, democracies require competitors for power to enter verbal combat, which from time to time may degenerate into a game or a fight. *The high test of a debate is whether each side addresses the other with understanding of the other's point of view.* Rapoport's book ends with a strong appendix in which he imagines how a capitalist might portray the best possible case for communism, and a communist the best possible case for capitalism.

The psychosocial virtue commended in Rapoport's third model is *empathy,* a virtue at once both intellectual and emotional. To be sure, advocates of hegemony can "use" empathy for dominating their subjects. Traders look for exchanges that can serve their own interests, but they also profit from appreciation of the interests of others. Without giving up their points of view, integrationists believe in searching for agreement on the nature of common and differing interests and value perspectives. If they enter debate, they do so with the fullest possible commitment to discovering why the others speak and act as they do. In this they share the wisdom of political leaders in Moscow and Washington in 1962: What is the meaning of each other's gestures toward war and peace?

The political and moral wisdom in Rapoport's third model, however, calls for a fourth model, which might be tagged *dialogue.* Debate is close to dialogue but with a crucial difference. Debates sometimes come to naught because the debaters share few if any common assumptions about what counts for truth and proof. Common ground is likely to elude the process, leaving the debaters farther apart than ever. A grain of truth about truth in so-called postmodernism is that many a truth-claim is specific to the interest, power, time, circumstance, and viewpoint of the claimant. If this assumption is empirically valid, the widest gaps in human communication are unbridgeable. We can shout at each other across the gaps but we cannot "communicate."

Whatever the future of postmodernism as an academic theory, it offers limited help to any leader with responsibility for building bridges between strangers, enemies, or other antagonists. Across chasms of noncommunication, what bridge can be built? The first pilings in such a bridge may have to be sheer hope that the bridge is possible. Tutu's word is the right one: moral-religious hope rather than empirical-rational optimism based on "the facts." Commenting on the Good Friday Agreement that produced a new parliamentary setting for Protestant-Catholic conflict in Northern Ireland, former Irish prime minister Garrett Fitzgerald reflected, at a conference in Oxford in September 1998, that the two sides had different understandings of what they had signed. They launched upon a new nonviolent search for a commonality that still lay shrouded in ambiguity. Willingness to live in ambiguity, he said, was a requirement for peace in Northern Ireland.

This is to say that hope for peace is the ingredient that undergirds and promotes political dialogue, the process by which two or more human agents search together for a commonality that "does not yet appear."[41] For a definition of real dialogue, Richard Rubenstein quotes Martin Buber — "entering a realm where the law of the point of view no longer holds." In their courage to risk dialogue, participants reach out for something that will bind them beyond the limits of their respective points of view. Senator George Mitchell, the

---

41. See Romans 8:24 and Hebrews 11:1–3.

American who helped catalyze the Good Friday peace agreement in Northern Ireland, testified that his role was to "keep the two sides talking to each other long enough until they finally heard each other" and discovered a way into political peace that took account of their differing memories, fears, interests, and assumptions. As in most negotiations, the parties sit down at table with at least a glimmering hope that "something good will come of it." Even if they glimpse that good in the abstract — peace, justice — they do not yet know how to realize it in concrete conflict.[42]

In the fearful incident remembered at the beginning of this essay — the Cuban Missile Crisis — Kennedy, Khrushchev, and their advisers entertained inaccurate impressions of where, if at all, each was willing to compromise. Their tortured, ten-day dialogue taught each leader something about the interests and intentions of the other. Their mutual, stubborn, fragile hope for avoiding nuclear war finally won the day — by a hairbreadth. Lebow and Stein summarize the lessons of the crisis:

> The resolution of the missile crisis stands in sharp contrast to its origins. The confrontation occurred because of the inability of either superpower to empathize with its adversary and to predict its likely response to their actions....
>
> Diplomacy triumphed over force because of mutual learning. Three reinforcing factors were responsible. [First and] most importantly, leaders had time to learn....

---

42. This is the view of P. M. Fitzgerald, expressed in the above-mentioned Oxford conference. The agreement permitted all parties to promote differing interpretations of what they had promised each other. Debate on the meanings of the agreement is now proceeding in the new parliament in a process resembling that of all democratic bodies, as constituents ask each other what their adopted "constitution" really means.

Second, the principals acquired crucial new information during the crisis, and "a third stimulus to learning was the threat of war," which persuaded each leader to "blink" — to draw back from positions previously thought inviolable.

> By Saturday night, war was no longer an abstract concept but a real fear. McNamara recalls that when the Ex Comm [executive committee] meeting ended on Saturday evening, he returned to the Pentagon and watched a spectacular sunset over the Potomac. He wondered how many more sunsets he was destined to enjoy. Soviet accounts reveal that Khrushchev and his advisors suffered similar angst. There is an old saying that nothing so concentrates the mind as the thought of execution. In this instance, it inspired a creative search for accommodation as the would-be victims sought desperately to cheat the hangman.[43]

The Contribution of the Churches to Global Peacemaking

If the collective human capacity to kill our own species is to be "cheated" in the years ahead, we must all find effective ways, short of killing, to live with each other and with our conflicts. Christianity has contributions to make to this hopeful future. It is not the only religion with a contribution to make, and world religions altogether cannot achieve a "just and lasting peace."[44] But new patterns of thought and institutionalized collaboration among the leaders of religion,

---

43. Lebow and Stein, *We All Lost the Cold War,* 144–45.

44. Worth remembering is the Commission on a Just and Lasting Peace organized toward the end of World War II by the Federal Council of Churches and chaired by future Secretary of State John Foster Dulles. Some members of this commission were also members of the so-called Calhoun Commission which, in early 1946, concluded that the dropping of the atomic bombs in 1945 had been unnecessary for ending the war with

government, commerce, and culture are more promising than the efforts of any leadership group working in isolation from the others.

I conclude this essay with treatments of two issues. First, what does the recent historical record of the Christian churches suggest about their possible future contributions to new levels of global peace, to the curtailment of violence within and between nations? And second, what intellectual-moral perspectives might the churches contribute to international debate about the uses of violence for the prevention or containment of violence?

Historians are clear that religion, including Christianity and its institutions, has a mixed record in supporting or inhibiting war.[45] It has been *least* effective in curtailing the organized violence of war:

- when its leaders have been so solidly allied with powerful political elites that the latter's decisions for war automatically acquire religious legitimation. The American entry into World War I promptly acquired such legitimation. Stalin asked the Russian Orthodox Church for support in the Soviet war against the Germans, and the Orthodox promptly offered it in the name of Russian nationalism.

- when a theology of "two kingdoms" or the like insulates the internal ethics of the religious institution from an ethic applicable to the political institution, which is permitted to go to war uncriticized. Lutheran Germans mounted little or no criticism of their government's entry

---

Japan. The phrase "just and lasting peace," of course, comes from Lincoln's Second Inaugural.

45. I have a more extensive summation of these "pluses and minuses" in "Religion and Violence Prevention," in *Cases and Strategies for Preventive Action,* ed. Barnett R. Rubin, published jointly by the Twentieth-Century Fund and the Council on Foreign Relations (New York: Century Foundation Press, 1998), 169–95.

into both world wars. Their classic "two-kingdom" ethic had helped form a habit of passivity toward government.

• when religious thinkers enter the debate on the use of political violence so belatedly that the nation is on the cusp of war by the time they consider opposing it. There was both church and labor union opposition to the internment of Japanese Americans in February 1942, but the inherent anti-Asian racism had not been notably challenged in the western American states.

• when, before or during war, the internal rhetoric of religious leaders either sanctions or fails to criticize popular images of the "inhuman" enemy. During the Pacific war there was only muted opposition in the churches to popular racist images of the Japanese.

• when, without taking sides in a conflict, religious institutions fail to offer "neutral ground" on which antagonists can meet for dialogue. When they finally did so, leaders of the three major religions in Bosnia had already witnessed many months of war.

• when the internal culture of the religious body so consistently mandates the muffling and bypassing of conflict in its own ranks that it lacks experience for resolving conflict in the secular arena. Hostilities based on religious conviction can oscillate between conceptual standoffs and outbreaks of near-violence. In either case, dialogue never occurs. Church congregations can be training grounds for conflict resolution, but they can also provide education in fighting.[46]

---

46. Michael Ignatieff writes soberly about "the narcissism of minor differences" in the context of recent Balkan wars. People often want to keep an identity that hinges on the preservation of at least some differences, no matter how minor. Threat to those differences from close neighbors may provoke more hostility than threat from afar. Thus, family and local church

On the other hand, over the centuries religion has demonstrated power to prevent and curtail deadly conflict:

- when its leaders have refused to equate the cause of the
  religious faith with any collective cause. When, for example, American churches have been wise enough about
  the First Commandment to refuse to display American
  flags in their sanctuaries.

- when, in religious leaders' relation to political elites,
  they have conceived their role as neither chauvinistic
  nor dualistic but as "critical support" and, on occasion,
  as "loyal opposition." This was the case among some
  church critics of the Vietnam War, matched by the witness of many Vietnam veterans. Many veterans received
  little credit from members of the peace movement for
  being loyal Americans as well as war opponents.

- when internally and publicly, religious rhetoric does not
  describe "the enemy" as "inhuman." Kosuke Koyama
  testifies that in 1942, when he was twelve, he attended
  a church-membership class in his Tokyo congregation,
  whose pastor said: "You must remember that the God
  and Father of Jesus loves Americans, too."

- when in their roles as educators, leaders draw on perspectives and sources of knowledge that counter information on which government and public media may be
  depending; when, for example, the intimate acquain-
  tance of church personnel with foreign cultures counters
  the stereotypes of political propaganda. In 1983, the
  Presbyterian Church (USA) sent two delegations to
  revolution-torn Central America. They came back with
  perspective and knowledge of those countries that was

---

quarrels can be the most vicious of all. See Ignatieff, *Warrior's Honor,*
34–71.

superior, in my estimation, to what we were being told by the U.S. State Department.

- when in its liturgies, preaching, and public pronouncements the religious community repents of its own contributions to past conflicts and undertakes support of both religious and secular efforts to prevent such conflicts in the future. Among other illustrations: the critique of the Hiroshima atomic bombing by a group of eminent Protestant theologians in March 1946; the wide church support of the founding of the United Nations; and much current American church support of the International Criminal Court.

- when its leaders, as they seek to erode public and church acceptance of the concept of *sacred violence,* refuse to offer religious justification even for the "good" side of conflict. Church criticism of loose U.S. gun-control law is up against quasi-sacred views of the U.S. Constitution and alleged Second Amendment legitimation of personal gun possession.[47]

- when leaders consistently urge their own constituents to study and practice nonviolent approaches to potentially deadly conflict, with emphasis on the crucial difference between violent and nonviolent "resistance." Many white churches, especially in the South, were slow to understand the difference as practiced by participants in the civil rights movement. Those whites who did learn the difference formed a cadre of good teachers inside some congregations.

- when, even in the midst of war, leaders continue to listen to the legitimate interests of all parties, maintaining

---

47. See the discussion below of the Presbyterians' 1998 General Assembly.

a reputation for truth-seeking and truth-telling at a critical distance from government propaganda.[48] Both the Roman Catholic bishops in Rhodesia and the Quakers in Biafra were important listeners to both sides of those conflicts.

• when, at the conclusion of violent conflict, religious bodies call for collective forms of repentance, forgiveness, and reconciliation on all sides, in ways that lay groundwork for the prevention of such conflicts in the future.[49] Practitioners of this role should not be dismissed as irrelevant, even though more accomplished in humanitarian relief than in violence prevention. The difference between the Versailles Treaty and the Marshall Plan is instructive. Although the relief efforts of churches after war are sometimes derogated as mere ambulance work, no one should forget that some wars are grounded in the postwar suffering of defeated peoples.

The Most Difficult Ethical Question

Religion's refusal to offer unambiguous justification of killing is critical in all the above strategies, but the adjective "ambiguous" keeps the door open to the question that many, including me, would prefer to consider closed: In the modern world, for now and the foreseeable future, is there a religiously legitimate role for *the use of violence in preventing or curtailing violence?* How some Christian ethicists and

---

48. Illustrations of each of these "minuses and pluses" are abundant. On the positive side, see Johnston and Sampson, *Religion: The Missing Dimension in Statecraft,* for examples from the post–World War II era.

49. On the mobilization and implementation of these ideas for dealing with the legacy of resentment and hostility in the aftermath of violent collective conflict, see my book, *An Ethic for Enemies: Forgiveness in Politics* (New York: Oxford University Press, 1995, 1997).

some Christian denominations are dealing with this difficult question is worth open-ended pursuit.

My denomination, the Presbyterian Church (USA), has hosted only a small minority of pacifists. The denomination has usually taken an Augustinian-Calvinist-Niebuhrian view, seeing violence as tragic but necessary for legitimate social purposes. Rather consistently it has resorted to the ancient doctrine of the just war. In this light, a pair of actions by the General Assembly in June 1998 took on more significance. On the one hand, by a vote of 393–120, which rejected a floor protest on behalf of Second Amendment rights, the body called on American Presbyterians "to intentionally work toward removing handguns and assault weapons from our homes and our communities." Not only did this resolution take a step toward a denominational policy of nonviolent resistance to armed assault, it endorsed a classic view that sees government as the only legitimate user — for purposes of law and order — of violence. Further, the resolution said that a situational common good trumps the individualistic American claim to "the right to bear arms." Among the ingredients of that common good is the life of children, fourteen of whom die every day in the United States from gunfire accident and murder. The murder rate in the United States earns the country an unenviable international record. Most American murders occur with guns. Tiny Northern Ireland, wracked for thirty years by politically driven hostilities and deaths, had a murder rate approximately half that of the United States.

Remarkably enough, this 1998 church assembly paid careful attention not only to individual acts of murder but also took up collective response to "administrative massacre." In our time, the term has come to characterize events such as the Holocaust and those in Cambodia, Bosnia, and Rwanda.[50]

---

50. See Mark Osiel, *Mass Atrocity, Collective Memory, and the Law* (New York: Transaction Publishers, 1998), a wide-ranging argument for

When can violence for the restraint of violence be ethically justified? This 1998 assembly debated and passed a long resolution on this question, titled "Just Peacemaking and the Call for International Intervention for Humanitarian Rescue."[51]

At the heart of the resolution, which runs fifteen double-column pages, are seven criteria for justifying external intervention in any region threatened by administrative massacre. The criteria display both kinship to and distinction from the classic ones treated in just war theory under the headings of *jus ad bellum* (morally just conditions in which force may be permissible) and *jus in bello* (morally just constraints of violence in the midst of conflict). To be justified such intervention:

1. should respond to genuine human need "that cannot be met by other means."

2. should "have a reasonable chance of alleviating the conditions it seeks to overcome."

3. must "not cloak the pursuit of the economic or narrow security interests of the intervening powers."

4. "should have international auspices."

5. "should advance the general welfare of all the inhabitants of the region and not become a tool by which powerful elites, either domestic or foreign, further cement their power."

6. "should involve the minimum degree of coercion necessary to achieve the purposes of the action."

---

an international court able to try political leaders responsible for organized killings, whose scale and intent distinguish them radically from individual acts of murder.

51. Quotations come from this document as printed in the *Minutes of the 210th General Assembly of the Presbyterian Church* (Louisville: Office of the General Assembly, 1998). This same assembly restated its advocacy of worldwide nuclear disarmament.

7. "should target political-military authorities when it resorts to sanctions, not broad population groups."

In the context of much serious wrestling over the past fifteen years with war and peace, this Presbyterian proposal demonstrates qualified respect for the use of violence in human affairs. Like the just-war doctrine, it sees armed interventions as a "last resort," but it strengthens the "lastness" of the resort by identifying preferable economic and political strategies. Early in the 1998 document is a quotation from a 1988 General Assembly policy paper, "Christian Obedience in a Nuclear Age":

> Christian obedience demands that we move toward [God's gift of] peace in all possible ways: by extending the rule of law, advocating universal human rights, strengthening the organs of international order, working for common security and economic justice, converting industry to peaceful production, increasing understanding of and reconciliation with those we identify as enemies, developing just peacemaking skills, constructing concrete manifestations of just peace across barriers of conflict and injustice, and other means.[52]

Among the "other means" the 1998 resolution endorses are individual protests against war represented by pacifism and conscientious objection. But in an early paragraph whose tinges of tragedy and compromise echo Niebuhrian "Christian realism," the resolution calls its central argument a "fourth position" in the history of Christian ethics. "Just peacemaking," unlike crusade, pacifism, and just war,

> agrees with the pacifists that war is contrary to God's will for humanity and cannot ever find war to be morally just. However, it simply realizes that there are times

---

52. *Minutes of the 200th General Assembly* (1988), pt. 1, 450.

when the powers and structures of human life are so threatened by the policies or actions of an international outlaw that there is no other course of action to take but, in great agony and without a sense of righteousness, to restrain an evil threat by military means.[53]

The ethical standards enunciated here may be considered a shift in emphasis in this denomination's traditional support of the just-war ethic. Supporters and critics of the resolution have observed that it is an elaboration of the just-war ethic and not a fourth position. The resolution invites the Presbyterian Church to do more collective thinking about these issues into the twenty-first century, for, as it concedes, "Intervention is tricky business." It is not now and never will be a perfect art, as recent fumbling attempts by national and international bodies prove only too vividly. The ethic that warrants the occasional, limited use of violence for quelling violence will need a lot of tutoring from politicians, military leaders, and conflict-resolution experts if it is ever to become a true "fourth position" for Christians.

Can intervention be *successful* while observing the strictures of the seven criteria? The store of international experience is not large. Intervention really is tricky business. Recent examples are full of cautionary data. During the worst killings of Muslims by Bosnian Serbs in July 1995, a contingent of 310 Dutch soldiers, members of the United Nations peacekeeping forces, apparently stood by "within earshot" of the gunfire that slaughtered seven thousand Muslims in Srebrenica. Their task had been to protect tens of thousands of mostly Muslim refugees. More numerous and better-armed Serbian troops overwhelmed the Dutch, and promised NATO air support never arrived. Militarily the position of the Dutch was probably hopeless. Larger forces were required to counteract the

---

53. Ibid.

commission of a war crime taking place before their eyes. Many in the Netherlands are still debating how the event could have turned out differently. One Dutch historian says that it is "the nation's greatest postwar trauma."[54]

A large American public experienced trauma of another sort in 1990 when American soldiers in Somalia began to be killed in a civil war they had been sent to suppress. When another nation's interest is at stake in its internal wars, every public has limits on its willingness to sanction such sacrifice. Perhaps the most notorious recent example of these limits has been Rwanda. U.N. military experts estimated that, with the intervention of five thousand to ten thousand peacekeeping troops early in the Rwanda tragedy, it might have been prevented. But this remains an untested hypothesis. Whose deaths can leaders most afford to risk in the eyes of their own constituents, and in what ratio to deaths prevented? It is an old question, as pertinent as ever in new global circumstances. "Greater love has no one than that one lay down one's life for a friend."[55] In a newly interconnected global society, whom do we risk our lives defending?

The Kosovo Test

As this is written, the world is testing the validity and practicality of "intervention as peacemaking," and the end of the test has not yet come. Will the Kosovo event strengthen or weaken the credibility of this revised just-war ethic?

Like most ethical criteria, none of the seven proposed in the Presbyterian resolution can be perfectly translated into political practice. But the Kosovo intervention seems to pass muster with most of them:

54. Jos Palm as quoted by Marlise Simons, "Bosnia Massacre Mars Do-Right Self-Image the Dutch Hold Dear," *New York Times*, September 13, 1998, 8.
55. John 15:13.

1. Tagged by the new statutes of the International Criminal
Court as a war crime, "ethnic cleansing" entered the vocabu-
lary in the Bosnian war. Among Balkan leaders, defenders of
the concept would claim that moving communities out of one
area into another is not the same as administrative massacre,
but in fact the line between the two has been egregiously violated by the Serbian government over the past six years. The
"cleansing" of Kosovo of its non-Serb population has produced "genuine human need" among hundreds of thousands
of human beings. Could their need be met by nonviolent pressures on a strong Serbian government? In the wake of the
government's behavior over the past seven years, it is hard to
believe that the answer could be other than "no."

Some of the strongest journalism on this issue has come
from Flora Lewis in Europe.

> [T]here is a new consensus [in Europe] that limits must
> be set on outrageous national behavior. The limits have
> not been well defined, but they are being drawn now . . .
> [that] there is a real feeling of need for minimal standards
> of how to treat people in Europe. . . . Europe's will, with
> America, to act at last is surely a sign that people can
> change, that this continent has had its fill of wars. It is
> a shame to have to bomb to prove it, but it must be
> proved. . . .
>
> Serbs ask: "Why us? What did we do to you, what did
> my children cowering in the cellar because of air raids do
> to you?" The Czech president, Václav Havel, has given
> the right answer. "What you have done to the Kosovars,
> you did to me . . . there is solidarity."[56]

---

56. Quotations from the *International Herald Tribune*, March 26 and
April 30, 1999. Similarly, in a broadcast on Czech television on April 12,
Havel said: "If anybody is being hurt, I am being hurt" (*International
Herald Tribune*, April 19, 1999).

So far, European leaders have not spoken much to why European governments responded with little apparent empathy for the 1994 mass murder in Rwanda. Critics of the Kosovo attacks are likely to say that this is the selective conscience of racism at work.

2. Does the Kosovo intervention have a "reasonable chance" of success? The precedent of Serb restraint in the face of United Nations–authorized air strikes in 1996 convinced many Western leaders that the answer was "yes." For the moment, the outcome of the Kosovo event is uncertain. Trustworthy information from both sides, which might help ethical judgments of the NATO attacks, is scarce. How many lives will have been saved at the expense of how many deaths? Will we ever know true statistics for wrestling with these ethically treacherous proportions? Has the war so strengthened the hand and the purposes of a Serbian dictator that, ironically, it has facilitated his policy of "cleansing" Kosovo? Will the legacy of new hostility between Kosovars and Serbs prevent any real "success" in compelling them to live together in Kosovo in some approximate peace?

3. Some European supporters have called the Kosovo war the first European war pursued by one side in defense of its "values" rather than its material and power interests.[57] Repentance for early inaction toward massacres in Bosnia and in Rwanda is evident, not to speak of a "what-if" scenario for the prevention of World War II. (Some scholars say, for example, that prompt French-British military response to Hitler's reoccupation of the Rhineland in 1936 would have

---

57. "So what makes this fight so different from all other fights? To begin with, this is a battle not even pacifists can resist: a war of conscience, not of interest. The attack on Yugoslavia is aimed at saving lives... " (Josef Joffe, editor of *Süddeutsche Zeitung*, *International Herald Tribune*, April 3–4, 1999, 8). There is "interest," however, in repressing rampant, violence-prone nationalism in all of Europe. Fear of return to that seedbed of continental war is in the background of most European support of the air war.

brought down his government.) Collective NATO motives
for the attack on Serbia come close to meeting this third criterion, for there is no indication that the nineteen members
of the alliance expected to gain territory, wealth, or power.
Of all the continent's political leaders, Britain's prime minister, Tony Blair, was the most forthright on the "conscience"
issue: "This is the first time that my generation has had to
come to terms with the fact that it is necessary to use force
on certain occasions to do what is right."[58]

4. The war as currently conducted has international auspices and international opposition. Future supporters and
critics of the intervention will make much of this distinction:
it is not a war of one nation against another, but an alliance
of nineteen nations arrayed against one nation. It is not a
war of "united" nations, either, hence the ambiguity of its
"international auspices." But the war is a new moment in
the history of Europe. The NATO initiative is a more broadly
international military effort than governments of Europe have
ever undertaken. American news reporting on Kosovo has
generally underplayed the significance of this development.
Critics of the NATO bombing underplay it also: they are swift
to blame the United States for the war policy and alleged war
crimes, when in all objectivity blame belongs, if it belongs, at
the doorsteps of nineteen national governments.

5. Will the Kosovo war end in reinforcing the power of Slobodan Milosevic? Will it "advance the general welfare of all
the inhabitants of the region"? By accelerating the forced emi-
gration of the Kosovo population and decreasing their chance
to return to their "normal" society, will the war end by inad-
vertently harming many people in the Balkans? The answers
to these questions remain uncertain.

6. The weapons of modern air war have been honed to

---

58. Writing in the *Washington Post* and reprinted in the *International
Herald Tribune*, April 19, 1999.

help discriminate between civilian and military targets. "Surgical strikes" to the contrary, however, there is little likelihood that the destructive power of these weapons will ever eliminate the killing of innocent people. So far we do not know how many civilians have been killed by air attacks on Iraq and Serbia. Nonetheless there is still room for the hazardous pragmatism that says, "With a few deaths, we protect many lives." Such a calculus seems inevitable for justifying war in the name of humanitarian purpose. The risk of paying too high a cost for achieving that purpose will always be part of any attempt to implement this principle of the just-war ethic. Ethically crucial is concern for limiting enemy deaths along with the deaths of allies.

7. The seventh criterion in the Presbyterian document — no harm to broad population groups — faces the difficult empirical question of whether it is possible to undermine the power of leaders without harming their constituents. Economic sanctions against South Africa probably harmed the white elite and helped bring down the government. So far the same cannot be said of Iraq and Serbia. The failure of economic sanctions against both Iraq and Serbia led to the "last resort" of military action. Targeting the guilty and sparing the innocent is an important principle in any form of justly punitive action. But the grim fact remains: however sophisticated, modern weapons of war are never perfectly discriminating. Furthermore, citizens of the twenty-first century must never forget that many a twentieth-century war ground to an end with the virtual abandonment of the discrimination principle. The names Stalingrad, Dresden, and Hiroshima will always provide such a reminder.

The lines between various kinds of violence in international conflict will never be easy to draw. It is not yet evident that economic sanctions in the twentieth century resulted in fewer deaths than air warfare. In the case of Iraq, for example, the United Nations has estimated that sanctions raised in-

fant mortality from 3.7 percent to 12 percent. The figures
represent an annual increase of forty thousand deaths among
children under the age of five, to which one might add fifty
thousand deaths of elderly adults.[59] Such statistics pose a disturbing ethical question which the power struggles of the
twentieth century will bequeath to the twenty-first: What
right and what power do foreign nations have to curb the
right and power of a national government to ignore the needs
of its own citizens?

Judging from one case is a weak test of the validity of any
ethic or political policy. The stakes in the Kosovo crisis are so
high, however, that any proponent of a just-war ethic must
be open to new reflection in light of the mixtures of good and
evil that may flow from Kosovo.

This means leaving essays like this one open-ended. The
Kosovo war is a test of the possible modern integration
of individual and collective moral responsibility, of collective agreement on international law and human rights, and
of institutional structures designed to serve these ends. The
complex facts about the war, its supporters, and its critics
suggest that the world of nations is only "slouching" toward
a peace on earth once promised at Bethlehem. We still live in
a violence-prone world.

The view of this essay is that Christians are not permitted to wait until God's final judgment to strive to overcome
our general propensities for killing each other. If we cannot
protect all our lives, we are obligated to protect all we can.
Perhaps the most questionable element in the U.S. military

---

59. John Mueller and Karl Mueller, "Sanctions of Mass Destruction,"
Foreign Affairs 78 (May–June 1999): 44–50. They estimate that air bombing killed two million civilians in the twentieth century, while many more
starved or otherwise died from the effects of economic sanctions. For example, 750,000 German civilians died from the economic blockade of
1914–18, and "economic sanctions may well have been a necessary cause
of the deaths of more people in Iraq than have been slain by all so-called
weapons of mass destruction throughout history" (48–49).

strategy in Kosovo was its insistence, for domestic political reasons, on bombing rather than ground troops as the way to halt Serb aggression. Sometimes only by the risk and loss of one life is another to be saved. Crusading zeal can warp this ethic into its opposite. Implemented with care, humility, and certainty about human fallibility, the ethic may yet offer some progress toward a truly global peace.

As the Kosovo event unfolds, one is tempted to add an eighth criterion to the Presbyterian seven: *Intervention for humanitarian purposes must cease once the action is clearly leading to another world war.* As this is written, one of the alarming potentials of the current intervention is the opportunity it is providing for powerful nations to manifest long-term, latent power competitions with little direct relevance to the interests at stake in Kosovo. One thinks of how the murder of one Austrian prince in Sarajevo set the spark to World War I. Whatever one might conclude about justice and injustice in the "microwars" of the late twentieth century, it is no longer possible to justify a world war by the old dictum of Clausewitz that "war is politics pursued by other means." Whether initiated by "international outlaws" or "civilized" nation-states, world war is now a formula for Pyrrhic victories. Avoiding the war that "ends all wars," because it will end the life of our planetary species, is a more urgent political hope than it has ever been in human history. Whatever the mix of justice and injustice in any human project, including war, none of us has a right to risk the destruction of the global village by well-intentioned attempts to save part of it.

– Chapter 5 –

FAITH, FEMINISM, AND THE FAMILY IN AN AGE OF GLOBALIZATION

Mary Stewart Van Leeuwen

The term "globalization" means many things, both in the church and in the world at large. Within the church, it can refer to worldwide ecumenical efforts to resolve matters of doctrine and service, to the global challenge of doing effective evangelism, or to expanding interfaith dialogue among adherents of the world religions. In academic and journalistic discourse, "globalization" most often refers to the worldwide spread of modernity in the form of democracy, urbanization, technical rationality, and market-oriented economics, and to the changes wrought by these forces on institutions such as government, the media, law, education, religion, and the family.

This chapter is an attempt to assess the global spread of modernity on gender and family relations, within a Reformed world- and life-view and also as mediated by the second wave of feminism, which has increasingly become one of many forms of "reflexive globalization." The latter term refers to social movements that respond critically to global outcomes of political, economic, technical, and cultural modernization, with a view to altering those outcomes. Thus, to the extent that it concerns itself with gender and family issues in global — and not merely Western — perspective, feminism is parallel in form, though different in focus, to other forms of global activism, such as the peace movement, the environmental movement, and certain forms of religious fundamentalism. Paradoxically, each of these movements criticizes certain aspects of modernity, while availing itself of many other aspects in the process of disseminating its agenda and realizing its goals.[1] In this chapter I will examine ways in which feminist theory and activism in part affirm, help develop, and distort the longer tradition of Christian theologizing about family life.[2]

A Theological Framework: Family as a Mixed Blessing

I approach the topic of family, feminism, and globalization as a Calvinist Christian influenced by the work of Abraham Kuyper (1837–1920), but concerned to extend his thinking in a more gender-egalitarian direction.[3] From this perspective, three theological themes are particularly relevant. The first is the concept of the *cultural mandate* — the idea that God is sovereign over all spheres of society and thus that service to God may take place in all areas of culture. The second is the affirmation that certain human activities and in-

---

1. Tony Spybey, *Globalization and World Society* (Cambridge, England: Polity Press, 1996), chap. 1. See also Ulrich Beck, Anthony Giddens, and Scott Lash, *Reflexive Modernization* (Stanford, Calif.: Stanford University Press, 1994).

2. For a more detailed account of Protestant family theology over the past few centuries, see Max L. Stackhouse, *Covenant and Commitments: Faith, Family, and Economic Life* (Louisville: Westminster/John Knox Press, 1997).

3. Kuyper articulately represents motifs in this area that can also be found in other traditions and figures. See, for example, the concept of "departments of life" in the work of Lutheran Ernst Troeltsch; "sectors of society" in the Catholic socialist Antonio Gramsci; "spheres of justice" in the writings of Jewish philosopher Michael Walzer; and particularly the role of such differentiations in official Roman Catholic teachings on "subsidiarity," as we will shortly see.

stitutions — including marriage and family — are at one and the same time *blessed in creation* and *distorted by sin*. The third is the conviction that Christ's redemptive work both *reaffirms* and *relativizes* family as a locus of human loyalty. If contemporary Christian thinkers are to help shape a global civilization that honors God and promotes gender and generational justice they need to keep these themes in fruitful tension, both in their theological analysis and in public-policy recommendations addressing the challenges of globalization.

Gender, Family, and the Cultural Mandate

Kuyper advanced the idea of the cultural mandate in order to challenge a dichotomous thought pattern shared by certain expressions of both Catholic and evangelical pietism — namely, the assumption that certain spheres of human functioning (such as prayer, devotions, and religious study and observance) were "sacred," while others (such as science, business, politics, and family) were "secular" and therefore of secondary importance to the Christian life or even detrimental to it. By contrast, Kuyper insisted that all of life was blessed by God in creation, and that all the activities proper to life were to be developed and redeemed according to norms that could be discerned in the Hebrew and Christian scriptures. Thus he advanced a theological rationale for robust Christian investment in the family, the academy, the arts, the marketplace, and the political forum.[4] At the same time he tended

---

4. See for example Kuyper's 1898 *Lectures on Calvinism: The Stone Lectures at Princeton University* (Grand Rapids, Mich.: Eerdmans, 1961), and also James D. Bratt, ed., *Abraham Kuyper: A Centennial Reader* (Grand Rapids, Mich.: Eerdmans, 1998). On the continuing relevance of Kuyper's thought for social analysis and public-policy debate, see Luis Lugo, ed., *Religion, Pluralism, and Public Life: Abraham Kuyper's Legacy for the Twenty-first Century* (Grand Rapids, Mich.: Eerdmans, forthcoming), and also the April 1996 (vol. 31, no. 1) issue of the *Calvin Theological Journal*, particularly the article by James Skillen, "From Covenant of Grace to Equitable Public Pluralism: The Dutch Calvinist Contribution" (67–96).

strongly toward another dichotomy common to nineteenth-century middle-class thinking — namely, that women were fitted, by God and by nature, mainly for participation in the domestic sphere, and men for the more public arenas of intellectual, political, and ecclesiastical achievement.[5] Kuyper thus effectively dichotomized the cultural mandate by gender, and read this dichotomy back into the scriptures. He also assumed an unchanging norm of male leadership in all spheres, whether home, church, or any other institutions of public life.

But when we turn to Kuyper's primary sources we find a rather different picture. The *locus classicus* for the doctrine of the cultural mandate is Genesis 1:26–28:

Then God said, "Let us make humankind in our image, according to our likeness; and let them have dominion over the fish of the sea, and over the birds of the air, and over the cattle, and over all the wild animals of the earth, and over every creeping thing that creeps upon the earth." So God created humankind in his image, in the image of God he created them; male and female he created them. God blessed them, and God said to them, "Be fruitful and multiply, and fill the earth and subdue it; and have dominion over the fish of the sea and over the birds of the air and over every living thing that moves upon the earth." (NRSV)

The primal story does not have God saying to the first female, "Be fruitful and multiply," and to the first male, "Subdue the earth." Both mandates — generativity and accountable dominion — are given to both members of the original pair.[6]

---

5. See Mary Stewart Van Leeuwen, "Abraham Kuyper and the Cult of True Womanhood: An Analysis of *De Eerepositie der Vrouw*," *Calvin Theological Journal* 31 (April 1996): 97–124, and idem, "The Carrot and the Stick: Abraham Kuyper on Gender, Family, and Class," in Lugo, *Religion, Pluralism, and Public Life*.

6. For a more detailed exposition of this theological framework, see

Made jointly in the image of God, women and men were commanded to unfold the good potential of creation in all areas of life. And so the primal male is placed in the garden to "till it and keep it" (Gen. 2:15) and, in another reflection of God-imaging capacities, has the task of drawing up a taxonomy of the garden's creatures (2:19–20). As he does so, God recognizes that "it is not good that the man should be alone" but that no creature named by the man is "a helper fit for him." So the "bone of his bones" is used by God to form the first woman. To her the man is thereafter to "cling," leaving his father and mother, and "becom[ing] one flesh" (2:18–24).

Once together, they are to exercise fidelity and mutual aid in the context of complementary sexuality. Some gender-hierarchical interpreters have argued for Adam's "headship" over Eve on the basis of his naming her in Genesis 2:23. But the classic Hebrew naming formula (the one used by Adam as he "named" the animals) consists of *calling* a person, an animal, or a place *by name*. Upon seeing the woman for the first time, the man does not "call her by name." Significantly, this does not happen until Genesis 3, when the fall has wrought its distortions on their relationship. In Genesis 2 he merely "calls" or "recognizes" her as "woman." Old Testament scholar Phyllis Trible writes: "In calling the woman, the man is not establishing power over her, but rejoicing in their mutuality. The man's poem ('Bone of my bones, flesh of my flesh, this shall be called woman') does not determine who the woman is, but rather delights in what God has already done in creating sexuality."[7]

Mary Stewart Van Leeuwen, *Gender and Grace: Love, Work, and Parenting in a Changing World* (Downers Grove, Ill.: InterVarsity Press, 1990), especially chaps. 2, 9, and 10.

7. Phyllis Trible, *God and the Rhetoric of Sexuality* (Philadelphia: Fortress Press, 1978), 100.

Woman is thus "the helper *corresponding* to the man,"[8] one beside whom he is to travel and labor, in response to God's call to responsible stewardship of the earth and the raising of heirs who will continue the task of being God's regents. Together women and men are to work out God's vision of *shalom* in ways that are sensitive to different settings and times in history, and to the life cycle of male and female human beings. This does not preclude the possibility that a gendered division of labor may be a just and satisfying way to organize a given family or culture at a specific time. But it does suggest that any construction of gender involving an exaggerated or inflexible separation of the cultural mandate by sex will eventually run into trouble, because it is creationally distorted and therefore potentially unjust toward both males and females. Generativity and accountable dominion together comprise a human — not a gendered — mandate.

Sphere Sovereignty, Subsidiarity, and the Family

Within this mandate marriage is portrayed in the Hebrew and Christian scriptures as part of God's creation order. That it was meant to be a one-flesh, monogamous union is affirmed in the creation accounts and reaffirmed in the Gospels (e.g., Mark 19; Luke 16) and in the Epistles (e.g., 1 Corinthians 5 and 7; Ephesians 5; 1 Timothy 3; Titus 1). Despite the relativization it undergoes in the New Testament economy of salvation (a point to which I will return shortly), marriage is part and parcel of what God approves for human life on earth. In biblical terms, it is one of several "powers" or creational structures that God establishes for human well-being, alongside such spheres of activity as law, government, commerce, art, and science. Each of these must be flexibly adapted to ensure justice and human flourishing in various historical

---

8. Ibid., 92. Or, as the NRSV translates the phrase, "a helper as his partner."

contexts; but each must still retain its basic creational shape and authority if that human flourishing is to occur.[9]

On this point, there has been a convergence of Catholic and Protestant thought since around the end of the nineteenth century, when both traditions responded to challenges of the industrial revolution such as urbanization, bureaucratization, the rise of factories, and the fragmentation of extended families. Abraham Kuyper coined the term "sphere sovereignty" to describe the right of God-ordained institutions or "spheres" — such as church, family, business, politics, science, and art — to develop as creationally intended without being overwhelmed by the state, ignored in the name of individual freedom, or merged into each other. In his account, none of the spheres of life is subordinate to any other, as the authority and task of each has been delegated by God alone. Perversion of the spheres can occur internally, as when there is corruption in government, abuse in the family, or exploitation of workers by business. It can also occur externally, as when the church tries to dictate what science can investigate, or when the state tries to replace the family.[10] But for Kuyper such perversions call not for the elimination of the affected or offending institutions, but their reform and renewal according to scriptural norms.

At about the same time Kuyper was writing about sphere sovereignty, Pope Leo XIII issued his social encyclical, *Rerum*

---

9. For a helpful analysis of this reading of the biblical language of powers, especially in a global theological context, see Lesslie Newbigin, *The Gospel in a Pluralist Society* (Grand Rapids, Mich.: Eerdmans; Geneva: World Council of Churches, 1989). For an application of Newbigin's analysis to gender and family, see Mary Stewart Van Leeuwen, "Principalities, Powers, and Gender Relations," *Crux: A Quarterly Journal of Christian Thought and Opinion* 31 (September 1994): 120–30.

10. See Kuyper, *Lectures on Calvinism,* and for a helpful contemporary interpretation of sphere sovereignty see Albert Wolters, *Creation Regained: Biblical Basics for a Reformational Worldview* (Grand Rapids, Mich.: Eerdmans, 1985).

Novarum (1891), which articulated the Roman Catholic notion of "subsidiarity." Like Kuyper's sphere sovereignty, the goal of subsidiarity was to defend both the right and the capability of families, businesses, and other institutions to do their assigned tasks without unwarranted interference from each other, from the state, or even from the church. Also parallel to Kuyper, the idea of subsidiarity holds that government exists to maintain a just balance among these institutions and when necessary should aid one or the other so that human flourishing can continue. When applied to the family, subsidiarity differs from Kuyperian sphere sovereignty in that it springs from a natural theology of kinship, marriage, and childbearing reaching back to Aquinas and Aristotle, whereas sphere sovereignty leans more on the idea of divine covenants established for each area of life.[11] In addition, Kuyper's spheres are horizontally related to each other on an equal basis, whereas subsidiarity presumes an organic and hierarchical system of institutions in which "lower" levels, such as the family, function with their own authority and capabilities until or unless they are unable to do so, in which case a "higher" institution such as church or government steps in to address distorted functioning and/or to dispense needed resources.

The unease that many Protestant and Catholic feminists experience in the presence of these concepts — sphere sovereignty and subsidiarity — stems from the historical fact that both Leo XIII and Kuyper tended to ignore certain issues of gender justice in their concern to maintain the functional integrity of families. Like Kuyper, Leo XIII believed in husbandly headship, albeit of a benign and self-sacrificing sort. And both tended to buy into the late-nineteenth-century bifurcation of the cultural mandate by gender: they regarded

---

11. For a further elaboration, see Don S. Browning et al., *From Culture Wars to Common Ground: Religion and the American Family Debate* (Louisville: Westminster/John Knox Press, 1997), especially chap. 8.

domesticity as normative for women and public achievement and authority as normative for men, a cultural attitude whose historical development I will trace later in this essay. But it is also possible to affirm the value of these two concepts for a Christian ethic of the family without endorsing a gendered division of labor, as I have tried to show in my brief exegesis of the creation story. And, as I will continue to argue below, it is possible to affirm the integrity of marriage and family as a sovereign sphere without buying into a theology of male headship.

Blessed in Creation, but Distorted by Sin

That both Kuyper and Leo XIII recognized the possibility of distorted sphere activity confirms that we cannot stop with a creational theology of marriage and family. Both thinkers would agree that the world, in all its splendid diversity, does in the final analysis belong to God. But the very same creational structures originally given for a just ordering of life are at the same time in the grip of powers that have not yet completely bowed the knee to Jesus Christ. They may seek to become principalities or authorities or dominions of their own. By God's intent, these powers or creational structures originate and are held together in Christ, as Paul reminds his readers in Colossians 1:15–16. But as Lesslie Newbigin points out, each and every creational element or power — including marriage and family — "can come to usurp the place to which they have no right, the place which belongs to Christ and to him alone. They can, as we say, become absolutized, and then they become demonic." [12]

Recognition of this tension between the createdness and the fallenness of the powers has made Protestant thinkers historically skeptical of a purely natural theology of the family. In Max Stackhouse's words,

---

12. Newbigin, *Gospel in a Pluralist Society*, 206.

the purposes intended by God are contorted, garbled, or made ambiguous in the actual operation of things. What we examine when we study what is "natural" is what is distorted, incomplete, or contingent, even if it bears traces of God's grace in its capacity to be reformed toward order, purpose, and reliable relationship. Thus, in most Protestant traditions, humans may — or even have a duty to — alter natural patterns of life to limit its defects...so that it may more nearly approximate grace-filled, right principles; good ends; and a viable civil society.[13]

Kuyper would certainly not have disagreed with this general theological point. However, when applied to the sphere of marriage and family, it is perhaps more sensitively rendered in the ethical thought of Emil Brunner, whose concept of the "orders" or "communities" of creation is similar to Kuyper's sphere sovereignty and Leo XII's subsidiarity. Writing in the early 1930s, Brunner recognized marriage and family as one of the orders of creation existing alongside the communities of labor, government, and culture (that is, the arts, sciences, and education).[14] Each of these, Brunner wrote, "are created by the natural psycho-physical powers of man [*sic*]...and may indeed exist and be known apart from faith." But, he hastens to add, "this does not mean that they have been created aright, in accordance with the divine will."[15] Thus,

Marriage is not a natural occurrence, but a moral act based on the foundation of a natural occurrence. Marriage does not consist in the mere fact that two persons feel that they are bound to each other in love; marriage

---

13. Stackhouse, *Covenant and Commitments*, 21–22.
14. Emil Brunner, *The Divine Imperative: A Study in Christian Ethics* (Philadelphia: Westminster Press, 1947).
15. Ibid., 335.

only exists where the divine order of marriage is recognized as binding in itself, and when two people know
that they are bound by it. . . . It is true, of course, that
marriage springs from [erotic] love, but its stability is
based not on love but on fidelity. Fidelity is the ethical
element which enhances natural love, and only by its
means does the natural become personal. . . . this alone
provides the guarantee to the other party which justifies
the venture of such a life companionship.[16]

Brunner is thus trying to find an intermediate space between a purely natural theology of the family and one which
is based simply on divine command. Natural passion is a necessary but not sufficient condition for marriage; it must be
enhanced by an ethic of fidelity and mutual sacrifice, rooted
in the grace of God. However, he is much less inclined than
either Kuyper or Leo XIII to assign women and men to different spheres of sacrificial service, or to read male headship
back into the creation order. Although he maintains a weak
notion of created inequality between the sexes, he insists it
must be "limited by the knowledge that Redemption has re-
moved this inequality and transcends it."[17] And although he
believes that women are physically, mentally, and spiritually
equipped for nurturing children in a way that men are not,
he also recognizes that women's specialization in domesticity
"is not merely the gift of the Creator, but also the product
of sin":

It is at this point also that the [Women's] Emancipation
Movement rightly intervenes. Woman has every right to
believe that the present individualization and differentiation of spheres, "hallowed" as it may appear to be by
centuries of tradition, has much more to do with mascu-

16. Ibid., 357–58.
17. Ibid., 380.

line violence and with feminine weakness and indolence that with the Divine order of creation. That is why it is absolutely impossible to put down in black and white, as a universal rule, which spheres of activity "belong" to woman and which do not. This can only become clear through experience, and for this experience first of all the field must be thrown open.[18]

Brunner's insight was more fully developed by feminist biblical theologians during the second wave of feminism beginning in the 1960s. They pointed out that in the biblical drama, it is when the members of the primal pair declare their independence from God — under the influence of the "enemy" who would usurp God's place — that the cosmic love story of mutuality and equality goes awry. The man's legitimate, accountable dominion degenerates into self-seeking domination, first of the woman then (as we see in the Cain and Abel story of Genesis 4) of other men. In the woman, creational sociability degenerates into social enmeshment. "Your desire shall be for your husband," God observes with regret in Genesis 3:16, "and he shall rule over you." As both Brunner and later feminist writers recognized, the woman's complementary flaw to the man's tendency to dominate is the temptation to cling to relationships even when they are warped by abuse and injustice.[19]

Thus, like all creational structures peopled by fallen human beings, marriage and family are the potential locus of much sin. In terms of biblical theology, *all* families are most accurately likened to the little girl of nursery-rhyme fame: when they're good, they're very, very good, and when they're bad,

---

18. Ibid., 375–76.
19. Judith Plaskow, *Sex, Sin, and Grace: Women's Experience and the Theologies of Reinhold Niebuhr and Paul Tillich* (Lanham, Md.: University Press of America, 1980). See also Van Leeuwen, *Gender and Grace*, chap. 2.

they're horrid. We have no theological brief to defend a romanticized view of marriage and family, in our own culture or any other. But, as I will argue later, neither are we justified in defending casual serial monogamy or an endless plurality of family forms. Moreover, at the level of public policy and theological ethics, a proper appreciation of marriage and family requires a capacity to discern the appropriate shape of social justice and well-functioning civil society for a given time and place. This will not be measured against some rigid, atemporal set of gender and familial roles, but according to a biblical vision of *shalom* which will necessarily play out somewhat differently in various cultures and historical periods. In sum, we must have both a hermeneutics of trust *and* a hermeneutics of suspicion toward marriage and family. Biblical wisdom comes in knowing when and how to invoke each.

Reaffirmation and Relativization

The Hebrew Bible is quite unsparing in its portrayal of the fallenness of marriage and family life. It presents us with accounts of rape, adultery, incest and — in the case of King Solomon — polygamy run wild. It adds accounts of further sins aimed at covering up sexual sins, such as David's plot to murder the husband of the woman he impregnated. None of these accounts is normative in character. They are meant to be an accurate portrayal of fallen men and women, warts and all. But they are also intended to show the Israelites that despite their special status as the nation by which the Messiah is to come, they cannot save themselves by trying to manipulate their family bloodlines. The Messiah comes in God's time and by God's means, and although his coming and preaching reaffirm the creational shape of family life, the biblical accounts also relativize it in the interests of bringing God's kingdom to completion.

The sovereignty of God and the relativization of marriage

and family are shown first in the manner of Jesus' coming. As summarized by Geoffrey Bromiley,

> The virgin birth, foreshadowed in Gen. 3:15 with its specific reference to the seed of the woman, forms the last and most extraordinary link in a series of unusual births that extends from Isaac to John the Baptist. During this period, children often come to aging parents, contrary to normal expectation. In some instances God chooses apparently unsuitable mothers, such as the foreigner Ruth and the adulteress Bathsheba. But now in the incarnation [God] sets aside not only marriage (except in a purely formal sense) but also the ordinary process of human reproduction to initiate the work which will undo the fall. "The power of the Most High" brings about this birth of the child that "is destined for the falling and the rising of many in Israel" (Luke 1:35, 2:34).[20]

In addition, Jesus' own life and teaching underscore that marriage and family now take back seat to the universal proclamation of God's salvation and the formation of a new "First Family" — a worldwide kingdom-building company, in which membership depends not on bloodlines, but on faith in the Messiah. Although he confirms God's intentions for monogamous marriage and performs his first miracle in the context of a wedding feast, Jesus proclaims that heavenly life will not include the marriage bond (Mark 12:25), and that his disciples must place marriage and family loyalty second to their allegiance to him (Luke 14:26). And he himself remains single, the better to carry out the unique — and uniquely self-sacrificing — task that is his.

None of this is a license to treat marriage and family obligations casually. Although Jesus' disciples do indeed "leave

---

20. Geoffrey W. Bromiley, *God and Marriage* (Grand Rapids, Mich.: Eerdmans, 1980), 35–36.

all to follow him," nowhere is there evidence that this meant literally hating or abandoning their wives. Indeed, in the New Testament Epistles, we learn that Peter and various other apostles took their wives with them on missionary journeys. Moreover, Jesus had sharp words for the Pharisees who tried to "make void the word of God" by siphoning off for supposedly religious purposes the economic support they owed their aged parents (Mark 7:9-13). What Jesus' teaching does affirm is that for all Christians the Body of Christ is First Family. "The biological family, though still esteemed and valuable, is Second Family. Husbands, wives, sons, and daughters are brothers and sisters in the church first and most importantly — secondly they are spouses, parents, or siblings to one another."[21]

And exactly as family is how the New Testament church behaves. Its central sacrament draws on the analogy of a family meal. It extends hospitality widely, knowing that the bond of baptism expressed in Galatians 3:26-29 has broken down barriers of class, sex, marital status, and ethnicity. This empathic solidarity, which embraces a wider and wider range of fellow Christians, is then meant to reach out to all humankind, since all are made in the image of God, and thus possess inherent dignity and worth. Moreover, in marriage even genital sexuality is to be placed in the larger context of kingdom service:

> Sexuality in the service of the kingdom ... is substantially freed of its destructive possibilities. It is freed from service to compulsive promiscuity, dissolution, or trivial hedonism, and instead binds one person to another in love and continuing commitment. On one level, married sexuality is simply enjoyment of God's gracious creation, male and female. But on another level, it is the base

---

21. Rodney Clapp, "Is the Traditional Family Biblical?" *Christianity Today* 32 (November 21, 1986): 24-28 (quotation from p. 26).

for a stable home from which to minister to the wider community.[22]

Convinced pluralists may insist that this normative vision, however cogently argued, is at most for Christians only. It is not to be enjoined or even recommended to others in an age when so many are convinced that all ethical visions are socially constructed and cultural relativism is the only moral absolute. But the longer tradition of Christian ethical reflection answers this challenge emphatically in the negative, for two reasons. First of all, however well-intended as a hedge against ethnocentrism, such cultural and moral relativism makes all that passes for religion, science, and ethics purely a matter of the power to mobilize group will. And in doing so, relativism makes vulnerable to abuse even (perhaps especially) those marginalized groups of people who have invoked it as a defense of their own lifestyle preferences.

This is not to say that human choice is to be routinely stifled, for "it is both rooted in the gift of the image of God, which is present in each person, and capable of being directed towards God and the right ordering of creation that God intended."[23] But whenever human will has rejected the content or even the existence of that right ordering, it "has brought moral disaster with it in every known experiment." Thus, we should not be surprised that an extreme bifurcation of the cultural mandate by sex in nineteenth- and twentieth-century America eventually led to two successive waves of feminism. At the same time, we should not be surprised that a remarkable mountain of data collected during the past thirty years of the divorce revolution shows that divorce is damaging to the

---

22. Ibid., 27. See also Rodney Clapp, *Families at the Crossroads: Beyond Traditional and Modern Options* (Downers Grove, Ill.: InterVarsity Press, 1993).

23. Stackhouse, *Covenant and Commitments*, 40.

well-being of children and adults alike (as we shall shortly discuss).

Hence there is a second reason for the church's refusal simply to hold its own standards up for its own people, exercising a bland live-and-let-live acceptance of all others. It is the conviction that God's creation structures are given to the human race as a whole, so it might flourish as it practices freedom within form, life within limits. Thus,

> The classical heritage has long recognized that nothing will suffice except an onto-theological view [for all of life].... The church is likely to continue to claim that the deepest ontic structure, given in creation; the purposive presence of a loving Creator and Redeemer in history; and the gift of the graced human consciousness to grasp the relation between these in the midst of time are together, necessary for life.... [T]his implies a distinction between the onto-theological (levels of life)..., which humans cannot substantially alter, and the phenomenological, which can be more easily constructed and deconstructed at will.[24]

Clearly the church has no brief to force such a vision on others in the service of setting up some kind of theocracy. But neither should it be satisfied with the vision of the "naked public square" required by the rationalist separation of (so-called) facts from values. The church must continue to preach and, more importantly, model its ontic vision for life so that its winsomeness, under the power of the Holy Spirit, will be persuasive to many. It may use this world- and life-view in good conscience as a benchmark against which to evaluate social theories which compete for attention in the academic arena and the public square. With this framework in mind, we are now ready to consider feminism and the family in global

---

24. Ibid., 40–41.

perspective. I begin with some observations on the origins and mixed outcomes of Western feminism.

A Historical Framework:
Feminism as a Mixed Blessing

In Iain Pears's complex thriller about seventeenth-century Restoration Britain, *An Instance of the Fingerpost*, one of the characters, an Oxford student, laments that it is becoming more and more difficult to find a good homemade ale. "Now that the men of business make beer and are trying to stop the women selling the ale they brew, I believe the great days of this country are over."[25] His complaint captures a major shift that began in early modern Europe and culminated with the rise of feminism first in the West, then globally.

Up through the late medieval period in Europe the gendered division between "public" and "private" spheres had little meaning. Although there were some clearly gendered "responsibilities," women as well as men had what we would now call public roles and authority. They practiced trades and skilled crafts in the lower classes (selling homemade beer among other things), worked as managers of estates and political brokers among the aristocracy, and headed charitable and financial institutions as heads of religious orders. The rationale for these activities had nothing to do with the modern concept of individual rights, which did not emerge until the eighteenth century. Nor did it have anything to do with the claim that women were the same as or equal in authority to men, since males had ruling authority in the church and were the heads of household in all classes unless displaced by death.

The public authority of women was instead undergirded by accepted notions of family and religious duty. The welfare and honor of both one's birth family and conjugal family

25. Iain Pears, *An Instance of the Fingerpost* (New York: Penguin Putnam, 1998), 225.

depended on each member being as successful as possible economically. In addition, the honor and claims of the church required both men and women to practice charity and to speak out against heresy and corruption. When done by women, these activities were regarded as natural extensions of motherhood — the provision of material and spiritual goods first for the immediate family, then the wider community. Thus the idea that domestic and public life were separate spheres, with women "naturally" fitted for the former and men for the latter, was generally not part of the medieval worldview.[26]

It was in the early modern period that the idea of separate spheres for women and men began to emerge in the West, in the context of gradual political centralization and the development of a distinct business class. As capitalist production techniques began to eclipse the medieval guilds, the latter defended themselves by restricting membership, limiting the number of masters, and shortening the time a widow could operate a shop after her husband's death. Women's legal status as witnesses and property owners was progressively curtailed, and the increasing formalization of education for physicians and scientists gradually pushed women out of all the practical professions except for midwifery. In addition, the locus of classical and theological training moved from monasteries to universities for the purpose of training male clerics, thus cutting off women religious from what was to become the educational mainstream.[27] As for lower-class women, for reasons of sheer survival they had to keep working in what

---

26. See Merry E. Weisner, "The Early Modern Period: Religion, the Family, and Women's Public Roles," in *Religion, Feminism, and the Family*, ed. Anne Carr and Mary Stewart Van Leeuwen (Louisville: Westminster/John Knox Press, 1996), 149–65.

27. See for example David Noble, *A World without Women: The Christian Clerical Culture of Modern Science* (New York: Oxford University Press, 1992).

was coming to be seen as the "public" arena, but the activities available to them became more marginal in both status and remuneration.

At the same time, an ideal of intimate family life began to form among urban middle-class men who possessed a comfortable discretionary income. Many of their wives accepted this and created a domestic culture that revolved around the nuclear family and the presumption that women were in need of protection from the increasingly masculine worlds of commerce, politics, and learning. The medieval notion that women were morally weaker than men was reversed, and their supposed moral superiority and domestic piety were now seen as the means of keeping adult men from being debased by the competitive public realm in which they had to operate. A bifurcation of the cultural mandate by sex became more rigid: women were increasingly seen as called to "be fruitful and multiply," while men were to "subdue the earth."

The evolution of this doctrine of separate spheres — also known as "the cult of domesticity" and "the cult of true womanhood" — was slower in the New World. Having to clear and farm large tracts of land necessarily meant that economic, domestic, and child-rearing functions remained combined within family units. Colonial nuclear families in North America were thus "highly multifunctional and relatively self-sufficient, serving as a workshop and business, school, vocational institute, church, welfare institution and even house of correction, as well as the seat of all domestic activities."[28] In addition, families were embedded in larger religious and governmental structures to which they remained accountable, and thus did not function in isolation.

But with the rise of industrialization and urbanization in the nineteenth century, households lost their role as produc-

---

28. David Popenoe, *Life without Father* (New York: Free Press, 1996), 87.

tive enterprises with a clear economic partnership between the sexes and the generations. Instead they became — as they had become in bourgeois Europe — specialized havens from the world at large, focusing on consumption rather than production, presided over by increasingly isolated and economically dependent wives, and supported by increasingly absent male breadwinners. This extreme division of labor sometimes led to men's resentment of having to shoulder the entire family financial burden, and to women's increased vulnerability to abuse.

By the mid–nineteenth century, the doctrine of separate spheres was an accepted societal norm. It was practiced by the rising middle classes and increasingly aspired to by others, despite the limiting roles it imposed on both women and men and the impracticality of realizing these roles in the poorer classes. At the same time, in reflexive response to these limitations, the term *feminism* emerged in the context of eighteenth- and nineteenth-century liberal ideals, with the accompanying challenge to extend "the rights of man" (in terms of franchise, property, and education) to women, too. Middle-class Anglo-American feminists challenged the doctrine of separate spheres by mixing this modern rhetoric of natural human rights with the earlier religious language of "calling" and "sacred cause." Many, especially in America, were best described as biblical feminists, because they used mainly exegetical arguments for more egalitarian families and churches where women and men would share privileges and responsibilities. Most were also domestic feminists, opposing divorce, contraception, and abortion as practices that did more to encourage male irresponsibility than women's opportunity, and basing their claim to expanded public roles less on their similarities to men than on their differences, including their supposed moral superiority.[29]

---

29. Hence the famous slogan of one domestic feminist organization:

Domestic feminists for the most part shared the traditional Protestant view of marriage as a creation-based, covenantal institution — a whole more than the sum of its parts, and a sexual community in which the nurture of children by procreation (or adoption) is a central function. But modernity also began to offer a competing model of marriage, drawn from the liberal political tradition that serves as a second source of Western feminism. Suspecting that the Protestant model of marriage was linked to men's domination of women, liberal feminists proposed an alternative model rooted in the language of individual rights and choice. In this model, marriage is not a covenantal bond rooted in creation, but simply a contract between sovereign individuals whose purpose is to maximize personal fulfillment, sexual and otherwise. It assumes a universe in which social order and obligation proceed not from creation norms, but from individual choice. It holds that rights are attached only "to free-floating individuals disconnected from their social context."[30] According to the liberal model, the church may treat marriage as a covenant for its own members, but the state should regard it simply as a legal contract between separate individuals from which certain joint benefits (such as health care and tax deductions) follow as long as the contract holds.[31]

Thus in their zeal to correct one distortion (the stifling and abuse of women in marriage), liberal feminists unwittingly

---

"Votes for women and chastity for men." See for example Nancy Cott, *The Grounding of Modern Feminism* (New Haven: Yale University Press, 1987). See also the chapters in Carr and Van Leeuwen, *Religion, Feminism, and the Family,* by Catherine Brekus, "Restoring Divine Order to the World: Religion and the Family in the Antebellum Woman's Rights Movement" (166–82), and by Margaret L. Bendroth, "Religion, Feminism, and the American Family, 1865–1920" (183–96).

30. David Orgon Coolidge, "The Dilemma of Single-Sex Marriage," *Crisis* (July–August 1996): 17–20 (quotation from p. 18).

31. See John Witte, Jr., *From Sacrament to Contract: Marriage, Religion, and Law in the Western Tradition* (Louisville: Westminster/John Knox Press, 1997).

promoted an opposite one — namely, the gradual ungluing of social bonds that are needed for individual and social flourishing. For it is fair to say that, especially with the advent in the 1970s of no-fault divorce — which in effect permits *unilateral* divorce — the liberal model has eclipsed the covenantal model as the assumed framework for marriage in most Western democracies. Under its influence, the rate of divorce in the United States has risen tenfold during the twentieth century, with similar if less dramatic rises in other industrialized nations.[32] The rate of out-of-wedlock births has also risen steeply: in the United States it has gone from less than 8 percent overall in 1965 to nearly 30 percent in the late 1990s, and from 22 percent to almost 70 percent among African Americans.

Not only is the marriage bond capable of easy dissolution by either party, for any or no reason. By the late 1990s nonmarital births threatened to surpass divorce as the main cause of single parenthood in America. Because the divorce revolution began some thirty years ago in the industrialized world, social scientists now have a lot of data with which to evaluate these trends. Despite their differing political allegiances, most scholars agree that divorce and nonmarital parenthood — apart from accompanying effects of financial hardship — have enduring, negative consequences for both the children and adults involved. On average, both the children of divorce and those of never-married parents show more antisocial behavior toward peers and adults, more depression, and more learning problems than children from intact homes. They are one and a half to two times more likely to drop out of high school, to become teenage parents, and to be neither in school nor in the workforce as young adults. As older adults, they have less sense of psychological well-being, less marital

32. Andrew Cherlin, *Marriage, Divorce, and Remarriage*, 2d ed. (Cambridge: Harvard University Press, 1992).

satisfaction, heightened risk of divorce, and even a shorter life span.[33]

Another body of accumulating literature shows that divorce is not the panacea for adults in unhappy marriages that many assumed it would be thirty years ago. Second marriages (as well as those preceded by cohabitation) are at greater risk for breakup than first marriages entered traditionally. Until the second wave of Western feminism began to dismantle the doctrine of separate spheres in the 1960s, it is true that marriage was in many ways more advantageous for men than for women, both economically and psychologically.[34] But data collected since then show that, on the whole, marriage is associated with enhanced well-being for both wives and husbands, as compared to divorced, widowed, cohabiting, or never-married persons. On average, and controlling for age, class and education, married persons have better health, more wealth, and higher earnings. They also report more physical and emotional satisfaction with their sex lives than sexually active singles or cohabiting couples.[35]

None of the scholars involved in this research denies that

33. Judith S. Wallerstein and Sandra Blakeslee, *Second Chances: Men, Women. and Children a Decade after Divorce* (Boston: Houghton Mifflin, 1989); Eleanor E. MacCoby and Robert Monokin, *Dividing the Child: Social and Legal Dilemmas of Custody* (Cambridge: Harvard University Press, 1992); Sara McLanahan and Gary Sandefur, *Growing Up with a Single Parent: What Helps, What Hurts* (Cambridge: Harvard University Press, 1994); David Popenoe, Jean Bethke Elshtain, and David Blankenhorn, eds., *Promises to Keep: Decline and Renewal of Marriage in America* (Lanham, Md.: Rowman and Littlefield, 1996); Barbara Dafoe Whitehead, *The Divorce Culture* (New York: Knopf, 1997).

34. See for example Jessie Bernard, *The Future of Marriage* (New York: World Publishing, 1972).

35. Linda Waite, "Does Marriage Matter?" *Demography* 32 (November 1995): 483–507. See also her volume *The Case for Marriage* (Cambridge: Harvard University Press, 1999). See also David Popenoe and Barbara Dafoe Whitehead, *Should We Live Together? What Young Adults Need to Know about Cohabitation before Marriage* (New Brunswick, N.J.: National Marriage Project, 1999).

divorce may be a regrettable necessity in cases of chronic abuse, adultery, addiction, or financial irresponsibility. Most are also concerned to make divorce laws more just toward vulnerable spouses and children, and do not advocate a return to the days of fault-based divorce.[36] However, there has been a definite — and needed — return in Western social thought to a hermeneutics of trust regarding marriage as a positive social institution. But what do we find when we look outside the West, where the path toward both modernity and feminist awareness came later? This is the topic to which we now turn.

Modernity, Gender, and the Family in Non-Western Societies

The less-industrialized nations are precariously poised between pre-modern local, modern, and postmodern global forces. In Africa, India, and other parts of the developing world, the forces of modernity have changed gender and family relations in ways that mirror, with a predictable time lag, their effects in the West. It is, of course, a mistake to romanticize traditional gender relations in the traditional societies, which could be distorted by patriarchal heavy-handedness as much as they were in the pre-modern Western world. Against these patriarchal traditions, both feminist and human rights groups of various kinds have begun to develop in nearly every country, often using liberal, Marxist, or Christian-derived ideas to challenge local practices — developments that themselves are a manifestation of globalization. Still, we need to recognize that under the legacy of colonialism and modernity, many societies have gone from systems in which the cultural

---

36. See for example Amy E. Black, *For the Sake of the Children: Reconstructing American Divorce Policy,* Crossroads Monograph Series in Faith and Public Policy 1, no. 2 (Wynnewood, Pa.: Evangelicals for Social Action, 1995).

mandate was cooperatively carried out by women and men to systems in which the negative effects of the doctrine of separate spheres have played out in unanticipated ways.[37]

In many parts of the world under precolonial systems of gender complementarity, women usually had independent access to economic resources such as land, and were expected — like the women in pre-modern Europe — to provide certain goods and services to the immediate and extended family. But political scientist Jane Jaquette notes that

> as new technology is introduced, such as cash cropping, or as migration moves men out of subsistence production, women find their work devalued. This undermines the material foundation for reciprocal gender relations and undercuts the shared authority mandated by traditional norms. The result is not simply an increase in male control within the family... but an increase in male rates of desertion, as women must ask men to provide resources that they were formerly able to provide themselves.... Under colonialism and capitalism, men's preferential access to resources, including foreign assistance, left women worse off — not *better* off, as the conventional view has maintained.[38]

The "conventional view" to which Jaquette refers is the "economic-growth" development paradigm that held sway prior to about 1970. This paradigm obscured gender and family relations in two ways. First, economic growth was taken as the single, adequate index of development, as measured by rising GNPs and increasing industrialization. As used by

---

37. See for example Gordon L. Anderson, ed., *The Family in Global Transition* (Minneapolis: PWPA Books, 1997).

38. Jane S. Jaquette, "The Family as a Development Issue," in *Women at the Center: Development Issues and Practices for the 1990s,* ed. Gay Young, Vidyamali Samarasinghe, and Ken Kusterer (West Hartford, Conn.: Kumarian Press, 1995), 45–62 (quotation from 46–47, her emphasis).

most countries, the United Nations System of National Accounts (SNA) placed no economic value on unpaid domestic work, such as child care, cooking, and the gathering of fuel and water. Indeed, in some developing countries the SNA did not even include food produced by women for family consumption.

Second, the economic-growth paradigm paid almost no attention to gender inequities either in families or in public life. Western utility economists presumed the universality of male heads of households, and assumed that these males, given title to land and a chance to grow cash crops, would be altruistic agents of their entire family's welfare.[39] But in fact men frequently spent the resulting cash on consumer items for themselves rather than on basic necessities for their families. Meanwhile, women, deprived of enough land on which to raise food crops, often could not feed their families adequately. Thus women lost access to traditional modes of subsistence without being integrated into the cash economy, leaving them worse off — both materially and in terms of domestic bargaining power — than before the development schemes began. Far from lifting all boats in a gender- and generation-neutral fashion, the rising tide of development was leaving many women and children in poverty.[40]

Urbanization has brought additional stresses to family life in the two-thirds world. Couples have fewer children due to the economic nonutility of large families in nonagricultural settings. The language of familism and collectivism remains, but individuals take less and less responsibility for the extended kin circle that served as a social safety net in traditional

39. For example, Gary Becker, *A Treatise on the Family* (Cambridge: Harvard University Press, 1970).

40. *Human Development Report of the United Nations Development Program* (New York: Oxford University Press, 1995); Ester Boserup, *Women's Role in Economic Development* (London: George Allen and Unwin, 1970).

subsistence economies. Some rural areas, especially in Africa, have been virtually emptied of adult men, who have been migrating to cities in hope of paid work. They cannot or will not send meager proceeds home to family members already less able to farm effectively in their absence.

All of this gives more flexibility to men than to women in choosing domestic relationships, with the result that cohabitation — usually heterosexual, but in urban areas increasingly homosexual, too — competes with formal marriage, and women and children face higher rates of desertion.[41] Needless to say, the growing transience of sexual relationships has also contributed to the AIDS epidemic, particularly in sub-Saharan Africa. There is much more to be said about trends in gender and family relations in non-Western societies, but I will now attempt to integrate such observations with more global theories of family and economic development as nuanced by feminist perspectives.

Competing Models of Gender and Family Relations for the Twenty-first Century

So far we have seen that, despite differences in details and timing, the global reach of modernity has posed similar challenges to gender and family relations in both more- and less-industrialized nations. These include the breakdown of economic cooperation between sexes and generations, and the increasing institutionalization of marriage as seen in rising rates of divorce, temporary cohabitation, out-of-wedlock childbearing, male migration, and family desertion, and the growing acceptance of homosexuality as an alternative lifestyle. How nations respond to these associations will be strongly influenced by prevailing worldviews. In global per-

---

41. Anderson, *Family in Global Transition.*

spective, three separate visions of gender and family relations now compete for primacy.[42]

Restoring a Hierarchy of Separate Gendered Spheres

At one extreme are the forces of patriarchal reaction, which aim to reinstate varying degrees of male headship and a highly gendered public-private dichotomy. In the late 1990s, this option has been most dramatically exemplified in the parts of Afghanistan under control of the Muslim Taliban forces, whose view of male headship extends across all spheres of life. Under its sway, women are caught in an assortment of no-win dilemmas. They are banned from working in the public arena, even if they are war widows who are the sole support of their children. They cannot be treated by male doctors, yet only a few women doctors trained prior to the Taliban takeover have been allowed to continue practicing. Women can no longer attend school or university, and must be completely veiled and accompanied by a male relative when walking in public or risk suffering physical violence.

Although not recognized by the United Nations, the Taliban has been affirmed by at least three other Muslim states as the ruling power in Afghanistan. But its attempted enforcement of "gender apartheid" accords with neither Afghan nor Islamic traditions under both of which women could until recently attend school, earn and control their own money, and participate freely in public life. Although the Taliban rhetoric is that women will be better off under its system — protected by male relatives and rulers from the cultural and moral anarchy of modernism — the reality is an extreme distortion of the cultural mandate and an attempt to turn the tragedy of fallen gender relations, as summarized in Genesis 3:16 ("Your

---

42. This typology overlaps with a helpful analysis by Neil Gilbert in "Working Families: Hearth to Market," in *All Our Families: New Policies for a New Century,* ed. Mary Ann Mason, Arlene Skolnick, and Stephen D. Sugarman (New York: Oxford University Press, 1998), 195–216.

desire shall be for your husband, and he shall rule over you"), into an ethically normative pattern.

Moreover, we should note the explosion of evangelical, pentecostal, and fundamentalist Christian churches in many parts of the world, and that they are influenced by trends in similar churches in Western nations, and particularly the United States. In these churches, forms of "soft patriarchy" have emerged despite (or perhaps in reaction to) three decades of feminist-led gains for women. Thus in 1989 the conservative evangelical *Danvers Statement* declared that "Adam's headship in marriage was established by God before the fall, and was not a result of sin. . . . In the church, redemption in Christ gives men and women an equal share in the blessings of salvation; nevertheless, some governing and teaching roles within the church are restricted to men."[43] Likewise, almost a decade later American Southern Baptists amended their quasi-confessional Faith and Message Statement in 1998 to require wives to "submit graciously to the servant leadership of their husbands, even as the church willingly submits to the leadership of Christ." And the well-known parachurch men's movement known as Promise Keepers, while claiming to have no official position on male headship, allows both its chief spokesman, Bill McCartney, and its other writers and speakers to promote a benign form of husbandly leadership. At the same time, the organization has yet to devote any portion of its considerable annual budget to systematically evaluating how Promise Keepers affects the lives of women whose husbands are involved.[44]

---

43. *The Danvers Statement* (Wheaton, Ill.: Council on Biblical Manhood and Womanhood, 1989). However, the council stopped short of claiming these statements as essential Christian confessions, but instead called them "affirmations" and conceded "the genuine evangelical standing of many who do not agree with all of our convictions."

44. See Mary Stewart Van Leeuwen, "Servanthood or Soft Patriarchy? A Christian Feminist Looks at the Promise Keepers Movement," *Journal of Men's Studies* 5 (February 1997): 233–61, and "The Promise Keepers

The secular analogue of attempts to make fallen gender relations creationally normative is a simplistic but dis-
turbingly popular version of evolutionary psychology. While
most forms of Christian theology recognize that evolution
offers the best scientific account of much biological development, crude forms of evolutionary psychology theorize a
virtual one-to-one correspondence between certain gendered,
supposedly survival-relevant behaviors and certain genetic
patterns laid down in humans' primitive "environment of evolutionary adaptation." These behavior patterns include male
aggression which, rather than being seen as a social problem
in need of repair, is translated by popularizers of crude evolutionary psychology into "the inevitability of patriarchy."[45]
Also defended is a double standard of sexual behavior according to which men are naturally promiscuous and needful of a
succession of young and beautiful lovers, while women will
contentedly mate with older, unattractive — and even philan-
dering — men as long as these men have status and wealth to
bestow on their legitimate wives and children.[46]

More sophisticated evolutionary psychologists rightly
point out that humans' most important genetic legacy is a flexible cerebral cortex which allows us to be the culture-creating,
problem-solving, environmentally adaptive creatures we have
always been. "The variation is tremendous," observes evolutionary theorist Barbara Smuts, "and it is rooted in biology.

---

and Proof-Text Poker," *Sojourners* 27 (January–February 1998): 16–21. It
should be noted that the same Bill McCartney who endorses male headship in marriage has become a strong supporter of women in ordained
ministries.

45. For example, Steven Goldberg, *The Inevitability of Patriarchy* (New
York: William Morrow, 1974).

46. See for example David Buss, *The Evolution of Desire* (New York:
Basic Books, 1994); Robert Wright, *The Moral Animal* (New York: Vin-
tage, 1994); and John Marshall Townsend, *What Women Want, What Men
Want* (New York: Oxford University Press, 1998).

Flexibility is itself the adaptation."[47] This does not mean that human behavior is infinitely malleable; some of it (e.g., fluent language acquisition) is bounded by critical periods in development. Nor does it mean that genes and hormones count for nothing. What it does mean is that genetic and hormonal legacies flexibly interact with cognitive and social processes, with resulting cultural, gender, and generational diversity in the way our lives are lived.

If there are limits to that diversity, they are not always the limits crude evolutionary psychology would predict. For example, much has been made of psychologist David Buss's survey of mate preferences in some three dozen countries at various stages of development. Its findings are said to show the universality (and hence the putative "naturalness") of men's greater attraction to young and beautiful females, and women's to ambitious and financially successful males. But in fact, in all cultures sampled by Buss, this difference only appears well down on the list of traits both sexes rate as important. When asked what qualities they value *most* in potential mates, men and women alike rate love, dependability, emotional stability, and a pleasing personality as the most important four.[48] So distorted gender relations (often masquerading as "natural") are indeed part of our human legacy. But in this international study they are eclipsed by just those qualities — or at least ideals — called for in men and women alike by the cultural mandate: creative cultural adaptation in the context of mutual care and faithful monogamy.

---

47. As quoted in Natalie Angier, *Women: An Intimate Geography* (New York: Houghton Mifflin, 1999), 346–47. See also Smuts's "Male Aggression against Women: An Evolutionary Perspective," *Human Nature* 3 (1992): 1–44, and "The Evolutionary Origins of Patriarchy," *Human Nature* 6 (1995): 1–32.

48. David Buss, "Sex Differences in Human Mate Preferences," *Behavioral and Brain Sciences* 12 (1989): 1–49. See also Angier, *Women: An Intimate Geography*, especially chap. 18.

The Model of Functional Equality between the Sexes

Of course feminist social theorists of both sexes oppose any return to gender hierarchy, whether politically imposed or pseudoscientifically defended. A quite opposite vision, the "functional-equality model," draws on the tradition of liberal political theory and has been most fully implemented in the Scandinavian countries.[49] This model is organized around four doctrines or tenets.

First is the negation of gender roles, which are seen as accidents of socialization and whose elimination is regarded as essential for achieving gender and family justice. Second is the devaluation of domestic activities, which are regarded as tedious necessities to be evenly divided between spouses or absorbed into an infrastructure of services done by paid third parties. Third is a celebration of waged labor, which is assumed to bestow "autonomy and self-respect as it liberates women from the repressive confinement of child care and household chores. The assumption is that women can achieve self-determination in the labor market but not in the family."[50]

Finally, in keeping with other strains of liberal thought, the functional-equality model asserts that the individual rather than the couple or family should be the focus of welfare and development policy. Thus in 1991 the Group of Experts on Women and Structural Change of the Organization for Economic Cooperation and Development recommended that for both taxation and public-pension purposes, the individual should be the unit of assessment, regardless of marital status. Social welfare theorist Neil Gilbert summarizes the functional-equality model as characterized by

---

49. Neil Gilbert, *Welfare Justice* (New Haven: Yale University Press, 1995).

50. Gilbert, "Working Families: Hearth to Market," 195.

a family in which both spouses work, maintain separate accounts, pay separate taxes, and contribute more or less equivalent sums to their financial support. Household tasks and caring functions... are divided equally between husbands and wives, with each contributing the same amount of time... so that they do not fall back into the traditional division of labor.... [T]he domestic tasks and caring functions to which they cannot attend are performed through arrangements with state-subsidized or private service providers, for which any remaining charges are born equally by each parent. Extending into the realm of more intimate behavior, half the time she uses a diaphragm; the other half he uses a condom.[51]

This model of gender relations is, of course, light years away from both the Taliban and the double standard of crude evolutionary psychology. But we should note that it is hardly a mark of liberation for women — or men either — to be shunted from one set of restrictive options to an opposite but equally confining set. Gilbert rightly points out that the functional-equality model, for all its use of the language of individual freedom, may become at least as restrictive as the older patriarchal model in its pressure to make every family operate in the same way.

Thus, for example, in Sweden working couples can avail themselves of subsidized day care to a possible total of almost $12,000 per year, but do not have the choice of taking this subsidy as a cash grant to enable them to care for their children at home. Efforts to institute a child-care allowance for stay-at-home Swedish parents have been blocked by members of the Social Democrat party, who claim that this practice would inevitably cause a reversion to the practice of separate spheres for men and women. But the existing policy, however

---

51. Ibid., 196.

well-intentioned, arguably treats women as "male clones," and points to the need for a third way — one which takes account of the generically human character of the cultural mandate while acknowledging the differing life cycle challenges of men and women. In Betty Friedan's famous phrase, "There has to be a concept of equality that takes into account the fact that women are the ones who have the babies."[52]

The Social-Partnership Model

The third, or social-partnership model, challenges the individualism and the one-size-fits-all rigidity of the functional-equality approach while taking care to ensure that any marital division of labor does not render one spouse more vulnerable than the other. Thus, instead of tax-subsidized day care available on a take-it-or-leave-it basis, the social-partnership model calls for direct cash subsidies or refundable tax credits that can be used either to replace the outside wages of a stay-at-home parent, or to pay for child care supplied by others. (So far Finland is the only Western welfare state that allows such a choice.) With regard to retirement income, the model calls for both public and private pension accounts to be "credit-shared" between spouses. That is, contributions — whatever their source and amount — would go into one account over which husband and wife have joint title. Thus far only Canada and Germany have national legislation requiring spousal credit-sharing of public pensions, and only the latter extends this requirement to private pensions too.[53]

---

52. Betty Friedan, quoted in John Leo, "Are Women Male Clones?" *Time*, August 18, 1986, 63.

53. Credit-sharing of pensions may make little functional difference in marriages that last a lifetime, but constitutes an important safety net in cases of divorce where one spouse has had less independent earning capacity as a result of having been out of the labor force doing family work. These spouses — usually women — risk being impoverished after divorce if their access to the other partner's pension assets is not protected. Under the

The social-partnership model is neutral as to how couples divide waged work and domestic responsibilities. But its supporters acknowledge that time taken out of the waged labor force by either spouse (though more commonly the wife) will reduce any pension account that depends on accumulated time in the workforce. Thus, in addition to credit-shared pensions, advocates of this model call for homemakers' pension credits covering the years spent in nonwaged domestic activity. Among the industrialized nations, Austria, Britain, France, and Hungary have such policies, varying in the amount of public pension credited and the eligibility of persons by sex.

Of course, policies such as these take for granted that pension funds exist in the first place, and that couples have choice as to which of them will be in the waged workforce at various times in the family cycle. But in many less-industrialized nations the formal economy is so small that the pension and welfare subsidies presumed by both the functional-equality and social-partnership models are available only to a privileged few. Moreover, poverty is so widespread in some places that the idea of sequestering women completely from public waged work, as in the Taliban model, is simply laughable. With these differences in mind, researchers at the United Nations Development Program have put forth a normative vision of gender and family relations which can be applied to nations at *various* stages of modernization, and which draws both on the functional-equality and social-partnership models.

The Human-Capabilities Approach to Development

This model is based largely on theoretical work done by Martha Nussbaum of the University of Chicago and Indian-born Amartya Sen of Harvard, who won the 1999 Nobel

social-partnership model, spouses have legal title to an equal share of their combined pension credits both while married and in the event of a divorce.

Prize for his related work in welfare economics. The model rejects the older focus on GNP per capita as an adequate measure of development because of the way it masks inequalities in the actual production and distribution of wealth by class, gender, and ethnicity. But it also rejects the assumption that justice can be achieved by giving everyone exactly the same resources. For "if people are not given positive freedom to function and thus to make adequate use...of all those 'goods,' the mere fact of having them will not necessarily make their lives better."[54]

As an alternative, Nussbaum and Sen have advanced a "human-capabilities" approach to development.[55] Its foundation is a list of *basic limits and abilities* common to all human beings, and a higher-order list of *functional human capabilities.* Human limits, in this model, include embodiment, mortality, sexual desire, the need for food and shelter, and an extended period of childhood dependency. Human abilities include mobility, perception, imagination, practical and abstract reason, sociability, and play. Higher-order functional capabilities are stated generically enough to avoid charges of ethnocentrism, and to allow for some variation in the way each might play out in different settings. Hence they include "being able to live to the end of a human life of normal length," and "being able to use the senses, to imagine, think, and reason in a way informed and cultivated by an adequate education." They also include "being able to have attach-

---

54. Margarita M. Valdes, "Inequality in Capabilities between Men and Women in Mexico," in *Women, Culture, and Development,* ed. Martha Nussbaum and Jonathan Glover (Oxford: Clarendon Press, 1995), 426–32 (quotation from p. 426). Thus, for example, equal access to education for girls and boys is a necessary but not sufficient condition of just development if the same education increases young men's economic and vocational choices while being treated merely as a refining process for women who otherwise remain economically dependent on male relatives.

55. Martha Nussbaum and Amartya K. Sen, eds., *The Quality of Life* (Oxford: Clarendon Press, 1993)

ments to things and persons outside oneself," "being able to laugh, play, and enjoy recreational activities," and "being able to form a conception of the good and engage in critical reflection about the planning of one's life."[56]

Although there is no mention of religion, even as a needed "higher-order functional human capability," Nussbaum and Sen's argument has echoes of the Catholic concept of subsidiarity, initiated by Pope Leo XIII. As pointed out earlier, subsidiarity justifies the relative autonomy of family, commerce, science, and the arts on the grounds that each has creationally rooted "capabilities" to carry out its tasks, with interference and/or aid from government and religious authorities only when internally or externally caused distortions or imbalances arise. These echoes are not coincidental, for both Nussbaum and Leo XIII are appealing to Aristotelian notions "of basic needs, of fulfilling goods, and well-ordered societies, and of human happiness,"[57] filtered further in Leo's case through the theology of Thomas Aquinas. But as we will see later, Nussbaum's rendering of human capabilities is weakened by an individualist bias that has also caused some other feminists to assume that family integrity and justice for women are mutually incompatible. Before dealing with this weakness, however, we need to appreciate the useful ways in which Nussbaum and Sen's approach has been applied to gender relations and gender justice on a global scale.

The development question that needs to be asked of *all* nations, according to this approach, is: Where are men, women, and children with respect to having not just their lower-order needs, but their higher-order capabilities, met? In Nussbaum's words, "Have they been put in a position of

---

56. See Martha Nussbaum, "Human Capabilities," in Nussbaum and Glover, *Women, Culture, and Development*, 62–104.

57. Lisa Sowle Cahill, *Sex, Gender, and Christian Ethics* (Cambridge: Cambridge University Press, 1996), 36.

mere human subsistence, or have they been enabled to live well?...and what costs are we willing to pay to get all citizens above the threshold, as opposed to leaving some below and allowing the rest a considerably above-threshold life quality?"[58] In an attempt to answer these questions on a global scale in the 1990s, the United Nations Development Program (UNDP) used the human-capabilities model to develop three indices of human well-being that allow for cross-national and cross-gender comparisons. These are the Human Development Index (HDI), the Gender-Related Development Index (GDI), and the Gender Empowerment Measure (GEM).

The Human Development Index is a tripartite measure of human flourishing which uses available cross-national statistics on *life expectancy, educational attainment,* and *real income.* The resulting score, which can vary between .000 and 1.00, shows the distance a given country is from predefined standards for these three development ideals, which are meant to represent the first level of capabilities identified by Nussbaum and Sen.[59] Using the HDI as a common metric allows information to emerge that was obscured by older, purely monetary measures of development. Most notably, the rank-order of nations' real GDP per capita is *not* a reliable predictor of its HDI. Reasonable — and rising — HDI indices have been attained by countries with modest levels of income. Conversely, steep GDP growth does not automatically translate into "people benefits" as measured by the HDI. The 1991 UNDP report concluded that "it is often the absence of polit-

---

58. Nussbaum, "Human Capabilities," 87.
59. More specifically, the three components measure, for any given country or subgroup within it, (*a*) life expectancy at birth; (*b*) educational attainment, with this measure divided between rate of adult literacy and combined primary, secondary, and tertiary school enrollment; and (*c*) real income in "purchasing power parity dollars" (PPP), adjusted for the diminishing utility of income levels higher than $5000 in 1992 dollars. See *UNDP Human Development Reports, 1990, 1994,* and *1995* for accounts of the ongoing refinement of these measures.

ical will, and not always the lack of financial resources, that is responsible for human neglect."[60] And it seems intuitively obvious that when a nation's GDP is used more for guns than for butter — or more to shore up a kleptocracy than to improve literacy — it will be at best a crude measure of human flourishing.

The weakness of the HDI is that it is not broken down by gender. As a result, the UNDP went on to develop two specifically gender-based measures, the GDI and the GEM. A given country's Gender-Related Development Index is basically its HDI discounted for gender inequality, as it compares women's with men's average life expectancy, education, and income. Like the HDI, it can range between .000 and 1.00, with the latter figure representing perfect gender equality on the three original measures.

By 1995, comparative GDI measures were able to cover 130 nations at varying stages of modernization, and to reveal patterns not shown either by the older GDP measures or the newer HDI measures. These patterns showed that even at the end of the twentieth century, "no society treats its women as well as its men."[61] And as with the HDI, there are surprises: in 1995 tiny Barbados, in eleventh place, ranked above Great Britain in thirteenth, and comparatively small and poor sub-Saharan nations such as Botswana, Zimbabwe, and Swaziland ranked above larger nations such as Egypt and India. Gender equality can be pursued — and has been — at all levels of national income. What it requires is a firm political commitment, not enormous monetary wealth.

Both the HDI and the GDI measure basic level human ca-

---

60. As quoted in the *UNDP Human Development Report 1995*, 29.

61. *Human Development Report 1995*, 75. The 1995 average GDI for a sample of 130 nations was .60, with only 32 countries' GDI value above .80.

pabilities. But according to Nussbaum and Sen's model, these capabilities mean little if they do not translate into influential participation in the public spheres of society. Consequently, in 1995 the UNDP began using a third device, the Gender Empowerment Measure (GEM), to assess women's potential and actual participation in the public realm. This is again a composite index, which includes (*a*) women's per-capita income; (*b*) the proportion of those holding professional/managerial or administrative/technical jobs who are women; and (*c*) the proportion of those holding seats in the national parliament who are women.

By comparing countries' ranking on the GDI and the GEM, one can see which nations have not just strengthened women's basic capabilities through access to education, health, and basic income, but which nations have opened up opportunities for women to advance in the public spheres of business, industry, education, and politics. Almost no country's GEM is as high as its GDI, showing that, globally, women's empowerment in the public sphere lags behind their access to basic capabilities. Among the industrial nations, the Scandinavian countries have the smallest GDI/GEM gap — as one might expect, given their general commitment to the functional-equality model of gender and family relations. Others — such as France, Japan, and Greece — have wide disparities between GDI and GEM measures.[62] And although some developing countries — particularly in the Arab world and the Far East — have very low GEMs, others outrank some Western democracies. For example, Costa Rica and Cuba had higher 1995 GEM values than Japan or France.[63]

---

62. Greece, for example, had a 1995 GDI of .825, but a GEM of only .343.

63. *Human Development Report 1995*, 82–86. For those who might be curious, the same report ranked the United States second from the top in its HDI, fifth from the top in its GDI, and eighth from the top in its GEM.

Recovering the Idea of Family as a Creational Sphere

The UNDP's application of the human-capabilities model presumes a normative vision for human life that rejects both reactionary patriarchalism and complete cultural relativism. The measures incorporated into the HDI, the GDI, and the GEM presume certain universal standards for human flourishing and gender justice, broadly enough defined to allow for variation in the way these are worked out cross-culturally. The resulting data permit useful cross-national, cross-regional, and cross-time comparisons, including progress toward gender equity in what Nussbaum and Sen call basic and higher-level capabilities.

But the human-capabilities approach should be assessed as much by what it does not say as by what it does say. More specifically, the model gives implicit preference to the functional-equality model of family and gender relations, in at least two ways. First, in choosing to focus on women's progress in the *public* sphere, the GEM ignores the possibility that women might be able to attain equity in a *home-based* setting, if that is where they choose to work. More important, in choosing to focus on cross-gender inequality, important as this is, both the GDI and the GEM render family units invisible.

More specifically, it is significant that Nussbaum includes sexual *desire* as an irreducibly human experience but not sexual *dimorphism,* although surely one of the most inescapable features of humans (as of all mammals) is that they reproduce sexually by assortative mating of male and female chromosomes. Despite her admirable determination to assert universal norms of gender justice, Nussbaum seems quite prepared to ignore sexual complementarity and parental attachment as limiting features of family life, even though she acknowledges the lengthy period required for human development to adulthood. As ethicist Lisa Sowle Cahill has noted, Nussbaum deals with kinship "only indirectly, and in ways

which tend to minimize its social content, and to present it
rather in terms of bodily realities (especially of individual
bodies) and of freely chosen interpersonal relationships."[64]
This liberal bias also leads Nussbaum to exclude religion as
a universal human reality, even as she allows for religious
freedom. Cahill rightly notes that neither of these omissions
serves women well, since kinship and religion are both universal orders of human functioning and potent sources of both
oppression and empowerment for women, and so must be
dealt with accordingly.

Happily, some agencies, notably the U.S. Agency for International Development (USAID) have been more favorable
to the idea of using intact families as the unit of analysis
for development theory and practice.[65] This has been resisted by some feminists on the grounds that it would once
again submerge women's specific needs under the banner
of family welfare and would again render women's family
work invisible and uncompensated. But Jane Jaquette argues
that a social-partnership approach is preferable to the individualism of the functional-equality model, because despite
their struggle for gender justice within families, most women
understandably resist being told that their commitment to
husbands and children is simply the result of pre-feminist false
consciousness. Jaquette also believes that a family-centered
approach can lead to successful development projects and can
preserve gender and generational equity *provided* that intra-
family practices concerning income and power are accounted
for alongside the goals of economic development and family
preservation.

What is needed is an analysis of family dynamics which
shows when members are in fact maximizing the collective

---

64. Cahill, *Sex, Gender, and Christian Ethics,* 59.
65. U.S. Agency for International Development, "The Family and Development Initiative" (Washington, D.C.: USAID, 1990).

good, and when some members are being rendered systematically vulnerable. We have already noted that in developing countries men's control over family labor and earnings is often used to enhance their own comfort and prestige at the expense of other family members. Women, by contrast, devote proportionately more time — as well as any income they generate — to collective family needs rather than to their own individual use.[66] Women, in general, "internalize family welfare rather than personal welfare...in a way that men do not."[67] In addition, women are often held culturally responsible for the success of the marriage and children, and also have fewer opportunities to enter and succeed in the public arena of waged work.

Hence women are less able than men simply to walk away from a family situation that becomes distorted and unequally burdensome. What Amartya Sen has called the "breakdown position" — the point where a spouse can decide to leave the marriage — is "strongly asymmetrical in favor of men, both culturally and economically."[68] Any development scheme is likely to founder if it ignores this reality or does nothing to counter it by increasing women's resources, whether in training, access to credit, or access to needed tools, land, and other materials.

It might be thought that giving women access to such resources actually weakens family ties by equalizing women's ability to abandon households and to function as purely self-interested individuals. But Jaquette and others argue just the opposite: it is the *failure* to ensure women's access to such

---

66. Lawrence Haddad, John Hoddinott, and Harold Alderman, eds., *Intrahousehold Resource Allocation in Developing Countries: Models, Methods, and Policies* (Baltimore: Johns Hopkins University Press, 1997).

67. Jaquette, "Family as a Development Issue," 53.

68. Ibid., 53. See also Amartya Sen, "Gender and Cooperative Conflicts," in *Persistent Inequalities: Women and World Development*, ed. Irene Tinker (New York: Oxford University Press, 1990).

resources that contributes to family disintegration. As Sally Bould observes,

> The western ideology of the male head as the primary provider not only denies the actual or potential contribution of women, but also inhibits the development of new norms of reciprocal economic obligations appropriate to new conditions. Men may become contemptuous of women's work and deny its importance. . . . Problems arise [leading men to flee their family responsibilities] when economic obligations for the family fall entirely on the man, [especially] in a situation where low wages and unemployment prevent their fulfillment.[69]

The solution to these distortions is not always and everywhere to promote women's waged work, as in the functional-equality model. But a just family policy will always emphasize reciprocal obligations between men and women. These cannot obtain if women simultaneously lose their access to traditional resources and are denied access to new resources so that their productivity can match that of men in degree, if not in kind.

In addition, just family relations require perceptual changes on the part of all family members as to what women really do contribute. Thus the 1995 UNDP report encourages nations to estimate the monetary value of unpaid household labor "not because this is the only way to value these activities, [but] to make economic valuations more accurate and comprehensive [and to ensure that] the fruits of society's total labor are more equitably shared."[70] Respect for women's con-

---

69. Sally Bould, "Development in the Family: Third World Women and Inequality," in *Women and Work in the Third World: The Impact of Industrialization and Global Economic Interdependence,* ed. Nagat M. El-Sanabary (Berkeley, Calif.: Center for the Study, Education, and Advancement of Women, 1983), 29.

70. *UNDP Human Development Report 1995,* 98.

tributions and entitlements is also raised when women are involved in other spheres of civil society, such as service clubs, mutual aid societies, arts groups, and religious organizations. Indeed, rather than underwriting culturally ephemeral notions of male headship and female passivity, churches in both developed and developing countries should be advancing a model of cooperative spousal contribution more in keeping with the spirit of the cultural mandate.

Theological Themes Once More

Our survey of feminism and the family in global perspective leads us back to the three theological themes with which we began. The sexual and affectional drives and the practices of marriage and family are among the "powers," "spheres," or "orders" built into creation, and within them humans are called to exercise God's cultural mandate in the form of responsible dominion, just relationships, and caring generativity. The formation of families by faithful spouses thus has great potential to be a positive activity under God's blessing. So we should not be surprised that women (not to mention men) in both developed and developing countries tend to reject any ideology which practices an undiluted hermeneutic of suspicion toward marriage and family.

At the same time, we have seen that the feminist hermeneutic of suspicion is often justified. Whenever there is an extreme dichotomization of the cultural mandate by gender, the result is usually an increase in male irresponsibility or heavy-handedness, and a corresponding increase in the vulnerability of women and children. Thus, from a Reformed Christian perspective, nuanced by insights from others, the most promising vision of gender and family relations is a version of the partnership model to which is added a strong ethic of lifelong monogamy. In industrialized countries, the partnership model allows spouses flexibility in the division of waged and unwaged labor, while ensuring that the fruit of their joint labor is equitably shared and that economic compensation of some sort accrues to spouses who take time from the waged workplace to specialize in domesticity. In less-industrialized countries dependent on external development aid, the partnership model can work equally well, provided that both visible and invisible productivity of family members is accounted for, and that the economic expectations of both men and women are backed by development resources that allow both to have a true stake in the production and enjoyment of family wealth.

In terms of the biblical drama, because all humans live eschatologically in the era of "the already but the not yet," we have no warrant to claim that a return to Eden is possible in gender and family relations or in any other sphere of human activity. But because God's creation orders persist and Christ's redemptive work has broken the hold of powers which distort them, we can be confident that substantial healing is possible if God's people work in the power of the Spirit and use the gifts God has bestowed to help all humans live out the cultural mandate.

The bottom line is thus neither a hermeneutics of trust nor suspicion toward marriage and family, but a hermeneutics of hope. When gender and family relations are bad, we are called to bend them back toward their creational shape, knowing — as we have seen throughout this chapter — that this calls for historical and cross-cultural discernment at the public-policy level. But under a hermeneutics of hope this effort, while never-ending, is entirely worthwhile, because the God of creation has not left us without guidance, and the Christ of redemption has not left us without power. And both have promised that when marriages and families are good, they're very, *very* good.

– Chapter 6 –

PUBLIC THEOLOGY, HOPE, AND THE MASS MEDIA

CAN THE MUSES STILL INSPIRE?

David Tracy

Introduction

Theology has relationships with several extratheological disciplines, especially philosophy, history, and literary theory.[1] Max Stackhouse is surely correct, however, to insist that theology also pay attention to the social sciences and the overwhelming issue of globalization. Hence my assigned topic on the mass media. I make no claim to expertise in the vast social-scientific literature on the mass media. However, like many theologians I have found it necessary to appeal, at times, to various social sciences for clarification, development, correction, or support of my own more properly theological concerns. In the three sections of this paper, therefore, I give examples in which a particular social-scientific perspective is helpful for theological concerns:[2] first, on the crucial notion of "reason" or "rationality" as related to the social-scientific

1. On the issues for the public character of fundamental theology, see the indispensable work of René Latourelle and Rino Fischiella, *The Dictionary of Fundamental Theology* (New York: Crossroad, 1994); see also Gerald O'Collins, *Fundamental Theology* (New York: Paulist, 1981).
    2. For an important and erudite if, in my judgment, exaggerated Christian theological critique of the social sciences and their use by theologians, see John Milbank, *Theology and Social Theory: Beyond Secular Reason*

debate in Jürgen Habermas on "modernity"; second, on the
positive side of contemporary mass media, the retrieval of
an understanding of religion as manifestation and participation by both empirical social-scientific work as well as by
social-scientific debate on postmodernity; and third, on the
profound dangers we now face as theologians from the leveling of all traditions (this is the negative side of the Information
Revolution) and the need for genuinely theological images,
inevitably eschatological, of hope.

Moreover, I have deliberately chosen different kinds of
social science and social theory to suggest an equally important methodological point: theologians can and should learn
from both highly empirical forms of social science as well
as from more critical and hermeneutical social theories (like
the very different theories of Jürgen Habermas, Anthony Giddens, David Lyon, Mark Poster, James Buchanan, or Gianni
Vattimo). In sum, the use of examples from different social-
scientific thinkers shows how a theologian can and should
maintain a theological center of gravity while remaining open
to learning from any social-scientific source or method available for theological conversation (i.e., any method beyond
the purely positivistic). Kenneth Burke's wise pluralistic rule
applies: "Use all that can be used."

Example One: Rationality and Modernity
and the Import of Jürgen Habermas for Theology

There is no lack of critical theory in many forms of theology
but there is often a lack of critical *social* theory.[3] To put the
problem in more categorical terms, without a critical *social*

(Oxford: Blackwell, 1990). Space does not permit a discussion of this work
which I discuss in my forthcoming book *On Naming and Thinking God*.

3. This section is an abbreviated version of a much larger analysis and
critique of Habermas's social theory which I undertook in "Theology, Critical Social Theory, and the Public Realm," in *Habermas, Modernity, and
Public Theology*, ed. Don S. Browning and Francis Schüssler Fiorenza (New

theory, the linkage between debates on reason or rationality in theology (e.g., on faith and reason) and between debates on modernity (and postmodernity) are difficult if not impossible to clarify. That methodological failure has important substantive consequences: first, the central category of "reason" or "ratio" or "rationality," a category essential to *any* theology reflecting on the contemporary intellectual situation, is in danger of becoming trapped in a purely "culturalist" or even "idealist" horizon unless the theologian can show the links between the cultural resources of a situation and the materialist (economic, social, political, and technological) conditions of a society. Many theologies, at their best, have shown how to employ critically the symbolic resources of both the tradition and the cultural situation (including, of course, the arts — the "Muses") for the public realm. But most theologians pay too little attention to the materialist embedding of all symbolic resources (the Muses) in the kind of society within which we find ourselves. In the West, for example, society is largely constituted by a democratic polity, a capitalist economy, and an ever more bureaucratized political administration as we face the complex dilemma of globalization.

Jürgen Habermas's critical social theory,[4] among others, provides a good example for theologians of how to analyze and test the nature of social systems as they relate to con-

York: Crossroad, 1992), 19–43. See also the articles there by Helmut Peukert, Francis Schüssler Fiorenza, Matthew Lamb, and Fred Dallmayr and the response by Jürgen Habermas. See also Edmund Arens, *Habermas und die Theologie* (Düsseldorf: Patmos Verlag, 1989); Paul Lakeland, *Theology and Critical Theory: The Discourse of the Church* (Nashville: Abingdon, 1990); Helmut Peukert, *Science, Action, and Fundamental Theology* (Cambridge, Mass.: MIT Press, 1986).

4. See especially Jürgen Habermas, *The Theory of Communicative Action,* trans. Thomas McCarthy, 2 vols. (Boston: Beacon Press, 1984, 1986). Also *Der philosophische Diskurs der Moderne: Zwölf Vorlesungen* (Frankfurt am Main: Suhrkamp, 1985); in English, *The Philosophical Discourse of Modernity: Twelve Lectures,* trans. Frederick G. Lawrence (Cambridge, Mass.: MIT Press, 1987).

temporary notions of rationality: the economy and political administration and their media of money and power; their necessary use of purposive, technical rationality in modern globalized technology, including mass media; and their invasion, if unchecked, of the communicative rationality necessary to social action in the life-world of the society, especially the public realm. Indeed, to understand why the "public realm" has become so impoverished and why the life-world has been "colonized" by the systems of the economy, political administration, and postmodern technology demands a social analysis that can show how in developed modern globalized societies the communicative rationality of the "citizen" can gradually be effected by the purposive rationality of the client and the consumer of mass media. At the same time, Habermas's critical social theory shows the vestiges of communicative rationality in the various realms (ethical, political, religious, and aesthetic) of the life-world as well as in the "new movements" of resistance to its colonization. Without such empirically testable hypotheses of both system and life-world and their complex interactions, the theologian is left with either purely culturalist modes of analysis or merely impressionistic sketches of the dilemma of rationality in all disciplines in our globalized and technological situation.

All the familiar cultural and implicitly sociological themes of modern philosophy and theology — either the "possessive individualism" of Bellah et al., the "Dialectic of the Enlightenment" of Adorno and Horkheimer, the "iron cage" of Max Weber, the triumph of "calculative reason" of Heidegger, or the "postmodernity" of Lyotard — are, one and all, not merely general (and often valuable) cultural insights but proposals for understanding our complex society in the process of globalization. As such they must be as open to empirical testing as all other sociological proposals. But these proposals can only be tested properly by a theory which could combine empirical testing with the demands of critical reflection —

more exactly, by a mode of dialogical reflection that can clarify the limits and possibilities of reason and thereby help to emancipate us from systemic illusions (e.g., sexism, racism, classism, elitism).

As critical theory, Habermas's theory challenges both positivism and empiricism by insisting with hermeneutics, language philosophy, and pragmatism that human action is intrinsically interactive and communicative and thereby reflective. As social theory, Habermas's theory challenges any purely culturalist or idealist mode of inquiry with the call to test all cultural theories sociologically.[5] As critical social theory, therefore, any theory on the nature of rationality in our society must be, in Habermas's phrase, reconstructive: that is, one that can defend philosophically a theory of communicative rationality and link that philosophical theory to a reconstructive, empirical, testable sociological hypothesis on the nature of modernity and postmodernity as they have been institutionalized in the distinct rationalization processes of both the social systems (especially the global economy and technology) and the life-world of social action (communicative rationality) in our societies.

On the philosophical side, the temptation of many forms of modern philosophy has been to defend rationality from the viewpoint of a philosophy of consciousness. From Descartes through Kant to Husserl to most forms of contemporary transcendental philosophy, this "turn to the subject" has been the great hope of modern reason and much modern liberal theology. But here, as Plato with his model of reflection-through-dialogue and Aristotle with his analyses of forms of argument would have known, the turn to the subject's

---

5. For early work (and bibliographies) see Thomas McCarthy, *The Critical Theory of Jürgen Habermas* (Cambridge, Mass.: MIT Press, 1978). For later work see (with bibliographies) Stephen K. White, *The Recent Works of Jürgen Habermas: Reason, Justice, and Modernity* (Cambridge: Cambridge University Press, 1988).

consciousness does not suffice. No modern philosophy of consciousness seems able to account for the interactive, dialogical character of our actual uses of reason in linguistic, communicative exchange. It cannot avoid monological defenses of reason or even (witness Husserl) adequately account for intersubjectivity.

As with communicative reason, so with social action: social action is, by definition, interactive; as Max Weber sometimes acknowledged, if communicative at all, social action can be construed as dialogical interaction. Habermas's work over the years, from his initial formulation of knowledge and constitutive interests, through his theory of the ideal speech situation, to his theory of communicative action, has focused on this interactive, dialogical, and linguistic character of reason.

By his critical use of Austin, Searle, and Strawson, Habermas also takes advantage of analytical philosophy to clarify the conditions of possibility for all communicative action, namely, comprehensibility, truth, rightness, sincerity. By his reformulations of Weber on "rationalization processes" and of Lukács and Adorno/Horkheimer on reification, Habermas has also managed to free both Weber and the early Frankfurt school from their own implicitly monological categories. Thereby does he retrieve the dialogical, interactive character of the Hegelian-Marxist tradition. At the same time, Habermas's reconstruction of both Weber's "rationalization" hypothesis and Adorno/Horkheimer's formulation of the "Dialectic of Enlightenment" has emancipated these positions from their temptations to a totalizing cultural pessimism, by showing how, on the basis of their own analyses, there is no "inevitability" to Weber's "iron cage" of modernity. In sum, Habermas, by his reconstruction of sociological theory as both social system and social action, presents a plausible and testable critical social theory. The heart of this theory is the claim that the problem of modernity is not one of the inevitable triumph of technical reason but of "selective rationality." Attention to the purposive-technical rationality in the social systems of modernity has provided a selective, one-sided account of rationality that ignores the character of that communicative rationality necessary to all social reason — and surely to what "media" were intended to be.

This one-sided, selective development of purposive rationality in the social systems of our society — including, especially, modern global communications systems — accounts for the perilous dilemmas in the public realm, as distinct from, for example, the problems of the eighteenth century. In Western societies, the entire life-world, including the public realm, has been subject to an "internal colonization" as the systems of late-capitalist economics, political bureaucratic administration, and modern global technologies have increasingly (but not completely) colonized the life-world; hence, the "citizen," who, by definition, must be involved in communicative action, can become a mere "producer," a "client," and a "consumer."

The only plausible defense of the kind of rationality appropriate to the public realm, and thereby to the "reason" needed for an effective contemporary fundamental theology, is a defense not of purposive rationality but of communicative action — action directed to mutual understanding and demanding reciprocity. The importance of the linguistic turn from earlier modern philosophical paradigms of the subject's consciousness can scarcely be overemphasized. For if the only philosophical defense of communicative rationality is provided by a transcendental philosophy of consciousness, then privatization of resources of communicative action in the public realm (ethics, politics, aesthetics, and theology itself) increases.

The solitary thinker may be under the illusion that language is only an instrument for expressing her or his conscious insights. The speaker or listener in dialogue can be under no such illusion. For language is not an instrument of a-linguistic consciousness, but the necessary medium for all interactive understanding, including the speaker's own personal, but not private, reflections. Habermas, learning from the linguistic turn of hermeneutics, analytical philosophy, and Peircean pragmatism, therefore developed his theory of communicative rationality. His fundamental argument is familiar and, in my judgment, sound: anyone who communicates with the purpose of establishing mutual understanding implicitly affirms the validity of the claims put forward. In every case, it is necessary to understand the kind of argument needed to redeem any claim and to be willing to redeem the claim, if challenged.

Like Aristotle, Habermas is chiefly concerned to clarify the nature of argumentation and thereby the distinct kinds of argument needed for the principal spheres of modern inquiry. Like the earlier critical theorists of the Frankfurt school, Habermas seeks to clarify how reason, as reflective, is both enlightening and emancipatory. In his model, reason functions as reason only through the persuasive force of the best argument. All critical theory is designed to unmask any coercive use of power, whether imposed externally as in totalitarian states or internally as in the neuroses and psychoses unmasked by psychoanalytical and feminist theories. Like any social theorist, Habermas must also show how different notions of rationality are embedded in different practices and institutions, especially in a complex modern society constituted by both internally regulated social systems (e.g., the economy and administration of global media) and the communicatively rational life-world of social action. Hence there is need, as in all social theory, to show the exact relationships in our globalized society between social system and social action. Habermas attempts to demonstrate how a theory of communicative action can account for the gains provided by systems theory (Parsons and Luhmann) without reducing social actions (as communicative action) to purely systemic, and hence purposively rational, action.

This is undoubtedly an ambitious, complex, and impressive research project. I am in fundamental agreement with Habermas's basic philosophical arguments on communicative rationality. As stated above and in my own work on dialogue, argument, and hermeneutics, Habermas argues persuasively for the four criteria (comprehensibility, truth, rightness, sincerity) entailed in every act of communicative rationality. He argues just as persuasively for the democratic implications of all communicative rationality, namely, equality and mutual reciprocity demanding individual dignity. As to his reconstructive social theory on the relationships of social system and social action in modern society, I can only state my necessarily tentative agreement with its general hypothesis — that the problem of reason or rationality today demands both a social theory attentive to and appropriate to the systems analysis of modern social systems, especially the economy and global communications systems, as well as an analysis of the communicative action entailed by all social action in the life-world. His central social theory does seem to clarify how the problem of modernity — including the problem of rationality in our contemporary globalized situation, which has been named either late modernity or postmodernity — is one of a selective and one-sided use of a purposive rationality appropriate for social systems like global communications technology, but inappropriate for, indeed devastating for, the communicative rationality necessary for a proper understanding of "reason" in any contemporary theology or philosophy.

Such critical social theory frees analysts from the temptations of total cultural optimism and total cultural pessimism by showing the nature of the problem of reason in our society and in our theologies as one of selectivity, not inevitability. Many social theories of mass media thereby also analyze the vestiges of reason in the practices and institutions of the life-world. For there is evidence that the life-world, although often devastatingly colonized by the purposive rationality appropriate to the globalizing social systems of mass media, is not simply Weber's "iron cage." At the same time, Habermas's social theory helps to clarify the reasons for and promise of various "new movements": for example, various liberation movements, the surprising resurgence of religion, and the ecological movement. All these movements provide hope by resisting the increasing colonization of the life-world as well as by implicitly affirming the need for communicative action and thereby the role of the "Muses" in a contemporary globalized world. All these movements give us realistic hope — a classic theological virtue — that can be brought to bear on contemporary discussions of reason, faith, and hope at the same time that the theologian strives to give the reasons for the hope that lies within us. In sum, social-scientific debates on modern communication technology can illuminate the formulations of "reason" in any contemporary theology.

Example Two: Debates on Postmodernity and the Recovery of Religion as Participation

I have defended the notion elsewhere (against Habermas) that we live more in a postmodern, not late modern, age.[6] This is not the place to rehearse those arguments. However, this much needs emphasis: this often inchoate category "postmodern" means, for the purposes of this essay, the emphasis across theology, philosophy, the humanities, and especially the social sciences on otherness and difference. "Postmodern" represents an insistence that modern rationality did enact a strategy of containment toward all who were other and different, who did not fit the modern foundational project of rationality. This same narrowness is often present

---

6. See also John B. Thompson and David Head, eds., *Habermas: Critical Debates* (Cambridge, Mass.: MIT Press, 1982); Seyla Benhabib, *Critique, Norm, and Utopia: A Study of the Foundations of Critical Theory* (New York: Columbia University Press, 1988).

implicitly in some contemporary theories of globalization, which reflect far too little on global technology's monological force and thereby on its ignoring of cultural difference and otherness. This postmodern release of "subjugated" knowledges (Foucault) insists that the issues of gender, race, and class be addressed. The postmodern insistence on the other and different implies an ethics of resistance in much postmodern thought to the leveling effects of much mass media. Postmodernity is first an ethical or cultural category and, increasingly, a religious and theological category for thinkers like Michel de Certeau, who combine theology and Foucault-like social science and write of the radical love mystics and apophatic mystics. However, postmodernity is also a multifaceted social-scientific notion that helps to interpret many major social and cultural changes occurring at the end of the twentieth century: especially the globalization of all social systems from the economy through culture and politics and religion, and the extraordinary pace of technological change, especially in communications.

It is impossible in this brief space to discuss all these conflicting interpretations on the social-scientific meanings of late modernity/postmodernity and their relevance to globalization theories and to how social-scientific debates on technology and globalization relate to cultural (including theological) debates on otherness and difference. I shall confine myself, therefore, to one example of how the new technologies and their attendant social world may be related to the widespread social and intellectual recovery of religion as participation or manifestation.

The new, participatory technologies of the global communications network are changing many social-scientific readings of our situation. Our situation is no longer adequately described simply as "postindustrial," as in social-scientific hypotheses of "late modernity" (again, as in Habermas), but is more radically "postmodern." Here the cultural postmodern emphasis on diversity, difference, and otherness surprisingly meets a new technologically informed sense of participation. This sense, in turn, as some social scientists now observe,[7] has given rise to a new sense of human participation in nature, the cosmos, the emerging global community and, at the limit, the divine. It is this new participatory sensibility, at once surprising and heartening, that, although in danger of proving merely virtual, deserves attention from theologians.[8] This sensibility can be seen most clearly in the ecological movement — based, after all, on the sense of radical human participation in nature, the cosmos and, often, the divine — and in the new postmodern, that is, ecological, holistic understanding of the natural sciences. Indeed, the latter serves as an intellectual link between the debates on otherness and difference in the cultural sciences and the debates on the ambiguity of participation (merely virtual or also actual?) in modern global technology.

The natural sciences in our day — or at least the postmodern, ecological sciences, as Frederick Ferré and Stephen Toulmin have argued — are singular among the disciplines for highlighting not just difference and otherness but also

---

7. For some of Andrew Greeley's important social-scientific studies of the Catholic religious sensibility, see *Religion as Poetry* (New Brunswick, N.J.: Transaction, 1995); *The Catholic Myth* (New York: Scribner's, 1990); "Theology and Sociology," *Journal of the American Academy of Religion* 59 (winter 1991): 643–52.

8. For some representative studies of globalization, postmodernity, and social science, see David Lyon, *Postmodernity* (Minneapolis: University of Minnesota Press, 1994); David Harvey, *The Condition of Postmodernity* (Oxford: Blackwell, 1990); Scott Lash, *Sociology of Postmodernism* (London: Routledge, 1990); Bryan Turner, ed., *Themes of Modernity and Postmodernity* (London: Sage, 1990); Simon Nora and Alain Minc, *L'Informatisation de la société* (Paris: La Documentation Française, 1980); Mark Poster, *The Mode of Information: Poststructuralism and Social Context* (Cambridge, England: Polity Press, 1990); Mike Featherstone, *Consumer Culture and Postmodernism* (London: Sage, 1991); and the forthcoming book of James Buchanan, *Wages into the Abyss*.

a new felt sense of participation in nature. Ecological science, in my judgment, is ahead of most other postmodern cultural thought, yet curiously harmonious with much postmodern technological communications culture, in providing a non-Romantic sense of our participation in nature as the key factor demanding new ethical, philosophical, and theological reflection.

If, therefore, radical diversity, including not only cultural and political and religious diversity but also biodiversity, is grounded in a radically new sense of participation in nature — often encouraged paradoxically by modern, seemingly virtual, participatory technology like the Internet — then this becomes an occasion to recover too often forgotten, marginalized resources in the Western theological and philosophical traditions. These resources include, especially, religion as participation or manifestation.

There are various ways to make useful distinctions among the most basic forms of religious expression. When one wishes to highlight the reality of the participation of human beings in the cosmos and, in Jewish and Christian faith, in relationship to God, the most basic distinction is that between religion as manifestation and religion as proclamation.

Religion as manifestation signifies radical participation of any person in the cosmos and in the divine reality. The sense of God's radical immanence in both cosmos and self is strong, along with the felt relationship among self, nature, and the divine. In religion as proclamation — and the three great prophetic and monotheistic traditions of Judaism, Christianity and Islam are all proclamation traditions in their prophetic core — a sense of God's transcendent power is also a source of the divine disclosure, which occurs principally in history, not nature. In religion as proclamation there is a new sense of distance between God and human beings and a powerful interruption of the once powerful, indeed radical, sense of belonging to or radical participation in the cosmos.

The sense of participation in nature does not die in prophetic traditions, as the Jewish liturgical year, the Christian
sacraments, or Islamic ritual make clear. The prophetic traditions, however, with their strong sense of God's transcendence
and of ethical responsibility before God in the struggle for justice and liberation from oppression, have their own ways of
relating to moments like the ecological crisis. These are usually straightforwardly ethical-political ways, as the Christian
theologies of "stewardship" and the promising use of the Reformed Christian "covenantal" theologies (Stackhouse et al.)
brilliantly show.

Many indigenous religious traditions, however, have never
lost the earlier sense of radical participation in nature and
the cosmos. Those traditions, once simply named "pagan"
by Jews, Christians, and Muslims, have returned to haunt
the always ethical conscience of the prophetic, proclamation-
oriented traditions like Jewish Kabbalistic mystical traditions
in relationship to the ethical monotheism of Judaism. There
has also been a return of the repressed other, the so-called
"pagan" manifestation of a *felt* relationship uniting self, cosmos, and God, including a sense of human beings' radical participation in nature. Then there is an answer to the telling question of Mircea Eliade: With all the talk of creation and sacrament, do Jews, Christians, and Muslims actually *feel* the world
as God's creation? Buddhists have taught Christians to see
Francis of Assisi as, in one way, the most radical religious figure
in the West. He can now be seen as the most radical religion-
as-manifestation figure in the West, having broken through
the anthropocentrism of most Western religion to recover a
sense of the radical participation of all creatures in the divine.

In the Catholic theological tradition, Bonaventure's joining of this new Franciscan sensibility toward nature with
Neoplatonic philosophy, Augustinian interiority, and love-
mysticism remains one of the most promising syntheses in
the Christian theological tradition. It is promising for a con-

temporary theology directed to this new sense of radical participation, just as Reformed covenantal theologies are, in my judgment, the most promising proclamation-oriented syntheses for Christian ethical responsibility in our globalized situation. The Muses may sing more beautifully in the Franciscan manifestation traditions, but their splendid tunes of our radical participation in one another, in creation, and in God will receive ethical-political responsibility from uniting to the less Muse-oriented covenantal traditions. Together they will form a Christian contribution usable, in principle, to all theorists in the contemporary situation of globalization.

But Bonaventure is only one among several promising Christian theological syntheses of God-self-cosmos. It is difficult to overemphasize how central what might be named "felt synthesis" was for most ancient and medieval thinkers. I agree fully with Louis Dupré in his *Passage to Modernity* that the most important and widely overlooked consequence of modernity — which he dates as early as the nominalist crisis of the fourteenth century and the humanist creativity of the fifteenth century — is the breakup of both the ancient and the medieval senses of a synthesis of God, self, and cosmos.[9]

Clearly all ancient and even most Jewish, Christian, and Islamic "felt syntheses" of God, cosmos, and self are expressions, religiously, of manifestation at least as much as proclamation. The ancients may indeed have had a sense of cosmos central to an understanding of the divine realm, to the gods, even Zeus (or Jupiter). The sense may have included human beings as a *microcosmos* related to and thereby participatory in the *macrocosmos,* and human reason as *logos,* intrinsically related to both the cosmic and the divine realms. The ancient synthesis — especially but not solely the Neoplatonic and the Stoic — was a felt synthesis of the intrin-

---

9. See especially Louis Dupré, *A Passage to Modernity* (New Haven: Yale University Press, 1995).

sic relationality of the cosmos, the divine, and self, and was grounded in various forms of religion as manifestation, that is, in senses of radical participation in the cosmos.

The proclamation-oriented monotheistic traditions did change but did not break this sense of felt synthesis and relation among God, self, and cosmos and of a radical participation of the self in the cosmos and in God. It is not so much the doctrine of redemption which prevailed, as it did in the prophetic, proclamatory Augustinian sense of the transcendent God at work mysteriously in history. Rather, both the patristic and medieval periods (even aspects of Augustine) were dominated by reflection on the doctrine of creation. How could any radically monotheistic tradition with its doctrine of a Creator God assume the continuance, in a new transformed form, of a synthesis of God-self-cosmos? This was the great challenge of our patristic and medieval ancestors. On the whole, they never lost a sense of radical participation and ordered relationship.

Especially through Platonic resources the medievals, even the champions of Aristotle like Aquinas, managed to maintain God's radical immanence in nature and humanity without loss of God's transcendence. Recall, for example, the subtlety of medieval discussions of formal and efficient causes. Recall, above all, how reason (*logos* or *intellectus*) for Christian thinkers like Anselm or Aquinas, or for Augustine before them, was never equivalent to modern rationality but was always understood — and, it seems clear, experienced — as radically participant in the divine and the cosmos. Human being, including human reason in participatory *logos,* was still *microcosmos* (as for the ancients) but was now also for the Christian *imago Dei,* another profoundly participatory notion.

Modernity clearly changed all this. No synthesis, ancient nor medieval, held any longer. As modernity advanced in seventeenth-century form, as the great modern scientific revolution, through a more reified eighteenth-century form, to the second scientific revolution of the twentieth century and the subsequent emergence of postmodern science and global participatory (again virtual/actual) technology, the sense of humanity's radical participation in an increasingly mechanized modern cosmos failed.

Each element in modernity was increasingly on its own. Cosmos became nature, and science adopted a dominating attitude toward nature (often encouraged by a reading of Genesis!). God withdrew from the synthesis into even greater transcendence and hiddenness. The self was largely deprived (in secular culture) of its former states as *microcosmos* and with only vague memories of its reality as *imago Dei*. The modern secular self became ever more autonomous and isolated from any sense of radical participation in the cosmos and radical felt relationship to God or Creator. Ancient and medieval reason-as-*logos,* moreover, retreated from radical participation in the cosmos and the divine into a narrower range of what would count as rational and thereby real. These pre-modern resources, kept alive in the theological traditions as powerful senses, in sacrament, ritual, art, and the use of the Muses in much theology, should now be retrieved anew for a postmodern hermeneutics of religion as participation, including what may be provided, however "virtually," by contemporary communication technology. Such, at least, is the possibility (no more, but also no less) opened by this second example of how contemporary social science can inform theology.

Theology would be foolish to ignore this new possible resource for religious retrieval or to fail to note the possible shift of many postmodern sensibilities from the largely nonparticipatory notions of religion of Western modernity to deeply participatory notions. There is also the possibility of employing that participatory sense in modern technology's openness to the Muses. This second example, however, may also suggest why it is difficult to be sanguine (as distinct from hopeful) about this new "possibility." The new global system often promotes, at one and the same time, instantaneous news and the leveling of otherness and differences through information technology that can seem at times merely virtual. There is the need to see the other side of the new communication technology and, hence, the need for a recovery of proclamation — first as explosive, fragmentary images of eschatological hope and then as a gathering of those fragments in a new global covenantal hope.

Images of Eschatological Hope: Fragments and Their Gathering into Covenant

We have seen positive possibilities of participation made real by modern communications. At the same time modern communication poses familiar problems. The first is the difficulty for a public realm if, as could happen, only technical reason were allowed. The second difficulty is that the participation and community made possible by modern communications may be merely virtual and may not provide the wisdom and traditions of genuine communities, as inspired by the Muses of participation and manifestation. These two difficulties are familiar and have been treated by many analysts, including myself in earlier papers on the public realm. The third difficulty is less familiar and more perplexing. Time changes us all, and in a situation of instantaneous communication it is difficult to see how temporality and community in their properly narrative forms can maintain the continuity needed for human communication. For that reason I would like to turn our attention to the possible import of focusing first on eschatological images as interruptive.

To understand our cultural situation rightly one must expand the cultural horizons of the contemporary discussion beyond a Western sense of centeredness and a Western sense of its own pluralism. We must do so in order to allow for a new global polycentrism. For there is no longer a Western cultural center with margins. There are many centers now, of which the West is merely one. Moreover, once one drops the Western grand narrative, sometimes unfortunately implicit in globalization theorists, the continuities in that narrative begin to dissolve. To observe that necessary disillusion, recall the now familiar postmodernity-versus-modernity debate. What can this contemporary debate — a debate on two essentialisms — now mean? It is not only that within Western culture itself there are now several postmodernities. There are also several modernities. Indeed, one can find in what is often named "postmodernity" as well as in the classical model of modernity itself — the classical Enlightenment — fragments of an earlier modernity which repressed the more flexible, more open, more fragmented culture of the fifteenth, sixteenth, and early seventeenth centuries. One can find elements of that creative period of early modernity before the reified model of the Enlightenment became the sole model of modernity.

Most forms of postmodernity, as I noted above, are explosions of once-forgotten, marginalized, and repressed realities in Enlightenment modernity: the other, the different, and the marginal disallow any totality system, including any Western globalization model.[10] These repressed elements were clearly far less marginal in early modernity, that too-seldom-studied singularity in most debates on modernity. The key phenomenon provoking new study is religion. Clearly it is time to reopen an otherwise exhausted debate on religion and modernity. It may well be, as several contemporary phenomenologists claim, that religion is the nonreductive saturated

---

10. For my own reading of the major issues on this side of postmodernity, see *Plurality and Ambiguity: Hermeneutics, Religion, Hope* (Chicago: University of Chicago Press, 1994); and *On Naming the Present* (Maryknoll, N.Y.: Orbis Books, 1994).

phenomenon par excellence. I am convinced that this is the case. And yet even before that contemporary case can be made it may be necessary to clear some further cultural debris.

Religion has always been the unassimilatable (as distinct from conquered and colonized) other of Enlightenment modernity.[11] Any saturated form of the religious phenomenon had to be marginalized by the Enlightenment. It could not fit what counted as rational. Other developments in Western culture fought this marginality of religion: the Romantic discovery of symbols and archaic rituals; the Western interest in Hinduism's excessive forms for the sacred; the Buddhist insistence on formlessness. Or consider Gershom Scholem's researches into Kabbalah. The scholarly recovery of Kabbalah undid the pretension of Judaism as simply a modern ethical monotheism. The fragments of the divine in Kabbalah and, as it turns out, in rabbinic exegesis itself undo that claim, as does the Jewish prophetic and apocalyptic discourse recovered by Levinas to help one understand, against the Enlightenment, how the ethics of the other, not the self, is first philosophy — an implication, as well, of all Jewish and Christian covenantal theology.

All of these religious phenomena, as distinct from the Enlightenment's notion of rational religion, are clearly other to the demands for intellectual closure in classical modernity.[12] Why otherwise the bizarre parade since the late seventeenth century of the modern ways of naming God? That series of "-isms" invented in modern philosophical and theological thought had little if anything to do with God as a religious phenomenon and religion as a saturated sacred phenom-

---

11. For my own hermeneutical analysis of religious revelation, see my essay for the conference, "Word, Language, and Religion," in the volume edited by Marco Olivetti, *Religione, Parola, Scrittura* (Rome: Archivio de Filosofia, 1992).

12. See Bernard Lonergan, *Method in Theology* (Philadelphia: Westminster Press, 1982).

enon. Those "-isms" were intended to classify and control the discussion of the ultimate religious other in any radically monotheistic reflection on God. But can the question of God really be controlled by the modern discussion of deism, pantheism, modern atheism, modern theism, or even, in the best achievement of modern Western religious thought, panentheism, from Bruno to Hegel to Whitehead?

Even before the "other" and the "different" became such central philosophical, cultural, ethical, and religious categories, Western thinkers sensed the temptation to reduce all reality to more of the same.[13] Modern global communications both encourages and disallows that temptation. The new phenomenologists,[14] especially in France — Jean-Luc Marion, Jean Louis Chretien, Michel Henry, and many others — following the earlier lead of Paul Ricoeur and Emmanuel Levinas, find saturated religious phenomena (spirit, gift, liturgy, covenant) demanding careful phenomenological description. They demand description precisely as saturated auratic phenomenon and as the most rigorous analytical demands; they provide an unthought and unexpected possibility for modern minds,[15] namely the realm of the impossible — true justice in the world (covenant) — and another realm of available participatory manifestations (liturgy). The strategies are many and sometimes mutually contradictory in the new attempts at understanding religion. Religion and philosophy have found

---

13. On hermeneutics see Hans-Georg Gadamer, *Wahrheit und Methode* (Tübingen: J. C. B. Mohr, 1965); Martin Heidegger, *Zur Sache des Denkens* (Tübingen: Max Niemeyer Verlag, 1969); Paul Ricoeur, *Hermeneutics and the Human Sciences* (Cambridge: Cambridge University Press, 1981); Hans Robert Jauss, *Toward an Aesthetics of Reception* (Minneapolis: University of Minnesota, 1982).

14. As representative of the new phenomenologists, see Jean-Luc Marion, *God without Being* (Chicago: University of Chicago Press, 1995).

15. For an excellent study of pre-modern resources for this issue, see Pierre Hadot, *Exercises spirituels et philosophie antique* (Paris: Etudes Augustiniennes, 1987).

each other again as fragments that do not and no longer wish to form a modern totality, but that may be able to order the fragments internally as worship and externally, that is, publicly, as covenant. But what of theology? Is it still as Walter Benjamin once suggested, "wizened and best kept out of sight"? Its opportunities in the contemporary communication saturation are strong if it will, in a first step, allow its truly saturated auratic, sacred elements-become-images to undo any temptation to totality in modern media.

It has become a truism by now that modernism, whatever else it is, prefers the unfinished, the syntactically unstable, the semantically malformed. What Walter Benjamin added to this familiar portrait is something like a theological theory of the modernist image.[16] The contemporary image is a fragment. History, including intellectual history, breaks up into images, as modern communication shows so well. Benjamin calls these images "dialectical" but it may be more accurate to name them "fragments," as saturated, auratic images available for and critical of modern global communication.

Above all one must avoid modernity's — not only mass media's — central temptation (not necessity): the drive to systematize, to render a totality system that makes everything simply more of the same. To render any totality system is to efface the distinct and potentially explosive image in favor of some larger conceptual architectonic of which the image is now made a part.

The image as fragment, as saturated and auratic — especially the marginal fragment that recalls forgotten, even repressed memories of the suffering of all victims and the forgotten and marginalized of the present — should be initially privileged over all other images, especially the image of

---

16. On the import of Walter Benjamin, see *On Walter Benjamin: Critical Essays and Reflections,* ed. Gary Smith (Cambridge, Mass.: MIT Press, 1988). See also the two volumes of Benjamin's own writings in the excellent new translations by Harvard University Press.

the contemporary "celebrity." In Christian theological terms this can read as an initial privileging of Mark's fragmentary, discontinuous, apocalyptic Gospel, grounded in fragments of the memory of suffering, over the Luke/Acts view of history as continuous realistic narrative.

In theological terms, a radically eschatological, indeed apocalyptic and messianic, understanding of history is now needed to critique prophetically the temptation to totality and to free the redemptive images of our past and present. New experiments in media (especially film and television) do attempt to let auratic, saturated, sacred images speak for themselves and thereby generate new tension and meaning as they work with and against every other image in a new constellation of images that does not yield to instantaneous closure.

We can and ethically should let go of the hope for any totality system, including any system lurking in globalization theories. We should focus initially on the explosive, marginal, saturated, and, at times, auratic fragments of our heritages. We should do this not merely in a neoconservative fashion, to shore up against our present ruin — although that, too, can be a noble response — but in a properly theological manner: blast alive the marginalized fragments of the past with the memory of suffering and hope; remove them from their seemingly coherent place in the grand narratives we have imposed; learn to live joyfully, not despairingly, with and in the great fragments we possess; allow the postmodern Muses (e.g., atonal music, rap, pop art, the new novel) to help us recover these explosive fragmentary images.

Sometimes this search — this intellectual and I do not hesitate to say, spiritual, search[17] — demands a destructive

17. For my own work in this area, see *Blessed Rage for Order: The New Pluralism in Theology* (Chicago: University of Chicago Press, 1995), especially the self-criticism in the new preface (1995); *The Analogical Imagination* (New York: Crossroad, 1982); *Plurality and Ambiguity; On*

moment of critique and radical suspicion of all totalities (including some globalization theories). This occurs by finding the spiritual fragments that expose any pretense to totality. Modern communications with its genius at images could clearly help this process — if it would allow more of its moral conscience to join with its technical expertise to free the saturated images our culture needs. Theology — if it focuses on its properly eschatological task in serving images of redemption and judgment — could surely help as well. That conclusion is at present neither a necessity nor even a plausibility. It is a hope grounded in the images of redemption and promise of our religious heritages.

Free the Muses to capture both needed images of participation in our religion-as-manifestation traditions and the explosive fragmentary images of the apocalyptic and prophetic proclamation traditions. Then one may find a new opening to a public theology for our globalized moment. That public theology could prove to be a covenantal (intrinsically open-ended and nontotalizing) theology correlated to globalization theories.[18] Then theologians committed to the ever-changing public realm may eventually be able to provide our culture with fragmentary images of both relationality-participation and description-proclamation. Once gathered through covenant, these images may prove to be the singular Jewish-Christian (and, in principle, Islamic) contribution to a genuinely public realm in our new global period.

Naming the Present; Dialogue with the Other (Grand Rapids, Mich.: Eerdmans, 1993). Further necessary documentation may be found in those works and the forthcoming *This Side of God* (Chicago: University of Chicago Press).

18. See the general introduction by Max Stackhouse.

SELECTED BIBLIOGRAPHY

Adams, James L. *Voluntary Associations*. Ed. J. R. Engel. Chicago: Exploration Press, 1986.

Albrow, Martin. *The Global Age: State and Society beyond Modernity*. Stanford, Calif.: Stanford University Press, 1997.

Anderson, Gordon L., ed. *The Family in Global Transition*. Minneapolis: PWPA Books, 1997.

Angier, Natalie. *Women: An Intimate Geography*. New York: Houghton Mifflin, 1999.

Annan, Kofi. "The Backlash against Globalism." *The Futurist* (March 1999).

Apel, K.-O. *L'Ethique à l'Age de la Science*. Lille: Presses Universitaires de Lille, 1987.

———. "How to Ground a Universalistic Ethics of Responsibility for the Effects of Collective Action and Activities." *Philosophica* 52 (1993).

———. "The Moral Imperative." *UNESCO Courier: A Window Open on the World* 45, nos. 7–8 (July–August 1992).

———. "A Planetary Macroethics for Humankind." In *Culture and Modernity: East-West Philosophical Perspectives,* ed. Eliot Deutsch. Honolulu: University of Hawaii Press, 1991.

———. *Selected Essays of K.-O. Apel*. Atlantic Highlands, N.J.: Humanities Press, 1996.

Arens, Edmund. *Habermas und die Theologie*. Düsseldorf: Patmos Verlag, 1989.

Arjun Appadurai, *Modernity at Large: Cultural Dimensions of Globalization*. New Delhi: Oxford University Press, 1977.

———. "The Production of Locality." In *Counterworks: Managing the Diversity of Knowledge,* ed. Richard Fardon. London: Sage, 1995.

Aristotle. *Nicomachean Ethics*. Translated by T. Irwin. Indianapolis: Hackett, 1985.

Arrighi, G., and B. Silver. *Chaos and Governance in the Modern World System*. Minneapolis: University of Minnesota Press, 1999.

Avineri, S. *The Social and Political Thought of Karl Marx*. Cambridge: Cambridge University Press, 1968.

Balasuriya, T. *Planetary Theology*. Maryknoll, N.Y.: Orbis Books, 1984.

Bale, Lawrence S., ed. *Envisioning a Global Ethic*. Philadelphia: Consortium for Interreligious Dialogue, 1995.

Barber, Benjamin R. *Jihad vs. McWorld*. New York: Times Books, 1995.

Barker, Ernest. *Traditions of Civility*. Cambridge: Cambridge University Press, 1948.

Barnet, Richard J., and John Cavanagh. *Global Dreams: Imperial Corporations and the New World Order*. New York: Simon and Schuster, 1994.

Beck, Ulrich. *The Reinvention of Politics: Rethinking Modernity in the Global Social Order*. Translated by Mark Ritter. Oxford: Polity Press, 1997.

Beck, Ulrich, Anthony Giddens, and Scott Lash. *Reflexive Modernization*. Stanford, Calif.: Stanford University Press, 1994.

Becker, Gary. *A Treatise on the Family*. Cambridge, Mass.: Harvard University Press, 1970.

Becker, L. C., ed. *Encyclopedia of Ethics*. New York: Garland, 1992.

Beitz, Charles R., et al., eds. *International Ethics*. Princeton, N.J.: Princeton University Press, 1985.

Bellah, Robert. *The Good Society*. New York: Vintage Books, 1992.

Bellah, Robert, et al. *Habits of the Heart*. Berkeley: University of California Press, 1985.

Benhabib, Seyla. *Critique, Norm, and Utopia: A Study of the Foundations of Critical Theory*. New York: Columbia University Press, 1988.

Berger, Peter, ed. *The Desecularization of the World: Resurgent Religion and World Politics*. Grand Rapids, Mich.: Eerdmans, 1999.

Bernard, Jessie. *The Future of Marriage*. New York: World Publishing, 1972.

Beyer, Peter. *Religion and Globalization*. London: Sage, 1994.

Black, Amy E. *For the Sake of the Children: Reconstructing American Divorce Policy*. Crossroads Monograph Series in Faith and Public Policy 1, no. 2. Wynnewood, Pa.: Evangelicals for Social Action, 1995.

Bock, Paul. *In Search of a Responsible World Society: The Social Teachings of the World Council of Churches*. Philadelphia: Westminster Press, 1974.

Bok, Sissela. *Common Values*. Columbia: University of Missouri Press, 1995.

———. *A Strategy for Peace: Human Values and the Threat of War*. New York: Pantheon Books, 1989.

Boserup, Esther. *Women's Role in Economic Development*. London: George Allen and Unwin, 1970.

Bould, Sally. "Development in the Family: Third World Women and Inequality." In *Women and Work in the Third World: The Impact of Industrialization and Global Economic Interdependence*, ed. Nagat M. El-Sanabary. Berkeley, Calif.: Center for the Study, Education, and Advancement of Women, 1983.

Bratt, James D., ed. *Abraham Kuyper: A Centennial Reader*. Grand Rapids, Mich.: Eerdmans, 1998.

Braudel, Fernand. *Civilization and Capitalism*. 3 vols. New York: Harper and Row, 1982–84.

Brecher, Jeremy, John Childs, and Jill Cutler, eds. *Global Visions: Beyond the New World Order*. Boston: South End Press, 1993.

Bromiley, Geoffrey W. *God and Marriage*. Grand Rapids, Mich.: Eerdmans, 1980.

Browning, Don S., and Francis Schüssler Fiorenza, eds.*Habermas, Modernity, and Public Theology*. New York: Crossroad, 1992.

Browning, Don S., et al. *From Culture Wars to Common Ground: Religion and the American Family Debate*. Louisville: Westminster/John Knox Press, 1997.

Brunner, Emil. *Christianity and Civilization*. New York: Scribners & Sons, 1947.

———. *The Divine Imperative: A Study in Christian Ethics*. Philadelphia: Westminster Press, 1947.

Buchanan, James. *Wages into the Abyss*. Forthcoming.

Bull, Hedley. *The Anarchical Society: A Study of Order in World Politics*. 2d ed. New York: Columbia University Press, 1995 (1977).

Burtless, Gary T., et al. *Globaphobia: Confronting Fears about Open Trade*. Washington, D.C.: Brookings Institution, Progressive Policy Institute, and the Twentieth-Century Fund, 1998.

Buss, David. *The Evolution of Desire*. New York: Basic Books, 1994.

————. "Sex Differences in Human Mate Preferences." *Behavioral and Brain Sciences* 12 (1989): 1–49.

Byrne, Peter. *The Moral Interpretation of Religion*. Grand Rapids, Mich.: Eerdmans, 1998.

Cahill, Lisa Sowle. *Sex, Gender, and Christian Ethics*. Cambridge: Cambridge University Press, 1996.

Cahill, Lisa Sowle, and James F. Childress, eds. *Christian Ethics: Problems and Prospects*. Cleveland: Pilgrim Press, 1996.

Caldwell, Sarah. "Transcendence and Culture: Anthropologists Theorize Religion." *Religious Studies Review* 28 (July 1999): 227–32.

Carr, Anne, and Mary Stewart Van Leeuwen, eds. *Religion, Feminism, and the Family*. Louisville: Westminster/John Knox Press, 1996.

Cherlin, Andrew. *Marriage, Divorce, and Remarriage*. 2d ed. Cambridge: Harvard University Press, 1992.

Clapp, Rodney. *Families at the Crossroads: Beyond Traditional and Modern Options*. Downers Grove, Ill.: InterVarsity Press, 1993.

Clapp, Rodney. "Is the Traditional Family Biblical?" *Christianity Today* 32 (November 21, 1986): 24–28.

Coolidge, David Orgon. "The Dilemma of Single-Sex Marriage." *Crisis* (July–August 1996): 17–20.

Comité Consultatif National d'Ethique. *Une même éthique pour tous*. Paris: Editions Odile Jacob, 1997.

Commission on Global Governance. *Our Global Neighborhood*. Oxford: Oxford University Press, 1995.

Conway-Turner, Kate, and Suzanne Cherrin. *Women, Families, and Feminist Politics: A Global Exploration.* New York: Haworth, 1998.

Cott, Nancy. *The Grounding of Modern Feminism.* New Haven: Yale University Press, 1987.

The Danvers Statement. Wheaton, Ill.: Council on Biblical Manhood and Womanhood, 1989.

Delmas-Marty, Mireille. *Vers un droit commun de l'Humanité: Entretiens avec Philippe Petit.* Paris: Editions Textuel, 1996.

de Mooij, M. *Global Marketing and Advertising: Understanding Cultural Paradoxes.* London: Sage, 1998.

Department of Public Information (DPI), United Nations. *The World Conferences: Developing Priorities for the Twenty-first Century.* New York, 1997.

Deutsche UNESCO-Kommission. *Wandlung von Verantwortung und Werten in Unserer Zeit* (Evolution of responsibilities and values today). Report of a colloquium organized by the German Commission for UNESCO, Freiburg im Brisgau, June 2–4, 1982. Bonn: Verlag Dokumentation Saur KG, 1983.

Diamond, Jared. *Guns, Germs, and Steel.* New York: W. W. Norton, 1998.

Dupré, Louis. *A Passage to Modernity.* New Haven: Yale University Press, 1995.

Elshtain, Jean Bethke. "International Politics and Political Theory." In *International Relations Theory Today,* ed. Ken Booth and Steve Smith. University Park: Penn State University Press, 1995.

Evans, Alice F., R. A. Evans, and D. A. Roozen, eds. *The Globalization of Theological Education.* Maryknoll, N.Y.: Orbis Books, 1993.

Falk, Richard, Robert C. Johansen, and Samul S. Kim, eds. *The Constitutional Foundations of World Peace.* Albany: State University of New York Press, 1993.

Falk, Richard, Samuel S. Kim, and Saul H. Mendlovitz. *Toward a Just World Order.* Denver: Westview Press, 1982.

Featherstone, Mike. *Consumer Culture and Postmodernism.* London: Sage, 1991.

Feinburg, John S., and Paul D. Feinburg. *Ethics for a Brave New World.* Wheaton, Ill.: Crossway Books, 1994.

Fisher, Julie. *Non-Governments: NGOs and the Political Development of the Third World.* West Hartford, Conn.: Kumarian Press, 1998.

Fleischacker, Samuel. *The Ethics of Culture.* Ithaca, N.Y.: Cornell University Press, 1994.

Frankena, William K. *Ethics.* Englewood Cliffs, N.J.: Prentice-Hall, 1973.

Fukuyama, Francis. *The End of History and the Last Man.* New York: Free Press, 1992.

———. *The Great Disruption: Human Nature and the Reconstitution of Social Order.* New York: Free Press, 1999.

———. *Trust: The Social Virtues and the Creation of Prosperity.* New York: Free Press, 1995.

Furet, François. *The Passing of an Illusion: The Idea of Communism in the Twentieth Century.* Trans. D. Furet. Chicago: University of Chicago Press, 1999.

Gadamer, Hans-Georg. *Wahrheit und Methode.* Tübingen: J. C. B. Mohr, 1965.

Galtung Johan. *The True Worlds: A Transnational Perspective.* New York: Free Press, 1980.

Gamwell, Franklin I. *The Divine Good: Modern Moral Theory and the Necessity of God.* San Francisco: HarperCollins, 1990.

Gellner, Ernest. *Nations and Nationalism.* Ithaca, N.Y.: Cornell University Press, 1983.

Gerle, Elizabeth. *In Search of a Global Ethics.* Lund: Lund University Press, 1996.

Gilbert, Neil. *Welfare Justice.* New Haven: Yale University Press, 1995.

———. "Working Families: Hearth to Market." In *All Our Families: New Policies for a New Century,* ed. Mary Ann Mason, Arlene Skolnick, and Stephen D. Sugarman. New York: Oxford University Press, 1998).

Goldberg, Steven. *The Inevitability of Patriarchy.* New York: William Morrow, 1974.

Gorbachev, Mikhail. *The Search for a New Beginning: Developing a New Civilization.* Translated by P. Palazchenko. San Francisco: HarperSanFrancisco, 1995.

Goulet, Denis. *Development Ethics: A Guide to Theory and Practice.* New York: Apex Press; London: Zed Books, 1995.

Grachev, Andrey, and Vladimir Lomeiko. *The Meeting of Civilisations: Conflict or Dialogue?* Reflections based on the Tbilisi International Forum, "For Solidarity against Intolerance, for a Dialogue between Cultures," July 13–15, 1995. Paris: UNESCO Editions, 1996.

Greeley, Andrew. *The Catholic Myth.* New York: Scribner's, 1990.

———. *Religion as Poetry.* New Brunswick, N.J.: Transaction, 1995.

———. "Theology and Sociology." *Journal of the American Academy of Religion* 59 (winter 1991): 643–52.

Gruppe von Lissabon. *Grenzen des Wettbewerbs, die Globalisierung der Wirtschaft und die Zukunft der Menschheit.* Translated by Vicente Colon and Katrin Gruber. Munich: Luchterhand, 1997.

Gustafson C., and P. Juviler, eds. *Religion and Human Rights: Competing Claims.* New York: M. E. Sharpe, 1999.

Habermas, J. *Der philosophische Diskurs der Moderne: Zwölf Vorlesungen.* Frankfurt am Main: Suhrkamp, 1985; in English, *The Philosophical Discourse of Modernity: Twelve Lectures.* Trans. Frederick G. Lawrence. Cambridge, Mass.: MIT Press, 1987.

———. *The Theory of Communicative Action.* Vol. 1: *Reason and the Rationalization of Society.* Vol. 2: : *Lifeworld and System: A Critique of Functionalist Reason.* Boston: Beacon Press, 1984, 1987.

Haddad, Lawrence, John Hoddinott, and Harold Alderman, eds. *Intrahousehold Resource Allocation in Developing Countries: Models, Methods, and Policies.* Baltimore: Johns Hopkins University Press, 1997.

Hadot, Pierre. *Exercises spirituels et philosophie antique.* Paris: Etudes Augustiniennes, 1987.

Harvey, David. *The Condition of Postmodernity.* Oxford: Blackwell, 1990.

Heelas, Paul, Scott Lash, and Paul Morris, eds. *Detraditionalization: Critical Reflections on Authority and Identity.* Oxford: Blackwell, 1996.

Heidegger, Martin. *Zur Sache des Denkens*. Tübingen: Max Niemeyer Verlag, 1969.

Hellyer, Paul. *Stop: Think*. Toronto: Chimo Media, 1999.

Himmelfarb, Gertrude. *One Nation, Two Cultures*. New York: Vintage, 1999.

Hobbes, T. *Leviathan*. Chicago: Encyclopaedia Britannica, 1978.

Hobsbawm, Eric. *The Age of Extremes*. New York: Vintage Books, 1996.

Hobsbawm, Eric, and Terence Ranger, eds. *The Invention of Tradition*. Cambridge: Cambridge University Press, 1983.

Hoffman, Stanley. *Duties beyond Borders: On the Limits and Possibilities of Ethical International Politics*. Syracuse, N.Y.: Syracuse University Press, 1981.

Hude, H. *Ethique et Politique*. Paris: Editions Universitaires, 1992.

Human Development Report of the United Nations Development Program. New York: Oxford University Press, 1995.

Huntington, Samuel P. *The Clash of Civilizations and the Remaking of the World Order*. New York: Simon and Schuster, 1996.

ICPQL. *Caring for the Future*. Report of the Independent Commission on Population and Quality of Life. Oxford and London: Oxford University Press, 1996.

Jack, Homer A. *Religion in the Struggle for World Community*. New York: World Conference on Religion and Peace, 1980.

Jacobson, H. K. *Networks of Interdependence: International Organisations and the Global Political System*. New York: Knopf, 1979.

Jameson, Fredric, and Masao Miyoshi, eds. *The Cultures of Globalization*. Durham, N.C.: Duke University Press, 1998.

Jaquette, Jane S. "The Family as a Development Issue." In *Women at the Center: Development Issues and Practices for the 1990s*, ed. Gay Young, Vidyamali Samarasinghe, and Ken Kusterer. West Hartford, Conn.: Kumarian Press, 1995.

Jauss, Hans Robert. *Toward an Aesthetics of Reception*. Minneapolis: University of Minnesota, 1982.

Johnson, Glen M. "Writing the Universal Declaration of Human Rights." In *The Universal Declaration of Human Rights: 45th Anniversary (1948–1993)*. Paris: UNESCO, 1994.

Johnson, James Turner. *The Quest for Peace: Three Moral Traditions in Western Cultural History.* Princeton, N.J.: Princeton University Press, 1987.

Jonas, Hans. *Das Prinzip Verantwortung: Versuch einer Ethik für die technologische Zivilisation.* Frankfurt: Insel, 1979.

Jouvenel, Bertrand de. *The Art of Conjecture.* Translated by Nikita Lary. New York: Basic Books, 1967.

Juergensmeyer, Mark. *The New Cold War: Religious Nationalism Confronts the Secular State.* Berkeley: University of California Press, 1993.

Kaplan, Robert D. *The Coming Anarchy: Shattering the Dreams of the Post Cold War.* New York: Random House, 1999.

Kennedy, Paul. *Preparing for the Twenty-first Century.* New York: Random House, 1993.

Kessler, Diane, ed. *Documents from the WCC Eighth Assembly in Harare* (December 3–14, 1998). Forthcoming.

Kidder, Rushworth M. *How Good People Make Tough Choices.* New York: William Morrow, 1995.

———. *Shared Values for a Troubled World.* San Francisco: Jossey-Bass, 1994.

Kidder, Rushworth M., and W. Loges. *Global Values, Moral Boundaries: A Pilot Survey.* The Institute for Global Ethics, State of the World Forum, San Francisco, October 3–6, 1996. Bet Schuman, 1997.

Kim, Yersu J. "The Idea of Cultural Identity and Problems of Cultural Relativism." Occasional Paper No. 40, the Woodrow Wilson Center for Scholars. Washington, D.C., 1990.

———. "Universality as a Regulative Ideal." In *Universalismus, Universalität,* ed. M. Buhr, E. Chitas, and M. Fisher. Salzburg: CEPI, 1998.

Kim, Yersu J., ed. *An Emerging Theology in World Perspective.* Mystic, Conn.: Twenty-third Publications, 1988.

King, Alexander, and Bertrand Schneider. *The First Global Revolution: A Report by the Council of the Club of Rome.* New York: Pantheon Books, 1991.

Korten, David. *When Corporations Rule the World.* West Hartford, Conn.: Kumarian Press, 1995.

Küng, Hans. *Christianity and the World Religions: Paths to Dialogue with Islam, Hinduism, and Buddhism.* New York: Doubleday, 1986.

————. *A Global Ethic for Global Politics and Economics.* New York: Oxford University Press, 1998. First published as *Weltethos für Weltpolitik und Weltwirtschaft.* Munich: Piper, 1997.

————. *Global Responsibility: In Search of a New World Ethic.* New York: Crossroad, 1991.

————. *Towards a Planetary Code of Ethics: Ethical Foundations of a Culture of Peace.* Paris: UNESCO, 1996.

Küng, Hans, ed. *Yes to a Global Ethic.* New York: Continuum, 1996. First published as *Ja zum Weltethos: Perspectiven für die Suche nach Orientierung.* Munich: Piper, 1995.

Küng, Hans, and Jürgen Moltmann, eds. *The Ethics of World Religions and Human Rights.* London: SCM Press, 1990.

Küng, Hans, and Karl-Joseph Kuschel. *A Global Ethic: The Declaration of the Parliament of the World's Religions.* New York: Continuum, 1993.

Kuyper, Abraham. *Lectures on Calvinism: The 1898 Stone Lectures at Princeton University.* Grand Rapids, Mich.: Eerdmans, 1961.

Lakeland, Paul. *Theology and Critical Theory: The Discourse of the Church.* Nashville: Abingdon, 1990.

Landis, David. *The Wealth and Poverty of Nations.* New York: W. W. Norton, 1998.

Lash, Scott. *Sociology of Postmodernism.* London: Routledge, 1990.

Laszlo, Ervin, et al. *Goals for Mankind.* New York: E. P. Dutton, 1977.

Latourelle, René, and Rino Fischiella. *The Dictionary of Fundamental Theology.* New York: Crossroad, 1994.

Leo, John. "Are Women Male Clones?" *Time,* August 18, 1986, 63.

Levinas, E. *Ethique et Infini.* Paris: Fayard, 1982.

Lippman, Walter. *Essays in Public Philosophy.* Boston: Little, Brown, 1955.

Litonjua, M. D. "Global Capitalism." *Theology Today* 56, no. 2 (July 1999): 210ff.

Lonergan, Bernard. *Method in Theology.* Philadelphia: Westminster Press, 1982.

Lovin, Robin. *Reinhold Niebuhr and Christian Realism.* New York: Cambridge University Press, 1995.

Lugo, Luis, ed. *Religion, Pluralism, and Public Life: Abraham Kuyper's Legacy for the Twenty-first Century.* Grand Rapids, Mich.: Eerdmans, forthcoming.

Lütterfelds, W., and Th. Mohrs. *Eine Welt-eine Moral? Eine Kontroverse Debatte.* Darmstadt: Wissenschaftlische Buchgesellschaft, 1997.

Lyon, David. *Postmodernity.* Minneapolis: University of Minnesota Press, 1994.

Lyotard, François. *Moralités Postmodernes.* Paris: Galilée, 1993.

MacCoby, Eleanor E., and Robert Monokin. *Dividing the Child: Social and Legal Dilemmas of Custody.* Cambridge: Harvard University Press, 1992.

MacIntyre, Alasdair. *After Virtue: A Study in Moral Theory.* Notre Dame, Ind.: University of Notre Dame Press, 1984.

———. *Three Rival Versions of Moral Enquiry: Encyclopaedia, Genealogy, and Tradition.* Notre Dame, Ind.: University of Notre Dame Press, 1991.

———. *Whose Justice? Which Rationality?* Notre Dame, Ind.: University of Notre Dame Press, 1988.

Mackie, John. *Ethics, Inventing Right and Wrong.* New York: Penguin, 1977.

Mahbubani, Kishore. "The Pacific Way." *Foreign Affairs* 74 (January–February 1995).

Mann, Thomas. "The Collectivist Betrayal." *The UNESCO Courier: A Window Open on the World* 47 (May 5, 1994): 44–45.

———. "The Downfall of Idealism." *The UNESCO Courier: A Window Open on the World* 47 (June 6, 1994): 46–47.

Marion, Jean-Luc. *God without Being.* Chicago: University of Chicago Press, 1995.

Markoff, John, and Veronica Montecinos. "The Ubiquitous Rise of Economists." *Journal of Public Policy* 13, no. 1 (1993).

Marpel, D. R., and T. Nardin, eds. *International Society: Diverse Ethical Perspectives.* Princeton, N.J.: Princeton University Press, 1998.

Mason, Mary Ann, Arlene Skolnick, and Stephen D. Sugarman, eds. *All Our Families: New Policies for a New Century.* New York: Oxford University Press, 1998.

Matilal, Bimal K. "Pluralism, Relativism, and Interaction between Cultures." In *Culture and Modernity: East-West Philosophical Perspectives,* ed. Eliot Deutsch. Honolulu: University of Hawaii Press, 1991.

McCarthy, Thomas. *The Critical Theory of Jürgen Habermas.* Cambridge, Mass.: MIT Press, 1978.

McKibben, Bill. *The End of Nature.* 10th anniversary ed. New York: Anchor Books, 1999.

McLanahan, Sara, and Gary Sandefur, *Growing Up with a Single Parent: What Helps, What Hurts.* Cambridge: Harvard University Press, 1994.

Midgely, Mary. *The Ethical Primate: Humans, Freedom, and Morality.* New York: Routledge, 1996.

Milbank, John. *Theology and Social Theory: Beyond Secular Reason.* Oxford: Blackwell, 1990.

Miller, Richard. *Moral Differences: Truth, Justice, and Conscience in a World of Conflict.* Princeton, N.J.: Princeton University Press, 1992.

Mitchell, Joshua. *Not by Reason Alone: Religion, History, and Identity in Early Modern Political Thought.* Chicago: University of Chicago Press, 1993.

Myklebust, O. G. *The Study of Missions in Theological Education.* 2 vols. Oslo: Egede Instituttet, 1955, 1957.

Nelson, N. *Morality: What's in It for Me?* Boulder, Colo.: Westview Press, 1991.

Nelson, Robert H. *Reaching for Heaven on Earth: The Theological Meaning of Economics.* Lanham, Md.: Rowman & Littlefield, 1993.

Neville, Robert Cummings, ed. *The Human Condition and Ultimate Realities.* 3 vols. Albany: State University of New York Press, forthcoming.

Newbigin, Lesslie. *The Gospel in a Pluralist Society.* Grand Rapids, Mich.: Eerdmans; Geneva: World Council of Churches, 1989.

Niebuhr, Reinhold. *The Nature and Destiny of Man.* 2 vols. New York: Charles Scribner's Sons, 1939–41.

————. *Structure of Nations and Empires.* New York: Charles Scribner's Sons, 1959.

Nielson, Kai. *Ethics without God.* New York: Prometheus Books, 1990.

Noble, David. *The Religion of Technology.* New York: Alfred Knopf, 1997.

————. *A World without Women: The Christian Clerical Culture of Modern Science.* New York: Oxford University Press, 1992.

Nora, Simon, and Alain Minc. *L'Informatisation de la société.* Paris: La Documentation Française, 1980.

Nussbaum, Martha. *Meaning and Method: Essays in Honour of Hilary Putnam.* New York: Cambridge University Press, 1990.

Nussbaum, Martha, and Amartya K. Sen, eds. *The Quality of Life.* Oxford: Clarendon, 1993.

Nussbaum, Martha, and Jonathan Glover, eds. *Women, Culture, and Development.* Oxford: Clarendon, 1995.

O'Brien, D. J., and T. A. Shannon, *Renewing the Earth: Catholic Documents on Peace, Justice, and Liberation.* New York: Doubleday, 1997.

O'Collins, Gerald. *Fundamental Theology.* New York: Paulist, 1981.

Pears, Ian. *An Instance of the Fingerpost.* New York: Penguin Putnam, 1998.

Peccei, Aurelio. *The Human Quality.* Oxford and New York: Pergamon Press, 1977.

Peukert, Helmut. *Science, Action, and Fundamental Theology.* Cambridge, Mass.: MIT Press, 1986

Plaskow, Judith. *Sex, Sin, and Grace: Women's Experience and the Theologies of Reinhold Niebuhr and Paul Tillich.* Lanham, Md.: University Press of America, 1980.

Pittman, Don A. et al. *Ministry and Theology in Global Perspective.* Grand Rapids, Mich.: Eerdmans, 1996.

Popenoe, David. *Life without Father.* New York: Free Press, 1996.

Popenoe, David, Jean Bethke Elshtain, and David Blankenhorn, eds. *Promises to Keep: Decline and Renewal of Marriage in America.* Lanham, Md.: Rowman and Littlefield, 1996.

Popenoe, David, and Barbara Dafoe Whitehead. *Should We Live Together? What Young Adults Need to Know about Cohabita-*

tion before Marriage. New Brunswick, N.J.: National Marriage Project, 1999.

Poster, Mark. *The Mode of Information: Poststructuralism and Social Context*. Cambridge, England: Polity Press, 1990.

Rabinowicz, W. *Universalisability*. Dordrecht, Netherlands: Reidel, 1979.

Rawls, John. *Political Liberalism*. New York: Columbia University Press, 1993.

———. *A Theory of Justice*. Cambridge: Harvard University Press, 1971.

Ricoeur, Paul. *Hermeneutics and the Human Sciences*. Cambridge: Cambridge University Press, 1981.

———. *Soi-Même comme un Autre*. Paris: Seuil, 1990.

Ritzer, George. *The McDonaldization of Society: An Investigation into the Changing Character of Contemporary Social Life*. Thousand Oaks, Calif.: Pine Forge Press, 1993.

Robertson, D. B., ed. *Voluntary Associations: A Study of Groups in Free Societies*. Richmond: John Knox Press, 1966.

Robertson, Roland. *Globalization: Social Theory and Global Culture*. London: Sage, 1992.

———. "Glocalization: Time-Space and Homogeneity-Heterogeneity." In *Global Modernities*, ed. Mike Featherstone, Scott Lash, and Roland Robertson. London: Sage, 1995.

———. "Religion and the Global Field." *Social Compass* 41, no. 1 (1994).

———. "The Search for Fundamentals in Global Perspective." In *The Search for Fundamentals: The Process of Modernisation and the Quest for Meaning*, ed. Lieteke van Vucht Tijssen, Jan Berting, and Frank Lechner. Dordrecht, Netherlands: Kluwer Academic Publishers, 1995.

———. "Values and Globalization: Communitarianism and Globality." In *Identity, Culture, and Globalization*, ed. Luiz Edwards Soares. Rio de Janeiro: UNESCO, 1997.

Robertson, Roland, and H. H. Khondker. "Discourses of Globalization: Preliminary Considerations." *International Sociology* 13, no. 1 (1998).

Rodrik, Dani. *Has Globalization Gone Too Far?* Washington, D.C.: Institute for International Economics, 1997.

Sandel, Michael. *Democracy's Discontent: America in Search of a Public Philosophy.* Cambridge: Harvard University Press, 1996.

Sanderson, Stephen K., ed. *Civilizations and World Systems.* London: Sage, 1995.

Sassen, Saskia. *Globalization and Its Discontents.* New York: New Press, 1998.

———. *Losing Control? Sovereignty in an Age of Globalization.* New York: Columbia University Press, 1996.

Schmidt, Helmut. Letter accompanying "A Declaration of Human Responsibilities, Proposed by the InterAction Council," September 3, 1997.

Schreiter, R. *Constructing Local Theologies.* Maryknoll, N.Y.: Orbis Books, 1985.

———. *The New Catholicity: Globalization and Contextuality.* Maryknoll, N.Y.: Orbis Books, 1996.

———. *Reconciliation.* Maryknoll, N.Y.: Orbis Books, 1992.

Schweiker, William. "Accounting for Ourselves: Accounting Practice and the Discourse of Ethics." *Accounting, Organizations, and Society* 18, nos. 2–3 (1993): 231–52.

———. "Power and the Agency of God." *Theology Today* 52, no. 2 (1995): 204–24.

———. *Power, Value, and Conviction: Theological Ethics in a Postmodern Age.* Cleveland: Pilgrim Press, 1998.

———. *Responsibility and Christian Ethics.* Cambridge: Cambridge University Press, 1995.

Schweiker, William, and C. Edward Arrington. "The Rhetoric and Rationality of Accounting Practice." *Accounting, Organizations and Society* 17, no. 6 (1992): 511–33

Sen, Amartya. *Development as Freedom.* New York: Knopf, 1999.

———. "Gender and Cooperative Conflicts." In *Persistent Inequalities: Women and World Development,* ed. Irene Tinker. New York: Oxford University Press, 1990.

Shafer, Ingrid. "Philosophical and Religious Foundations of a Global Ethic." Paper presented at the University of California, Berkeley, June 20–21, 1995.

Shapiro, Ian, and Lea Brilmayer, eds. *Global Justice.* Nomos 41. New York: New York University Press, 1999.

Sherman, Amy L. *The Soul of Development*. New York: Oxford University Press, 1997.

Shriver, Donald W., Jr. *An Ethic for Enemies: Forgiveness in Politics*. New York: Oxford University Press, 1995.

———. *Rich Man, Poor Man*. Richmond: John Knox, 1972.

Shriver, Donald W., Jr. John R. Earle, and Dean D. Knudsen *Spindles and Spires: A Re-Study of Religion and Social Change in Gastonia*. Atlanta: John Knox, 1996.

Sidgwick, Henry. *The Methods of Ethics*. 1st ed. London: Macmillan, 1874; 7th ed., 1907; reprint, Chicago: University of Chicago Press, 1962.

Sivaraksa, Sulak. *Seeds of Peace: A Buddhist Vision for Renewing Society*. Berkeley and Bangkok: Parallax Press, 1992.

Skillen, James. "From Covenant of Grace to Equitable Public Pluralism: The Dutch Calvinist Contribution." *Calvin Theological Journal* 31, no. 1 (April 1996): 67–96.

Smith, Gary, ed. *On Walter Benjamin: Critical Essays and Reflections*. Cambridge, Mass.: MIT Press, 1988.

Smith, W. C. *Towards a World Theology: Faith and the Comparative History of Religion*. Maryknoll, N.Y.: Orbis Books, 1981.

Smuts, Barbara. "The Evolutionary Origins of Patriarchy." *Human Nature* 6 (1995): 1–32.

———. "Male Aggression against Women: An Evolutionary Perspective." *Human Nature* 3 (1992): 1–44.

Stackhouse, Max L. *Covenant and Commitments: Faith, Family, and Economic Life*. Louisville: Westminster/John Knox Press, 1997.

———. *Creeds, Society and Human Rights: A Study in Three Societies*. Grand Rapids, Mich.: Eerdmans, 1984; reprinted: Parthenon Press, 1996).

———. *Ethics and the Urban Ethos*. Boston: Beacon Press, 1972.

———. "Human Rights and Public Theology: The Basic Validation of Human Rights." In *Religion and Human Rights: Competing Claims?* ed. Carrie Gustafson and Peter Juviler. New York: M. E. Sharpe, 1999, 12–30.

———. "Public Theology and Ethical Judgment." In *East and West, Religious Ethics: Proceedings of the Third Symposium* of *Sino-American Philosophy and Religious Studies,* Chinese edition ed. Zhang Zhegang and Mel Stewart. Beijing: University of Beijing, 1998; Eng. ed., *Theology Today* 54 (July 1997): 165–79.

———. *Public Theology and Political Economy: Christian Stewardship in Modern Society.* Grand Rapids, Mich: Eerdmans, 1987; reprinted, University Press of America, 1991. Korean ed., trans. Yung and Geun. Seoul: Logos Press, 1991.

———. "Theology and the Economic Life of Society in a Global Era...." In *Policy Reform and Moral Grounding,* ed. T. W. Boxx. Latrobe, Pa.: Center for Economic and Policy Education, 1996.

———. "The Vocation of Christian Ethics Today." *Princeton Theological Seminary Bulletin,* n.s., 16, no. 3 (1995): 284–312.

Stackhouse, Max L., with Peter Berger, Dennis McCann, and Douglas Meeks. *Christian Social Ethics and the Globalization of Economic Life.* Christian Ethics and Economic Life 1. Nashville: Abingdon, 1995.

Stackhouse, Max L., Tim Dearborne, and Scott Paeth, eds. *The Local Church in a Global Era.* Grand Rapids, Mich.: Eerdmans, 2000.

Stackhouse, Max L., with Dennis McCann, Shirley Roels, et al., eds. *On Moral Business: Classical and Contemporary Resources on Ethics and Economic Life.* Grand Rapids, Mich: Eerdmans, 1995.

Stackhouse, Max L., with Lamin Sanneh, Mark Heim, et al. *Apologia: Contextualization, Globalization and Mission in Theological Education.* Grand Rapids, Mich.: Eerdmans, 1988.

Swidler, Leonard, ed. *Toward a Universal Theology of Religion.* Maryknoll, N.Y.: Orbis Books, 1987.

Taylor, Mark C. *Erring: A Postmodern A/theology.* Chicago: University of Chicago Press, 1984.

Thompson, John B., and David Head, eds. *Habermas: Critical Debates.* Cambridge, Mass.: MIT Press, 1982.

Tinder, Glenn. *The Political Meaning of Christianity.* Baton Rouge: Louisiana State University Press, 1990.

Tomlinson, John. *Cultural Imperialism.* Baltimore: Johns Hopkins University Press, 1991.

Toulmin, Stephen. *Cosmopolis: The Hidden Agenda of Modernity.* Glencoe, Ill.: Free Press, 1990.

Townsend, John Marshall. *What Women Want, What Men Want.* New York: Oxford University Press, 1998.

Tracy, David. *The Analogical Imagination: Christian Theology and the Culture of Pluralism.* New York: Crossroad, 1981.

———. *Blessed Rage for Order: The New Pluralism in Theology.* Chicago: University of Chicago Press, 1995.

———. *On Naming the Present: God, Hermeneutics, and Church.* Maryknoll, N.Y.: Orbis Books, 1994.

———. *Plurality and Ambiguity: Hermeneutics, Religion, Hope.* Chicago: University of Chicago Press, 1994.

———. *This Side of God.* Chicago: University of Chicago Press, forthcoming.

———. "Word, Language, and Religion." In *Religione, Parola, Scrittura,* ed. Marco Olivetti. Rome: Archivio de Filosofia, 1992.

Trible, Phillis. *God and the Rhetoric of Sexuality.* Philadelphia: Fortress Press, 1978.

Turner, Bryan, ed. *Themes of Modernity and Postmodernity.* London: Sage, 1990.

U.S. Agency for International Development. "The Family and Development Initiative." Washington, D.C.: USAID, 1990.

Valdes, Margarita M. "Inequality in Capabilities between Men and Women in Mexico." In *Women, Culture, and Development,* ed. Martha Nussbaum and Jonathan Glover. Oxford: Clarendon Press, 1995.

van der Meer, Peter. *Religious Nationalism: Hindus and Muslims in India.* Berkeley: University of California Press, 1994.

van der Toorn, K., et al., eds. *Dictionary of Deities and Demons.* 2d ed. Leiden: Brill; Grand Rapids, Mich.: Eerdmans, 1999.

van Huyssteen, J. Wentzel. *Essays in Postfoundationalist Theology.* Grand Rapids, Mich.: Eerdmans, 1998.

Van Leeuwen, Arend Th. *Christianity in World History: The Meeting of the Faiths of East and West.* Trans. H. H. Hoskins. New York: Charles Scribner's Sons, 1964.

Van Leeuwen, Mary Stewart. "Abraham Kuyper and the Cult of True Womanhood: An Analysis of *De Eerepositie der Vrouw*." *Calvin Theological Journal* 31 (April 1996): 97–124.

———. "The Carrot and the Stick: Abraham Kuyper on Gender, Family, and Class." In *Religion, Pluralism, and Public Life: Abraham Kuyper's Legacy for the Twenty-first Century*, ed. Luis Lugo. Grand Rapids, Mich.: Eerdmans, forthcoming.

———. *Gender and Grace: Love, Work, and Parenting in a Changing World*. Downers Grove, Ill.: InterVarsity Press, 1990.

———. "Principalities, Powers, and Gender Relations." *Crux: A Quarterly Journal of Christian Thought and Opinion* 31 (September 1994): 120–30.

———. "The Promise Keepers and Proof-Text Poker." *Sojourners* 27 (January–February 1998): 16–21.

———. "Servanthood or Soft Patriarchy? A Christian Feminist Looks at the Promise Keepers Movement." *Journal of Men's Studies* 5 (February 1997): 233–61.

Van Leeuwen, Mary Stewart, et al. *After Eden: Facing the Challenge of Gender Reconciliation*. Grand Rapids, Mich.: Eerdmans, 1993.

Waite, Linda. *The Case for Marriage*. Cambridge: Harvard University Press, 1999.

———. "Does Marriage Matter?" *Demography* 32 (November 1995): 483–507.

Wallerstein, Immanuel Maurice. *The Modern World System*. 3 vols. New York: Cambridge University Press, 1974, 1980, 1989.

Wallerstein, Judith S., and Sandra Blakeslee. *Second Chances: Men, Women. and Children a Decade after Divorce*. Boston: Houghton Mifflin, 1989.

Walsh, Michael, and Brian Davies, eds. *Proclaiming Justice and Peace: Papal Documents from "Rerum Novarum" through "Centesimus Annus."* Mystic, Conn.: Twenty-third Publications, 1993.

Walzer, Michael. *Spheres of Justice: A Defense of Pluralism and Equality*. New York: Basic Books, 1983.

———. *Thick and Thin: Moral Argument at Home and Abroad*. London: Basic Books, 1983.

Warren, Heather A. *Theologians of a New World Order: Reinhold Niebuhr and the Christian Realists, 1920–1948.* New York: Oxford University Press, 1997.

Waters, Malcolm. *Globalization.* London and New York: Routledge, 1995.

Watson, James L. *Golden Arches East: McDonald's in East Asia.* Stanford, Calif.: Stanford University Press, 1997.

Weigel G., and R. Royal, eds. *A Century of Catholic Social Thought: Essays on "Rerum Novarum" and Nine Other Key Documents.* Washington, D.C.: Ethics and Public Policy Center, 1991.

Weisner, Merry E. "The Early Modern Period: Religion, the Family, and Women's Public Roles." In *Religion, Feminism, and the Family,* ed. Anne Carr and Mary Stewart Van Leeuwen Louisville: Westminster/John Knox Press, 1996.

White, Stephen K. *The Recent Works of Jürgen Habermas: Reason, Justice, and Modernity.* Cambridge: Cambridge University Press, 1988.

Whitehead, Barbara Dafoe. *The Divorce Culture.* New York: Knopf, 1997.

Williams, Bernard. *Ethics and the Limits of Philosophy.* Cambridge: Harvard University Press, 1985.

Wink, W. *Engaging the Powers: Discernment and Resistance in a World of Domination.* Philadelphia: Fortress Press, 1992.

———. *Naming the Powers: The Language of Power in the New Testament.* Philadelphia: Fortress Press, 1984.

———. *Unmasking the Powers: The Invisible Forces That Determine Human Existence.* Philadelphia: Fortress Press, 1986.

Witte, John Jr., ed. *Christianity and Democracy in Global Context.* San Francisco: Westview, 1993.

———. *From Sacrament to Contract: Marriage, Religion, and Law in the Western Tradition.* Louisville: Westminster/John Knox Press, 1997.

Wolters, Albert. *Creation Regained: Biblical Basics for a Reformational Worldview.* Grand Rapids, Mich.: Eerdmans, 1985.

World Commission on Culture and Development. *Our Creative Diversity.* Paris: UNESCO, 1995.

Wright, Robert. *The Moral Animal.* New York: Vintage, 1994.

Wuthnow R., and V. A. Hodgkinson, eds. *Faith and Philanthropy in America.* Baltimore: Jossey-Bass, 1990.

Young, Gay, Vidyamali Samarasinghe, and Ken Kusterer, eds. *Women at the Center: Development Issues and Practices for the 1990s.* West Hartford, Conn.: Kumarian Press, 1995.

Yutaka, Y. *Religions of the World.* Translated by C. Jin. Seoul: Bulgyo-Sidae-Sa, n.d.

INDEX

Adorno, Theodor, 234, 236
Agenda 21, 74–75
AIDS, 211
Alchemist, The (Jonson), 113
Alperovitz, Gar, 148n.9
American Council for the United
    Nations University, 91
Americanization, 62
Amnesty International, 85
Andropov, Yuri, 145n.4
annals schools, the, 32n.40
Annan, Kofi, 4–5
Anselm, 246
anthropology, 39, 148
antiglobalism, 61–62
Apel, Karl-Otto, 89, 94–95
Appadurai, Arjun, 124
architecture, 47
Ardrey, Robert, 156
Arendt, Hannah, 162n.38
argumentation, 238
Aristotle, 108n.3, 191, 221, 235,
    238, 246
Arrighi, Giovanni, 3–4
Association of Theological Schools,
    28, 30
Atlan, Henri, 89
Augustine, St., 111n.5, 113, 123,
    127, 246
authenticity, 63–64
authorities, the, 45–50

Baillie, Gil, 152
Bainton, Roland, 148–49n.12
Balasuriya, Tissa, 28
Balkan wars, 169n.46. *See also*
    Bosnia; Kosovo

Barth, Karl, 26n.27
Bellah, Robert, 9n.10, 32n.40, 234
Benjamin, Walter, 252
Berger, Peter, 6n.6, 32n.40
Berling, Judith, 29–30
Bexell, Göran, 92n.3
biodiversity, 243
Blair, Tony, 180
Bok, Sissela, 90, 93
Bonaventure, 244, 245
Bonhoeffer, Dietrich, 158
Bosnia, 169, 176–77
Bould, Sally, 228
Boulding, Kenneth, 161
Brandt Commission, 72
Braudel, Fernand, 32n.40
Bromiley, Geoffrey, 197
Browning, Don, 29
Brundtland Commission on Envi-
    ronment and Development,
    73
Brunner, Emil, 26, 26n.27, 193–95
Bruno, Giordano, 251
Buber, Martin, 165
Buchanan, James, 232
Buddhism, 15, 97, 244, 250
Bundy, McGeorge, 141
Burke, Kenneth, 232
business, 84–85. *See also* economics
Buss, David, 215
Byrne, Peter, 8n.8

Cahill, Lisa Sowle, 225–26
Caldwell, Sarah, 6n.6
Calvin, John, 114
Camus, Albert, 157

capitalism
demonization of, 109
globalization and, 5, 5n.5, 19–20
paradox of, 122
women's roles and, 202–3
child care, 217, 218
children, 206–7, 217, 218
Chretien, Jean Louis, 251
Christianity
corporations and, 128–34
economics and, 114–17, 134–37
on humans' relation to the right
and good, 13–14
nature and, 243–44
notion of the "world" proposed
by, 110–13
violence and, 168–72
See also church, the
Christian realism, 26, 175
Chrysostom, John, 113
church, the
corporations and, 133–34
global peacemaking and, 167–72
on marriage and family, 198–201
the rebirth of imagination and,
132–33
task of, vis-à-vis transnational
agents, 138–39
as transnational, 126–28
on violence, 172–77
See also Christianity
Churchill, Winston, 48
City of God, The (Augustine),
111n.5
Clausewitz, Carl von, 183
Clement of Alexandria, 113
Club of Rome Report, 70, 87
Cole-Turner, Ron, 47
collective memory, 66–67
commercialism, 118
Commission on a Just and Lasting
Peace, 167n.44
Commission on Global
Governance, 79–80

commodification
corporations and, 124
of persons, 108–9
of the poor, 122
of religion, 65–66
communications, 235–40, 241–48.
See also mass media; Muses,
the
communicative action, 237–38
communism, 24n.25
commutative justice, 136–37
conflict resolution, 161–67
Confucianism, 15
conscientious objection, 175
consciousness, 235–36
Constantine, 21
consumerism, 65–66
corporations. *See* transnational/
multinational corporations
covenant, 18, 113–14, 248–54
covenantal theologies, 244, 245
creation, 246
credit-sharing of pensions, 218,
218–19n.53
crime, 86
Cuban Missile Crisis, 140–42, 143,
166
cult of domesticity, 203
cult of true womanhood, 203
cultural mandate, the, 185, 186–89
culture
future of traditional, 67–68
globalization as promoting
traditional, 58–59
relativization and the threat to
local, 59–63
culture wars, 62–63

Dalai Lama, the, 48
Danvers Statement, 213, 213n.43
de Certeau, Michel, 241
"Declaration of Human Duties and
Responsibilities," 83–84

"Declaration toward a Global Ethic" (Parliament of the World's Religions), 80–81
Delphic method, the, 82–83, 96
deontology, 13
Descartes, René, 235
development
  challenges to positive evaluations of, 76
  and gender relations in the non-Western world, 209–10
  the human-capabilities approach to, 219–24
dialogue, 237–38
Diamond, Jared, 8n.9
distributive justice, 136–37
diversity, 96–99
divorce, 206–8, 218–19n.53
dominions, the, 50–52
Donne, John, 142
Dulles, John Foster, 167n.44
Dupré, Louis, 245
Durkheim, Émile, 66

ecological movement
  in the 1970s, 70
  participatory sensibility and, 242–43
  principles of, 74–75
  promise of, 240
  resurgence of, 48
  universal ethics and, 102
economics
  Catholic view of, 114–15
  cultural pluralism and, 117–19
  the dignity of persons and, 107–10
  integrated view of justice and, 135–38
  neoclassical, 126n.24
  overemphasis of role of, in globalization, 54–57
  the principalities and, 37

Protestant view of, 114
  recent Christian thought on, 115–17
  three current positions on the church and, 134–35
  war and, 161–62
  See also mammon; transnational/multinational corporations
economists, 56–57
education, 46
Edwards, Jonathan, 114
Eliade, Mircea, 144, 244
Ellul, Jacques, 47
empathy, 153–55, 164
Encyclopedia of Global Problems and Human Potential, 87, 101
end of history, the, 22
energies, moral or spiritual, 33–36. *See also* authorities, the; dominions, the; powers, the; principalities, the; spheres
engineering, 47
Enlightenment, the, 15, 21, 48, 249–50
Eros, 37, 42. *See also* sexuality
eschatology, 248–54
ethics
  economics and Christian, 134–35
  global, 80–81, 84–86
  theology's relation to, 7–8
  UNESCO's project on universal, 86–100
  universal, for the twenty-first century, 100–104
  on violence, 172–77
  See also norms; theological ethics; values
ethnic cleansing, 178
ethology, 9n.10, 11
ethos, 8–9, 9n.10, 10
European Union, the, 63
evangelical churches, 213
evolutionary psychology, 214–15

family
    the church on, 198–201
    the cultural mandate and, 186–
        89
    the Hebrew Bible on, 196
    history of changes in the modern
        Western, 203–8
    the human-capabilities approach
        to development and, 219–24
    Jesus on, 196–98
    models for the future of, 211–19
    natural theology of, 192–96
    in non-Western societies, 208–9
    recovering the idea of, as a
        creational sphere, 225–30
    sphere sovereignty and, 189–92
fascism, 24n.25
Fate of the Earth, The (Schell), 146
feminism
    critique of creation story by, 195
    the family and, 229–30
    in non-Western societies, 208
    origins and results of, 201–8
    reflexive globalization and,
        184–85
Ferré, Frederick, 242
Fights, Games, and Debates
    (Rapoport), 163
film, 253
finance, 84–85. *See also* economics
Fitzgerald, Garrett, 165
Fitzgerald, P. M., 166n.42
Foucault, Michel, 91, 241
Francis of Assisi, 150, 244, 245
Frankfurt school, 236, 238
French Revolution, 24n.25
Fried, Charles, 137
Friedan, Betty, 218
Fukuyama, Francis, 23n.23, 146
functional-equality model of re-
    lations between the sexes,
    216–18, 226
fundamentalism, 60–61, 78, 213
Furet, François, 24n.25

Gamwell, Franklin I., 8n.8
Gandhi, Mahatma, 48
gender apartheid, 212
Gender Empowerment Measure,
    222, 223, 224, 225
Gender-Related Development
    Index, 222, 223–24, 225
gender relations
    the cultural mandate and, 186–89
    the family and, 225–30
    the future and, 211–19
    the human-capabilities approach
        to development and, 219–24
    in non-Western societies, 208–11
Giddens, Anthony, 232
Gilbert, Neil, 216–17
Girard, René, 152
globality, 106. *See also*
    globalization
globalization
    attacks on, 5n.5
    beginnings of, 8n.9
    capitalism and, 4–5, 19–20
    collective memory and, 66–67
    covenantal theologies and, 245
    the crisis of values and, 72–76
    defined, 53–54
    different meanings of, 184
    history of theological and ethical
        discussion of, 21–24, 25–31
    the local as in tandem with,
        64–66
    overemphasis of the role of
        economics in, 54–57
    postmodernity and, 241
    poverty and, 77–78
    the principalities and, 37
    of problems, 70–72
    relativization and, 59–63
    the "table of values" of, 122–24
    theology's task vis-à-vis, 253–54
    three dominant responses to, 5
    traditional culture and, 58
    unfounded blaming of, 63–64

globaphobia, 60
glocalization, 56, 64–65
God
    and humans' relation to the right
        and good, 13–14
    modernity and, 247
    naming, 250–51
    nature and, 243–44, 246
    as outside valuation, 128
    synthesis of self, cosmos, and,
        245–46
    task of theological ethics vis-à-
        vis, 14–15
Golden Rule, the, 79
Goldhagen, Daniel, 157
good, the (moral principle), 12–15,
    130–31
Gramsci, Antonio, 185n.3
Gregory of Nyssa, 113
Group of Experts on Women
    and Structural Change of
    the Organization for Eco-
    nomic Cooperation and
    Development, 216
gun control, 173

Habermas, Jürgen, 94, 232–40
Hampshire, Stuart, 90
Hanafi, Hassan, 89
Havel, Václav, 178, 178n.56
Hegel, G. W. F., 23n.23, 236,
    251
Heidegger, Martin, 234
Hellyer, Paul, 5n.5
Henry, Michel, 251
heritage industry, the, 65
heroes. *See* leaders
Heschel, Abraham Joshua,
    156n.27
Himmelfarb, Gertrude, 10n.11
Hinduism, 15, 250
Hitler, Adolf, 149n.12, 179
Hobsbawm, Eric, 57, 69

Hollenbach, David, 116
Holy Spirit, the, 152–53, 155
homogenization, 55–56
homosexuality, 211
Horkheimer, Max, 234, 236
human-capabilities approach to
    development, 219–24, 225
Human Development Index, 222–
    24, 222n.59, 225
Human Quality, The (Peccei),
    70–72
human rights, 99–100
hunger, 154
husbandly headship, 191–92. *See
    also* male headship
Husserl, Edmund, 235, 236

Ignatieff, Michael, 169n.46
imagination, 132–33, 134
Independent Commission on
    Disarmament and Security
    Issues, 72
Independent Commission on
    International Development
    Issues, 72
indigenous peoples, 59
indigenous religions, 244
individualism, 66, 102–3
Institute for Global Ethics, 82–83
InterAction Council, 81–82
International Association of
    Evangelicals, 28
International Criminal Court, 171,
    178
International Monetary Fund, 5n.5,
    84–85, 108
Internet, the, 243
invention of tradition, the, 57–59,
    62
Invention of Tradition, The
    (Ranger), 57
Iranian Revolution, 60
Islam, 13, 212–13, 243–44

Jaquette, Jane, 209, 226, 227
Jesus
    on anger, 158
    on mammon, 112–13
    on marriage and family, 196–98
    nonviolence of, 152
    on peacemakers, 159
    on war, 159
Joffe, Josef, 179n.57
John Paul II, Pope, 27n.32, 116, 136
John XXIII, Pope, 27
Jonson, Ben, 113
Jouvenel, Bertrand de, 96
Jubilee Year, 137n.33
Judaism, 13–14, 243–44
justice
    the church and economic, 134
    current dominant positions on Christianity and economic, 134–35
    defined, 107
    integrated view of economic, 135–38
    universal ethics and, 103
"Just Peacemaking and the Call for International Intervention for Humanitarian Rescue," 174–76
just-war theory, 159, 173, 174, 175, 176

Kabbalah, the, 250
Kagawa, Toyohiko, 150
Kant, Immanuel, 235
Kennedy, John F., 141, 144n.2, 166
Kennedy, Robert, 142
Khrushchev, Nikita, 140–41, 144, 145n.4, 166, 167
Kidder, Rushworth, 82–83, 90
Kim, Y. J., 27n.32
King, Martin Luther, Jr., 49, 158
kingdom of God, the, 13
kinship, 225–26. *See also* family

Kosovo, 161, 177–83
Koyama, Kosuke, 51, 170
Krueger, David, 116
Küng, Hans, 27, 80–82, 89, 93
Kuyper, Abraham, 185, 185n.3, 186–89, 190–91, 193
Kyi, Aung San Suu, 49

labor, 136
Landis, David, 8n.9
languages, 126–27
law, the (profession), 46
leaders, 16–18, 48–49
League of Nations, the, 23
Lebow, Richard Ned, 166–67
Lee, Hong-Koo, 89
Leo XII, Pope, 193
Leo XIII, Pope, 115, 190–91, 221
Lesher, William, 28
Levinas, Emmanuel, 250, 251
Lewin, Kurt, 144
Lewis, Flora, 178
liberalism, 205–6
liberation theology, 27, 115, 135
Lifton, Robert, 144, 145, 151, 154–55, 157
Lincoln, Abraham, 168n.44
localization, 59, 64–66. *See also* glocalization
Lubbers, Rudd, 89
Lukács, Georg, 236
Lyon, David, 232
Lyotard, Jean-François, 91, 234

MacIntyre, Alasdair, 12n.12
Maier, Charles, 145
male headship, 212, 213. *See also* husbandly headship
mammon, 37, 112–13. *See also* economics
Mandela, Nelson, 49
Mao Tse-tung, 149n.12
Marion, Jean-Luc, 251

marriage
  changes in modern Western,
    203–8
  the church on, 198–201
  and family as a creational sphere,
    225–30
  the Hebrew Bible on, 196
  the human-capabilities approach
    to development and, 219–24
  Jesus on, 196–98
  models for the future of, 211–19
  natural theology and, 192–96
  in non-Western societies, 208–9
  scripture on, 189–90
Mars, 37, 42. *See also* violence; war
Marx, Karl, 23n.23, 122, 236
Marxism, 144n.2
mass media
  effects of, 43
  global academic and cultural
    conventions and, 85
  and images of eschatological
    hope, 248–54
  the principalities and, 37
  reason and, 239–40
  and the recovery of religion as
    participation, 240–48
  See also Muses, the
Matilal, Bimal K., 93–94
maximalist morality, 90–91
Mbiti, John, 51
McCann, Dennis, 116
McCartney, Bill, 213, 214n.44
"McDonaldization," 55–56
McKibben, Bill, 23n.24
McNamara, Robert, 167
Mead, G. H., 163
Médecins Sans Frontières, 85
medicine (as a profession), 46
Mikoyan, Anastas, 141, 144n.2
Mill, J. S., 9n.10
Milosevic, Slobodan, 180
Milton, John, 113
minimalist ethics, 90–91

missionaries, 16–18
Mitchell, George, 165–66
modernity
  and the breakup of the God-self-
    cosmos synthesis, 246–47
  main consequence of, 245
  rationality and, 236–37, 239
  religion and, 249–50
  the several forms of, 249
Moltmann, Jürgen, 48
money. *See* Mammon
monogamy, 229
Morris, Desmond, 156
Mueller, John, 182n.59
Mueller, Karl, 182n.59
multiculturalism, 62–63
multiculturality, 62, 63
Multilateral Agreement on
  Investment, 85
multinational corporations. *See*
  transnational/multinational
  corporations
Murray, Patrick, 122
Muses, the
  Christianity and, 245
  current influence of, 43
  the new movements and, 240
  postmodern form of, 253–54
  as a principality, 37, 39
  religion and, 44
  theology and, 233, 247
  See also mass media
Myklevust, Olav G., 26, 26n.26

nationalism, 5, 58–59
national states, 72
NATO, 179, 180
natural law, 18n.19
nature
  God and, 246
  indigenous religions and, 244
  modernity and, 247
  the participatory sensibility and,
    242–43

nature (continued)
    prophetic religions and, 243–44
    Protestantism on, 192–93
    resurgence of concern for, 48
    universal ethics and, 102
Nazism, 145, 155, 157
neo-Marxism, 32n.40
Neville, Robert Cummings, 6n.6
Newbigin, Lesslie, 192
new movements, the, 240
new world order, the, 21–24
Niebuhr, Reinhold, 15n.16, 26
Nietzsche, Friedrich, 23n.23
nongovernmental organizations
    (NGOs), 49, 78, 85
nonviolence, 151–59
norms, 10–11. *See also* values
North American Free Trade
    Agreement, 108
Northern Ireland, 165–66, 173
nuclear weapons
    argument for dropping, in 1945,
        148n.9
    cost of, 162n.37
    "religious" meaning of, 145–48
    Soviet leaders on, 145n.4
Nussbaum, Martha, 219–22, 224,
    225–26

Obenchain, Diane, 51
oil crisis, 70
Ojukwu, Emeka, 153
Organization for Economic Co-
    operation and Development,
    216
Osiel, Mark, 173–74n.50
Osmer, Richard, 46
other, the, 249–50, 251
Our Creative Diversity (World
    Commission on Culture and
    Development), 80
Our Global Neighborhood
    (Commission on Global
    Governance), 79–80

Pacem in Terris, 27
pacifism, 153, 175
Palme Commission, 72–73
Paradise Lost (Milton), 113
para-ecclesial groups, 49–50
Paris, Peter, 49
Parliament of Religions, 28
Parliament of the World's Religions
    (Chicago, 1993), 80–81
Parsons, Talcott, 32n.40
Pascal, Blaise, 157
Passage to Modernity (Dupré), 245
Patchen, Kenneth, 148
patriarchy, 212–13, 214–15
Paul VI, Pope, 27
peace
    churches and the making of,
        167–72
    conflict resolution and, 161–67
    theories on making, 159–61
Pears, Iain, 201
Peccei, Aurelio, 70–72, 101
pensions, 218–19
pentecostal churches, 213
Pérez de Cuéllar, Javier, 80
philosophy, 88–89
Phutthathat, 97
Plato, 14, 235
pluralism, 117–19
Polanyi, Michael, 120
Political Liberalism (Rawls), 97
political science, 37
poor, the, 109, 122, 136. *See also*
    poverty
pop art, 253
Populorum Progressio, 27
Poster, Mark, 232
postmodernism, 16, 165, 240–48,
    249
poverty, 77. *See also* poor, the
power, 162, 162n.38. *See also*
    powers, the
powers, the, 31–36, 36n.48
Presbyterian Church (USA), 173–76

principalities, the, 36–39
problems, global, 71–72, 101–3
productive justice, 136–37
Promise Keepers, 213
Protestantism, 27–28, 114, 192–93
psychology, 37, 214–15
public theology, 7, 43, 52
Puritans, the, 10n.11

Quakers, 153

Ranger, Terence, 57
rap music, 253
Rapoport, Anatol, 161–65
rational-choice theory, 126n.24
rationality, 232–40
Rauschenbusch, Walter, 115
Rawls, John, 97
reflexive globalization, 184–85
reformers, 16–18
regencies, 36n.48
relativism, 199
relativization, 59–63
religion
    commodification of, 65–66
    defined, 38
    disciplines that study, 38–39
    as a "dominion," 50–51
    future of traditional, 67–68
    globalization's promotion of
        traditional, 59
    Marxian view of, 144n.2
    modernity and, 249–50
    and positive analysis of
        globalization, 6
    as a principality, 43–44
    reason for resurgence of, 240
    recovery of, as participation,
        240–48
    roots of term, 38n.49
    as a sphere, 40–41
    as transnational, 126–27
    violence and, 143–51
Rerum Novarum, 190–91

Ricoeur, Paul, 251
right, the (moral principle), 12–15
"Rio Declaration on Environment
    and Development," 74–75
Robertson, Roland, 106, 107
Roman Catholic Church, 27,
    114–15
Roosevelt, Eleanor, 48
Rorty, Richard, 91
Rousseau, Jean-Jacques, 98
Royal, R., 27n.32
Rubenstein, Richard, 165
Rusk, Dean, 144
Rwanda, 177, 179

salvation, 111
sanctions, 181–82
Sanneh, Lamin, 51
Sassen, Saskia, 8n.9, 106, 107
Schell, Jonathan, 146–47, 148
Schmidt, Helmut, 81
Scholem, Gershom, 250
Schreiter, Robert, 29
Schweiker, William, 12n.12, 41–42
Schweitzer, Albert, 48
science, 47, 242–43, 247
scripture, 149–50, 187–88, 196–97
In Search of Wisdom for the World.
    See Club of Rome Report
self, the, 245–46, 247
Sen, Amartya, 219–21, 224, 225,
    227
separate spheres doctrine, 203–8,
    212–15
sexuality, 42, 198–99, 225. *See also*
    Eros
Shared Values for a Troubled World
    (Kidder), 82
Sharp, Gene, 152
Sherman, Amy L., 34n.46
Shriver, Donald, Jr., 28, 42
Silver, Beverly, 3–4
sin, 111, 111n.5
slavery, 109

Smith, Wilfred Cantwell, 28
Smuts, Barbara, 214–15
social-partnership model of gender
    relations, 218–19, 226, 229–
    30
social sciences
    and the recovery of religion as
    participation, 240–48
    theology and the rationality of,
    232–40
    See also specific social sciences
sociology, 39
Somalia, 177
South Africa, 158
spheres
    doctrine of hierarchy of gendered,
    212–15
    doctrine of men's and women's
    separate, 203–4
    overview of the, 39–45
    sovereignty and the, 189–92
sphere sovereignty, 189–92
Stackhouse, Max L., 9n.10, 19n.19,
    41n.50, 116, 192–93, 231,
    244
Stalin, Joseph, 149n.12
Star Trek, 160
"State of the Future," 91
Stein, Janice Gross, 166–67
Stimson, Henry, 147, 148n.9
subsidiarity, 185n.3, 189–92,
    221

table of values, the, 123–25,
    126
Taliban, the, 212–13, 219
Taylor, Charles, 97
technology, 47, 241–48. *See also*
    mass media
teleology, 13
television, 253
Teresa, Mother, 48, 150
Tertullian, 113
Thangaraj, Thomas, 51

theological ethics
    defined, 38
    "ethos" and, 8–9
    the tasks of, 9–18
theology
    current task of, 252–54
    ethics's relation to, 7–8
    globalization and, 25–31
    mass media and, 252
    nonviolence and, 151–59
    rationality, the social sciences,
    and, 232–40
    and recovery of religion as
    participation, 247–48
    See also theological ethics
Third Millennium Project, 83–84
Third World, the, 77
Thomas Aquinas, 114, 191, 221,
    246
Tillich, Paul, 115
Tocqueville, Alexis de, 122
Toulmin, Stephen, 242
tourism, 65
Tracy, David, 43
tradition
    collective memory and, 66–67
    globalization and the authenticity
    of, 63–66
    invention of, 57–59, 62
    reconstruction of, 67
transnational/multinational
        corporations
    and attacks on globalization,
    5n.5
    the church and, 127–28, 133–34
    defined, 119–20
    "locality" of, 125
    overview of social and cultural
    roles of, 120–25
    as presupposing human beings as
    historical agents, 125–26
    table of values and, 126
    the values of, 128–31
Trible, Phyllis, 188

Trinity, the, 155
Troeltsch, Ernst, 32n.40, 122, 185n.3
Troeltsch's paradox, 122, 130
Turnbull, Colin, 156
turn to the subject, the, 235–36
Tutu, Desmond, 49, 150, 158, 159, 165
two-kingdom ethic, 168–69
tyranny, 117–18, 130–31

UNESCO, 85, 86–100
UNICEF, 85
United Nations, the, 72–74, 85, 171
United Nations Development Program (UNDP), 222–23, 228
United Nations System of National Accounts, 210
"Universal Declaration of Human Responsibilities" (InterAction Council), 81–82
"Universal Declaration of Human Rights" (UN), 85, 99
Universal Ethics Project, 86–100
universality, 96–99
urbanization, 210–11
U.S. Agency for International Development (USAID), 226

Valencia Declaration, 83–84
values
    attempts to find universal, 78, 79–84
    corporations and the table of, 122–24
    response to the crisis in, 72–76
    theological ethics and, 10–11
    See also table of values, the
Van Leeuwen, Arend, 26, 27n.29
Van Leeuwen, Mary Stewart, 42
Vatican II, 27

Vattimo, Gianni, 232
Verhey, Allen, 46–47
Veritatis Splendor, 27n.32
Vietnam War, 170
violence
    antiglobalism and, 61
    approaches to the resolution of, 161–67
    Arendt on, 162n.38
    churches' role in curtailing, 168–72
    ethical question of using violence in curtailing, 172–77
    extent of twentieth-century, 143–44
    Kosovo as test case of resolving, 177–83
    religion and, 144–45
    scripture and, 149–50
    theology and a politics opposed to, 151–59
    theories on overcoming, 159–61
    See also Mars

Wallerstein, Immanuel, 32n.40, 54
Walzer, Michael, 90–91, 97–98, 117, 131, 185n.3
Wan, Sze-Kar, 51
war, 177–83. *See also* Mars; violence
Weber, Max, 32n.40, 121, 234, 236, 239, 240
Weigel, G., 27n.32
Wei-ming, Tu, 89
Wesley, John, 114
Westphalia, Treaty of, 58
Whitehead, Alfred North, 251
Wicca, 62
Willkie, Wendell, 143
Wilson, Woodrow, 58
Wink, Walter, 32–33, 32–33n.42, 152–53
Witte, John, Jr., 46

women
Brunner on the role of, 194–95
and the family as a creational
sphere, 225–30
feminism and the history of, in
the modern West, 201–8
the human-capabilities approach
to development and, 219–24
models for the future of, 211–19
in non-Western societies, 208–9
scripture on, 187–88
worldwide conference on, 76
See also feminism
"world," the
Christian conception of, 107
globalization and, 19–24

history of Christian thought on,
110–13
World at the Year 2000, The, 87
World Bank, 5n.5, 84–85, 108
World Commission on Culture and
Development, 80
World Conference of Associations
of Theological Institutions,
28
World Council of Churches, 28
World Missionary Congress (1910),
23
World's Parliament of Religions
(Chicago, 1893), 59
World Trade Organization, 84–85,
108